T0329151

POLITICAL BEHAVIOR in ORGANIZATIONS

To Drew, Douglas and Gizella, and Melanie and Will, and Andrew Drake.

POLITICAL BEHAVIOR in ORGANIZATIONS

ANDREW J. DuBRIN
Rochester Institute of Technology

Los Angeles • London • New Delhi • Singapore • Washington DC

For information:

SAGE Publications, Inc.
2455 Teller Road
Thousand Oaks, California 91320
E-mail: order@sagepub.com

SAGE Publications India Pvt. Ltd.
B 1/I 1 Mohan Cooperative
Industrial Area
Mathura Road, New Delhi 110 044
India

SAGE Publications Ltd.
1 Oliver's Yard
55 City Road
London EC1Y 1SP
United Kingdom

SAGE Publications Asia-Pacific
Pte. Ltd.
33 Pekin Street #02-01
Far East Square
Singapore 048763

Library of Congress Cataloging-in-Publication Data

DuBrin, Andrew J.
Political behavior in organizations/Andrew J. DuBrin.
p. cm.
Includes bibliographical references and index.
ISBN 978-1-4129-5461-7 (pbk.)
1. Organizational behavior—Textbooks. I. Title.
HD58.7.D85 2009
302.3′5—dc22 2008019318

08 09 10 11 12 10 9 8 7 6 5 4 3 2 1

Acquisitions Editor: Al Bruckner
Editorial Assistant: MaryAnn Vail
Production Editor: Carla Freeman
Copy Editor: Susan Jarvis
Typesetter: C&M Digitals (P) Ltd.
Proofreader: Penny Sippel
Indexer: Michael Ferreira
Cover Designer: Candice Harman
Marketing Manager: Jennifer Reed Banando

CONTENTS

PREFACE

Welcome to *Political Behavior in Organizations.* Organizational politics has been part of the study of organizational behavior and management for close to 40 years, and part of the research literature for much longer if power and influence are included. Some aspects of organizational politics are studied in a wide range of schools from career schools (also known as vocational-technical institutes) to MBA programs and doctoral programs. The time is therefore right for a textbook about political behavior in organizations that is a blend of theory, research, practical advice, cases, self-quizzes, and exercises.

PURPOSE AND GOALS OF THE BOOK

The purpose of *Political Behavior in Organizations* is to provide a guide to the effective use of organizational politics, with as many strategies and tactics as feasible based on scholarly research and theory. The book is therefore clearly a textbook, yet with an emphasis on application. The application emphasis is achieved primarily by presenting positive and ethical strategies and tactics for gaining political advantage.

Political Behavior in Organizations is designed to meet the needs of courses and seminars in organizational politics, and power and influence. The book could also serve as a second text in courses in organizational behavior or leadership that emphasized organizational politics. Researchers may be interested in the book as a source of additional research topics and hypotheses to pursue.

Many topics within the text are found in briefer form in chapters about organizational politics in organizational behavior, introduction to management, and leadership texts. Several of the topics mentioned in *Political Behavior in Organizations* are also found in the textbooks just mentioned, but our emphasis is different. We focus on the political aspects of these topics rather than duplicating the information found in textbooks about organizational behavior, introduction to management, or leadership. One example would be leader–member exchange (LMX) theory. Instead of reviewing the many findings on this topic, we focus on the aspects of LMX useful in building downward relations. Also, we describe the political aspects of organizational citizenship behavior (OCB) rather than presenting a summary of research about many aspects of the topic. And when we refer to organizational culture, we focus on the aspects directly related to political behavior in organizations rather than presenting an overview of culture.

Where appropriate, this text includes theory about political behavior in organizations that is infrequently found in organizational behavior or management texts. Among these theories are social network theory and the conservation of resources theory. Among the many topics found in *Political Behavior in Organizations* rarely found in organizational behavior or management texts are social capital, the alpha executive, the dependence perspective, nepotism, political blunders, social network analysis, and spin.

Another major purpose of our textbook is to place some focus and structure on the field of political behavior in organizations, or organizational politics. A recent Yahoo! search of the term "organizational politics" yielded 5.5 million entries, and a Google search yielded 2.9 million. According to the *Handbook of Organizational Politics,* more than 150 studies have been published in academic journals that have explored the meaning of this phenomenon along with its antecedents, implications, and significance for workers at all levels.

Another purpose of *Political Behavior in Organizations* is to emphasize the importance of this field for managers and professionals working in a variety of settings. Students with considerable work experience are the most likely to understand the relevance of studying political behavior in organizations. As a result, many people do not appreciate the importance of organizational politics until they have already missed out on career opportunities or failed to acquire the power they needed to attain their work goals. An intensive study of political behavior in organizations might help to resolve the problem of ignoring political factors until it is too late.

STRUCTURE OF THE TEXT

To achieve the purposes and goals of the text, it is divided into three parts and 10 chapters.

Part I is about the nature and context of political behavior in organizations. Chapter 1 describes that nature of organizational politics and contributing factors or causes. Chapter 2 deals with the organizational context, such as the culture and ethics of organizational politics.

Part II deals with the heart of political behavior in organizations: strategies and tactics of positive organizational politics, including developing interpersonal relationships. Chapter 3 is about major initiatives for acquiring power. Chapter 4 is about upward relations, or managing your boss. Chapter 5 is about lateral or coworker relations. Chapter 6 studies downward relations, or the more political aspects of dealing with subordinates. Chapter 7 deals with both standard influence tactics and some of those not ordinarily found in the professional literature, such as being an alpha executive and negotiating sensibly. Chapter 8 describes the most popular topic in organizational politics: the development of social networks.

Part III deals with the vital topics of negative tactics, blunders, and overcoming dysfunctional politics. Chapter 9 examines negative political tactics, including the ubiquitous backstabbing, and removing the opposition. Chapter 10 describes the control of dysfunctional politics, including how the perception of politics can be a negative force.

Each chapter contains a combination of information and suggestions based on journal articles, the business press, trade books, and the author's experience. The vast majority of examples and cases are based on information in the business press, with an emphasis on the *Wall Street Journal* and *BusinessWeek*. Each chapter contains the didactic features of learning objectives, an introductory case story, highlighted key terms, a self-assessment quiz, a summary, questions and activities, a case study, and a skill-building exercise. The text is supported by an instructor's manual and test bank and PowerPoint slides, all prepared by the author.

ACKNOWLEDGMENTS

A project as complicated as a textbook requires the cooperation of a group of dedicated and talented people. First, I thank the hundreds of managers, professionals, and students with whom I have discussed organizational politics. Second, I thank the following academic colleagues who offered suggestions for improving the plan for the text and then provided constructive feedback on the first manuscript:

Martha Andrews
University of North Carolina at Wilmington

Dennis P. Bozeman
University of Houston

Anthony T. Cobb
Virginia Tech

Abigail Hubbard
University of Houston

Christian Kiewitz
University of Dayton

B. Thomas Mayes
California State University, Fullerton

Stuart M. Schmidt
Temple University

Donald Vredenburgh
Baruch College

The editorial and production staffs at SAGE Publications and Ohlinger Publishing Services also receive my gratitude. These people include Al Bruckner, MaryAnn Vail, Erin Curtis, and Susan Jarvis. Writing without loved ones would be a lonely task. My thanks, therefore, also go to my family members—Drew, Douglas and Gizella, Melanie and Will, Rosie, Clare, Camila, Sofia, and Eliana.

—A. J. D.

PART I

THE NATURE AND CONTEXT OF POLITICAL BEHAVIOR IN ORGANIZATIONS

ONE

THE NATURE AND CAUSES OF ORGANIZATIONAL POLITICS

LEARNING OBJECTIVES

After studying this chapter and doing the exercises, you should be able to do the following:

1. Pinpoint several meanings of organizational politics, including positive and negative connotations.
2. Explain why knowledge about and skill in political behavior contributes to career advancement and organizational performance.
3. Identify major factors contributing to political behavior in organizations.
4. Differentiate between functional and dysfunctional organizational politics.
5. Be prepared to apply the framework for effective use of organizational politics.

Nicole Davis knows that her clients' bottom line and brand identity rely on her ability to "build a bridge between an inanimate object and what the object represents." Davis is the vice president of marketing and public relations for Goldstein Communications (www.goldstein.com), a full-service agency that specializes in marketing luxury jewelry and fashion. "Branding is a driving force," says Davis. "Consumers are not just buying that ring, they're buying into the lifestyle."

When Davis, 34, spots a trend in design that benefits her clients, she communicates it to magazine editors, retail store operators, TV producers, and fashion stylists, to accelerate buzz by getting jewelry placed on celebrities in photo shoots, music videos, and at award galas. She has provided jewelry for Renée Zellweger, Jamie Foxx, Elizabeth Hurley, and Oprah Winfrey.

Davis, a native of Kingston, Jamaica, is also account manager for Platinum Guild International USA (www.preciousplatinum.com), a marketing organization for platinum jewelry designers and manufacturers. And, while she affirms that purchases are often driven by emotion, she believes that buying luxury jewelry is also very much an investment. "Jewelry should be a lifetime purchase that can pass from generation to generation."

The York University psychology graduate was interviewed for a position in the public relations industry in 1997 when she landed in the luxury jewelry division of VNU Expositions. For two years, Davis served as account manager for the Couture Jewelry Collections Conference, which exposed her to many facets of show production.

She lists strong writing skills, event production experience, and the ability to build strategic relationships as highly desirable skills in her field. "You have to be a people person and able to tell a story in many different ways."[1]

The story about a jewelry-marketing and public relations professional hints at many factors associated with career success, including a good education, creativity, and passion for one's work. Furthermore, the vignette highlights the importance of being politically astute in order to succeed in organizational life. In this woman's case, building strategic relationships (or high-level networking) is a major political factor underlying her success. Our study of political behavior in organizations begins with an analysis of the meaning and nature of organizational politics, along with their importance, contributing factors to organizational politics, and a framework for using ethical political tactics. Subsequent chapters deal with other major aspects of political behavior in organizations.

THE MEANING OF ORGANIZATIONAL POLITICS

You have undoubtedly already read or heard something about, or watched a television show concerning the nature of, political behavior in organizations, organizational politics, or office politics. A recent insertion of "organizational politics" into the Yahoo! search engine yielded over 4.5 million entries. (Admittedly, there were a lot of duplications, advertisements, and irrelevant entries among them.) As with the terms "leadership" and "management," some clarification of the subject matter of this book is in order.

A starting point is the phrase chosen for the title of this text, **political behavior in organizations.** The term refers to a wide variety of behaviors, including organizational politics, influence processes, and power struggles to gain advantage or resources in the workplace. Yet, rather than agonizing over subtle differences between terms, "political behavior in organizations" and "organizational politics" should really be viewed as synonyms.

Before we present the definition of organizational politics that will be used in this text, recognize that dozens of definitions of the term have been proposed. However, according to a research handbook on the topic, organizational politics are generally regarded as a social influence process in which behavior is strategically designed to maximize short-term or long-term self-interest.[2]

The meaning of organizational politics has been perceived both positively and negatively, as shown in Exhibit 1.1. On the positive side, organizational politics can be regarded as wielding influence for the greater good, such as using your personal contacts in an organization to raise money for childhood leukemia. Or organizational politics can be regarded neutrally, as in the definition "power in action." Politics are used to apply power. From a negative viewpoint, organizational politics are perceived as a group of influence tactics used to serve self-interest. The popular meaning of "office politics" illustrates its negative meaning, conjuring up thoughts of kissing up to the boss, back-stabbing rivals, and being insincere to obtain what you want.

To help make the abstract concept of organizational politics more concrete, you are invited to take the accompanying self-quiz (Self-Assessment 1.1). At the same time, you will obtain a tentative measure of your tendencies toward engaging in political behavior in the workplace.

Rather than keeping dozens of definitions in mind for the same concept, our purposes will be served by defining **organizational politics** as informal

Exhibit 1.1 Representative Definitions of Organizational Politics

Positively Toned or Neutrally Toned

"Power in action."[3]

"Informal means of influence."[4]

"The readiness of people to use power in their efforts to influence others and secure personal or collective interests or, alternatively, avoid negative outcomes within the organization."[5]

"Political skill is an interpersonal style that combines social awareness with the ability to communicate well."[6]

"Political skill is the ability to effectively understand others at work, and to use such knowledge to influence others to act in ways that enhance one's personal and/or organizational objectives."[7]

"A style of interaction that allows you to read situations, interpret them, and exhibit the right kind of behavior to induce others to do what you want—and do it willingly."[8]

"Politics is the pursuit of power."[9]

"Procedures for promoting interests to allocate scare resources."[10]

Negatively Toned

"The management of influence to obtain ends not sanctioned by the organization or to obtain sanctioned ends through nonsanctioned influence means."[11]

"Actions by individuals which are directed toward the goal of furthering their own self-interest without regard for the well-being of others or their organization."[12]

"An intentional social influence process in which behavior is strategically designed to maximize short-term or long-term self-interests." [13]

"Playing the game—the practice of using factors other than good performance to improve one's stance in an organization."[14]

"Underhanded or advancing oneself by unscrupulous means."[15]

"Unsanctioned actions or those that deviate from formal or rational procedures."[16]

approaches to gaining power and advantage through means other than merit or luck. This definition helps emphasize that political behavior is not a substitute for good job performance or talent. Organizational politics help you capitalize on the talent and hard work that can lead to attaining organizational objectives.

SELF-ASSESSMENT 1.1

The Positive Organizational Politics Questionnaire

Answer each question "Mostly agree" or "Mostly disagree," even if it is difficult for you to decide which alternative best describes your opinion.

	Mostly Agree	Mostly Disagree
1. Pleasing my boss is a major goal of mine.	___	___
2. I go out of my way to flatter important people.	___	___
3. I am most likely to do favors for people who can help me in return.	___	___
4. Given the opportunity, I would cultivate friendships with powerful people.	___	___
5. I will compliment a coworker even if I have to think hard about what might be praiseworthy.	___	___
6. If I thought my boss needed the help, and I had the expertise, I would show him or her how to use an electronic gadget for personal reasons.	___	___
7. I laugh heartily at my boss's humor, so long as I think he or she is at least a little funny.	___	___
8. I would not be too concerned about following a company dress code, so long as I looked neat.	___	___
9. If a customer sent me a compliment through e-mail, I would forward a copy to my boss and another influential person.	___	___
10. I smile only at people in the workplace whom I genuinely like.	___	___

(Continued)

(Continued)

11. An effective way to impress people is to tell them what they want to hear. ___ ___
12. I would never publicly correct mistakes made by the boss. ___ ___
13. I would be willing to use my personal contacts to gain a promotion or desirable transfer. ___ ___
14. I think it is a good idea to send a congratulatory note to someone in the company who receives a promotion to an executive position. ___ ___
15. I think "office politics" are only for losers. ___ ___
16. I have already started to develop a network of useful contacts. ___ ___

Scoring and Interpretation: Give yourself a "+1" for each answer that agrees with the keyed answer. Each question that receives a score of +1 shows a tendency toward playing positive organizational politics. The scoring key is as follows:

1. Mostly agree
2. Mostly agree
3. Mostly agree
4. Mostly agree
5. Mostly agree
6. Mostly agree
7. Mostly agree
8. Mostly disagree
9. Mostly agree
10. Mostly disagree
11. Mostly agree
12. Mostly agree
13. Mostly agree
14. Mostly agree
15. Mostly disagree

1–6: Below-average tendency to play office politics

7–11: Average tendency to play office politics

12 and above: Above-average tendency to play office politics; strong need for power

Skill Development: Thinking about your political tendencies in the workplace is important for your career because most successful leaders are moderately political. The ability to use politics effectively and ethically increases with importance in the executive suite. Most top players are effective office politicians. Yet being overly and blatantly political can lead to distrust, thereby damaging your career.

THE IMPORTANCE OF POLITICAL BEHAVIOR FOR CAREER ADVANCEMENT AND ORGANIZATIONAL PERFORMANCE

One argument for the importance of understanding political behavior in organizations is that managers spend so much time dealing with politics. Several informal surveys have concluded that managers spend about 20% of their time dealing with company politics, or about one out of five working days.[17] A misleading conclusion about these surveys is that the term "politics" includes all types of conflict. Nevertheless, even if nonpolitical conflicts are excluded, managers invest considerable time in dealing with organizational politics.

Understanding political behavior in organizations is important for reasons beyond the fact that such activity is part of a manager's job. Here we look at some relevant research and opinions about how political behavior is related first to career advancement, and second to organizational performance.

How Interpersonal Influence Behavior Facilitates the Pathway to the Boardroom

As implied in the definition of organizational politics used here, a major purpose of political behavior is to gain advantage. Not every act of political behavior will achieve its end, yet it is widely accepted that being a skilled politician facilitates career advancement. Most books and articles about office politics offer the promise of career advancement for those who can develop political skills. As concluded in *Political Skill at Work,* "In today's organizations, career success depends more on political skill—the ability to influence, motivate, and win support from others—than on almost any other characteristic."[18]

A study about gaining entrance to the boardroom provides more specific evidence about the contribution of interpersonal influence behavior to career advancement. It is a widely accepted belief that a key path to the boardroom is membership in an exclusive club, attendance at a very selective prep school, an MBA from a highly ranked program, or a listing in the Social Register. A study by James D. Westphal and Ithai Stern explored how individuals—especially those without privileged backgrounds—gained access to the boardroom. They concluded that an alternate method of being chosen for a board position was *ingratiating behavior* toward the CEO and others who control appointments to a board of directors. As measured in the study, ingratiation comprised flattery, reinforcing the CEO's opinion, and doing favors of some kind.

The researchers analyzed survey data on influence behavior from a sample of 1,012 CEOs and other senior managers at 138 of the Forbes 500 companies. They found that senior managers who engaged in ingratiatory behavior toward their CEO were more likely to receive board appointments at other firms where their CEO served as a director. The same managers were also more likely to receive a board appointment at firms in which the CEO was indirectly connected to the board network.

A specific finding was that, during a 12-month period, challenging the CEO's opinion one less time, complimenting the CEO on his or her insight two more times, and doing one personal favor increased the chances of an appointment to a board where the CEO was already a director by 64%. The results of the study also suggested that interpersonal influence behavior substitutes to some degree for the advantages of an elite background or belonging to a majority demographic group.

Another conclusion reached by the researchers is that managers lacking an elite background who are part of a minority group or female must engage in a higher level of interpersonal influence behavior in order to have equal opportunity to obtain a board appointment.[19]

A possible misinterpretation of the study just cited is that ingratiating behavior is the primary reason why high-ranking managers obtain a seat on the board. All the participants in the study had already worked their way up into high-level positions in major business corporations. We therefore can assume they also had enough talent, and worked hard enough, to be high performers. Yet being deferent toward the CEO apparently helped senior managers capitalize on their good job performance.

Political Behavior and Organizational Performance

We generally think of an organization that is overly political as being ineffective. The power struggles between groups and executives competing for power may lower organizational performance. An example is found in some of the problems the Ford Motor Company faced during the 1990s and early 2000s. Finance and engineering teams frequently clashed over a requirement of the finance group that each new-car program cost less to engineer than the one it replaced. Such a requirement placed heavy pressure on the marketing groups, and led to conflict and power struggles. A product manager complained that the finance staff had the company by the throat.

A plan to completely modernize the highly profitable Lincoln Town Car was discarded because, among other factors, the engineers could not develop a cost-efficient way to redesign the doors.

The poor cooperation was also found in Ford's geographic divisions. A joke circulating around the company a few years ago was that if the head of Ford Europe said it was snowing, the head of Ford North America would put on his bathing suit. The North American and European groups were also engaged in power struggles over whether the 2003 Ford Focus should be refreshed or a completely new version built.[20]

The negative example just presented illustrates what can happen when leaders lack the power and influence to overcome squabbles. Ronnie Kurchner-Hawkins and Rima Miller explain that it is useful to think of positive political behavior as a skill set which leaders need to develop in order to positively influence their organizations and use power ethically to achieve results.[21]

In support of this idea, senior managers at Procter & Gamble are deluged with ideas for new products and the purchase of other companies to supplement the company's product lines. Such differences of opinions do not generate into petty power struggles partly because of the positive leadership climate within the company. As a result, Procter & Gamble continues to be a highly admired company.

Political skill contributes to organizational performance in another basic way. Managers and professionals who are politically skillful will often have higher job performance, which is the building block for organizational performance. For example, a project manager might use political skill to facilitate the manufacture of a major new piece of equipment that is in demand from several customers.

As part of a larger study with industrial sales representatives, Yongmei Liu and her coresearchers explored whether political skill predicts job performance. A finding relevant to the present discussion was that political skill is positively associated with job performance in terms of quantity of work output, quality of workout, and accuracy of work. The same relationship of political skill and job performance was found when the study was repeated with business students in an internship program, and with healthcare workers. Another finding of the study with the three groups was that political skill has a positive effect on a person's reputation and that a positive reputation also is associated with good job performance.[22]

FACTORS CONTRIBUTING TO POLITICAL BEHAVIOR IN ORGANIZATIONS

Understanding why political behavior in organizations is so widespread helps explain the nature of organizational politics. Various factors related to the nature of organizations contribute to political behavior, so it would be easy to blame (or credit) organizations for fostering organizational politics. However, many inner qualities of organizational members themselves contribute to a political environment. Here we look at major organizational and individual factors that contribute to—and sometimes cause—political behavior.

Organizational Factors

Many characteristics of, and conditions that exist in, organizations foster a political environment, as outlined in Exhibit 1.2. Several of these topics will be reintroduced at other chapters later in the book.

The Political Nature of Organizations

The most fundamental reason for political *behavior* in organizations is the political *nature* of organizations. Coalitions of interests and demands arise both within and outside organizations. Similarly, organizations can be viewed

Exhibit 1.2 Organizational Factors Contributing to Political Behavior in Organizations

1. The political nature of organizations
2. A competitive work environment
3. Hierarchical structures and downsizing
4. Built-in conflicts of interest
5. Subjective standards of performance
6. Environmental uncertainty and turbulence
7. Political behavior by senior management
8. Encouragement of admiration from subordinates

as loose structures of interests and demands which are in competition with one another for attention and resources. The interaction among different coalitions results in an undercurrent of political tactics, such as when one group tries to promote itself and discredit another.

Over 30 years ago, Jeffrey Pfeffer observed that organizations were more political than rational. Rational models of organizations, such as bureaucratic theory, assume that control devices such as rewards based on job performance or seniority, and rules for fair treatment of people, can eliminate self-interest in organizational decision making. Political models of organizations view organizations as pluralistic and divided into various interests, cultures, and subcultures.[23] The power struggles at the Ford Motor Company between finance and marketing illustrate vividly the political model just described.

One of the characteristics of the political model is the presence of struggle and conflict, with winners and losers. Some organizational members become so involved in the political model that they take joy in beating the competition—even if the competition is another unit in the same organization. A finance manager was asked how well his meeting went with the manufacturing group earlier that morning. He replied, "Fantastic. We really nailed those manufacturing types to the wall. They couldn't produce figures to justify purchasing the new IT system they wanted."

To reinforce further the idea that organizations are political in nature, it is helpful to recognize that people who work in organizations perceive them to be political. In one survey, 60% of the respondents agreed with the statement that "Most casual conversation appears to be about things I would consider as workplace politics."[24] ("Politics" in this context might include negative gossip about people.)

A Competitive Work Environment

Forces in the organization that breed competitiveness also foster political behavior. For instance, when a company hires a large number of ambitious people, these individuals attempt to outperform each other in order to achieve recognition and advancement. During job cutbacks, employees compete for the remaining positions. No matter why people feel compelled to compete with one another, they often resort to negative organizational politics to improve their competitive edge. An example would be sending an e-mail to a coworker (and a copy to his or her boss) with the following message: "We missed you at yesterday's meeting. Your input would have been valuable."

A competitive work environment also contributes to the presence of positive political behaviors. One key example is exerting effort to establishing good working relationships with other people in order to enhance their cooperation in achieving your work. If you have gone out of your way to cultivate a relationship with a tech-savvy coworker, that person might be willing to help you when you are faced with an urgent software problem. A related positive political tactic important in a competitive work environment is to build a network of contacts who can help you in a variety of ways, such as recommending you for promotion or task force assignments.

Hierarchical Structures and Downsizing

The very shape of large organizations is a fundamental reason why organizational members are motivated toward political behavior. A hierarchy, or pyramid, concentrates power at the top. Only so much power is therefore available to distribute among the people wanting more of it. In a true hierarchy, each successive layer on the organization chart has less formal power than the layer above it. At the very bottom of the organization, workers have virtually no power except for that provided by employment law, such as the right to form a labor union or not to be discriminated against. Because most organizations have fewer layers than previously, the competition for power has become more intense. Although empowerment may be motivational for many workers, it is unlikely to satisfy the quest to hold a formal position of power. Workers still struggle to obtain a corner office or cubicle.

Downsizing and team structures create even less opportunity for climbing the hierarchy, thus intensifying political behavior for the few remaining powerful positions. Worried about layoffs themselves, many workers attempt to discredit others so that the latter would be the first to go. Internal politics generally increase as good jobs, promotions, and bonuses become scarcer. Two business columnists made an observation several years ago that continues to be true in part: "The art of fawning over a boss may be more important now because of the stagnant economy and shortage of well-paying, full-time jobs."[25]

Built-In Conflicts of Interest

A conflict of interest occurs when a person's objectivity is compromised, such as when being asked for an honest opinion about the person who pays your salary. A bird analogy is in order: "Whose bread I eat, whose song I sing."

Lawrence B. Sawyer was among the early scholars to identify the political nature of internal auditing based on a conflict of interest. He noted that part of the street wisdom of internal auditing is to first let it be perceived that an internal audit can inflict harm. Sawyer then cautions as follows:

> That harm should be inflicted rarely because usually if we enhance a manager we have made a friend. If we diminish him or her, we have made a mistake. And street smarts tell us when to use honey and when to use acid. But the ability to pour acid, even though it is withheld, commands respect.[26]

In recent years, a series of financial scandals revealed a key weakness in the American business model: the failure of auditing systems to deliver true independence. The problem was found to be particularly acute when the outside auditor was a member of a firm that provided other lucrative financial services, such as investment banking, to the firm. Being a political animal, the auditor might minimize some of the brewing financial problems. A scholarly analysis of the subject suggested that auditors are often unaware of how morally compromised they have become because of conflicts of interest.[27] So much concern arose about conflicts of interest involving auditors that the government was prompted to pass the Sarbanes-Oxley Act of 2002, which established procedures for more objectivity and independence (less conflict of interest) in auditing.

Many other people besides auditors might behave politically when prompted by a conflict of interest. A compensation consultant paid by the CEO and the board might be prompted to find many valid reasons for concluding that the CEO merits an enormous bonus. Another example is the head of a staff group, such as facilities management, finding it easy to agree that top management's ideas for improving the facilities are quite sound. The worry here is that disagreeing with top management might result in the employee being replaced.

Subjective Standards of Performance

People often resort to organizational politics because they do not believe the organization has an objective and fair way of judging their performance and suitability for promotion. Similarly, when managers have no objective way of differentiating effective people from less effective employees, they will resort to favoritism. The adage "It's not what you know but who you know" applies to organizations lacking clear-cut standards of performance. Examples of relatively clear-cut performance standards include return on investment, units produced, and customer retention.

Environmental Uncertainty and Turbulence

When people, or the organizational subunits they represent, operate in an unstable and unpredictable environment, they tend to behave politically. They rely on organizational politics to create a favorable impression because uncertainty makes it difficult to determine what they should really be accomplishing.

The uncertainty, turbulence, and insecurity created by corporate downsizing is a major contributor to office politics. Many people believe intuitively that favoritism plays a major role in deciding who will survive the downsizing. In response to this perception, organizational members attempt to ingratiate themselves with influential people.

Political Behavior by Senior Management

Lower-ranking employees sometimes engage in political behavior because senior managers behave politically. When C-level executives are highly political, it contributes to a climate of acceptance for organizational politics. One of the most visible aspects of political behavior is favoritism in its many forms. When lower-ranking managers perceive that the practice exists among senior management of placing poorly qualified friends into high-paying positions, the lower-ranking managers are likely to follow suit.

Encouragement of Admiration From Subordinates

Most organizational leaders say they do not encourage kissing up, and that they prefer honest feedback from subordinates. Yet, without meaning to, these same managers and leaders encourage flattery and servile praise. Managers, as well as other workers, send out subtle signals that they want to be praised, such as smiling after receiving a compliment, and frowning when receiving negative feedback. Also, admirers are more likely to received good assignments and high performance evaluations. Executive coach Marshall Goldsmith explains that, without meaning to, many managers create an environment where people learn to reward others with accolades that are not completely warranted. People generally see this tendency in others but not in themselves.[28]

Individual Factors

Organizations should not receive all the blame, or credit, for politically motivated behavior in the workplace. Many workers would behave politically in almost any place they worked. Exhibit 1.3 outlines the individual factors within people that trigger organizational politics.

Exhibit 1.3 Individual Factors Contributing to Political Behavior in Organizations

1. The political side of human nature
2. Predisposing personality factors
   a. Need for power
   b. Machiavellian tendencies
   c. Self-monitoring trait
   d. Emotional insecurity
3. The desire to avoid hard work

The Political Side of Human Nature

A basic reason organizational politics are so widely practiced is that they simply reflect the reality of human nature. People are generally favorably biased toward people they know, like, and trust, even if they are trying to be impartial. As a result, an office buddy might be chosen over a slightly more qualified person to be invited to become a member of an elite task force.

Another part of human nature that breeds political behavior is the desire to be accepted. Many employees who practice politics in the office do not aspire to a high-level position or wish to attain much power. They simply want to be accepted and liked by others, as determined by the psychological need for acceptance. To accomplish this, they perform favors for coworkers and carry out relatively harmless ploys. Among these techniques are leaving a full candy dish for the enjoyment of coworkers, running errands for others during lunchtime, and bringing coworkers trinkets upon their return from a vacation.

Self-interest is a part of human nature that results in negative political behavior. Many people engage in organizational politics because they place their own welfare before that of coworkers or their employer. For example, a product manager might campaign for a bigger budget for a pet product that does not hold much promise for future sales. If she obtains the bigger budget, more money will be available for expanding her sphere of influence. If this product manager were more interested in the welfare of the company, she would want the increased budget to flow toward another product—one she does not manage—that would lead to a better outcome for the company.

Self-interest is also reflected when a CEO appoints friends on the board so the friends will approve an enormous compensation package for the CEO. The board members themselves will often be well compensated in addition to holding the prestigious position of "board member." Self-interest is at stake on the part of the CEO because some of his or her exorbitant compensation could be used to (a) pay dividends to stockholders, (b) lower the price on products or services, (c) pay higher wages to entry-level workers, and (d) preserve a few more jobs.

Predisposing Personality Factors

Several personality traits figure prominently in the display of political behavior on the job. Because personality is a stable and deeply ingrained part of people, these tendencies are likely to surface across different situations. Four such aspects of personality are mentioned here.

1. *Need for Power.* Organizational politics are also fostered by the need for power. Executives have much stronger power needs than others, and thus propel themselves toward frequent episodes of political behavior. Because executives are responsible for controlling resources, their inner drive to do so helps them in their jobs. A personalized power need is more likely to trigger political behavior than a socialized power need. The personalized power need focuses on self-interest, whereas the socialized power need focuses on gaining power to help others—for example, a manufacturing manager struggling to keep a plant open to salvage jobs for manufacturing employees.

2. *Machiavellian Tendencies.* Some people engage in political behavior because they want to manipulate others, sometimes for their own personal advantage. **Machiavellianism** is an attitude in which it is accept to treat people as a means to an end. A person with Machiavellian tendencies is said to represent the epitome of the negative organizational politician.[29] The term "Machiavellianism" can be traced back to Niccolo Machiavelli (1469–1527), an Italian political philosopher and statesman. His most famous work, *The Prince,* describes how a leader may acquire and maintain power. Machiavelli's ideal prince was an amoral, manipulating tyrant who would restore the Italian city-state of Florence to its former glory. Three hundred and sixty years later,

a study by Gerald Biberman showed a positive relationship between Machiavellianism and political behavior, based on questionnaires that measured these tendencies.[30] The questionnaire used in the study was an earlier version of the one you were invited to take earlier in this chapter.

3. *Self-Monitoring Trait.* Self-monitoring is considered to be one of the five major factors that help explain human personality. According to the construct (jargon for concept) of self-monitoring, people differ in the extent to which they *monitor* the public appearances of the self that they display in interactions with other people. Monitor in this sense refers to observation, regulation, and control.[31] High self-monitors tend to monitor and control the images that they present to better fit the social situation at the moment. High self-monitors act politically because they essentially tell people what they want to hear. Working for Apple, a high self-monitor might tell a manager, "I think it is fantastic how the iPod is distributing music to millions of people." If the same person then went to work for a music company, he might say to the manager, "I am concerned that the iPod is siphoning away so much money from the CD industry."

4. *Emotional Insecurity.* Some people resort to political maneuvers to ingratiate themselves with superiors because they lack confidence in their talents and skills. A pension fund manager who has directed the firm toward investments with an annualized 15% return does not have to be overly political because he or she will have confidence in his or her capabilities. A person's choice of political strategy may indicate emotional insecurity. For instance, an insecure person might laugh loudly at every humorous comment the boss makes.

Desire to Avoid Hard Work

In an organizational subunit where people are not upwardly mobile (and/or waiting for retirement), political tactics are sometimes used to *avoid* work in contrast to striving for choice assignments and promotions. The rationale for this behavior is that "If you get in good with the boss, you won't have to work hard." An extreme example is that some highway construction workers do favors for their boss during the hot months so they will be permitted to nap in the cool concrete pipes during the working day. In general, using ingratiating behavior to avoid work is a ploy of the low work-motivated individual with a low need for power.

FUNCTIONAL VERSUS DYSFUNCTIONAL ORGANIZATIONAL POLITICS

In this text, we differentiate between positive and negative organizational politics, as suggested by Chapter 9, which looks at negative tactics and political blunders. A theoretical justification for this position is the concept of functional versus dysfunctional politics proposed by Russell Cropanzano and Alicia A. Grandey.[32] Politics will sometimes lead to positive outcomes for the organization, and sometimes to negative outcomes.

Functional politics are political behaviors that assist the organization to attain its goals. An example would be a middle-level manager enlisting the support of network members to help save the company enough money so a profit goal can be attained and a layoff avoided. *Dysfunctional politics* are political behaviors that inhibit the attainment of organizational goals. An example would be a manager hiring an unqualified job candidate over a qualified candidate primarily because the less competent candidate is a friend.

The theory under consideration goes on to explain that the same political behavior may be either functional or dysfunctional, depending on how it affects the organization. Assume that a CEO decides to relocate company headquarters to a more attractive building in a more luxurious setting. The result will be dysfunctional to the organization, and only satisfy the CEO's self-interest if the added expense of relocation and higher rent lowers profit. In contrast, if the relocation impresses a few potential customers enough to more than pay for the added expenses, the relocation activity becomes functional. It is also possible that the new location will attract talented people to the organization who will help the company to prosper.

The example just cited illustrates another part of the theory. Self-interest and organizational goals sometimes overlap. The CEO enjoys being in a prestigious new office building, and the organization also prospers. Another example is that backstabbing is usually a dysfunctional political behavior causing harm and stress to the person whose reputation was attacked. However, some individuals might actually enjoy the excitement of counterattacking a backstabber, and therefore profit from the apparently dysfunctional political behavior. The counterattacker wins and experiences an increase in job satisfaction, which in turn leads to a spurt in productivity. In Chapter 10 we will describe in more detail how employee perceptions of political behavior influence whether such behavior is functional or dysfunctional.

A FRAMEWORK FOR EFFECTIVE USE OF ORGANIZATIONAL POLITICS

As will be revealed throughout this book, hundreds of different political strategies and tactics exist, limited only by the imagination of the political actor. To help you capitalize on the potential power of organizational politics, Exhibit 1.4 presents a framework for its effective use.

Step 1 is to evaluate the culture and the situation. As described in Chapter 2, some organizational cultures tolerate more political behavior than others. In addition, some political tactics are more acceptable than others. For example, at the investment bank J. P. Morgan, hundreds of staff professionals want to be elected into partnership by the inner circle of powerful executives. At the same time, lobbying for partnership is frowned upon so the aspirant to partnership must find other ways of being noticed, including outstanding work performance and slowly building relationships with influential people.

Exhibit 1.4 A Framework for Effective Use of Organizational Politics

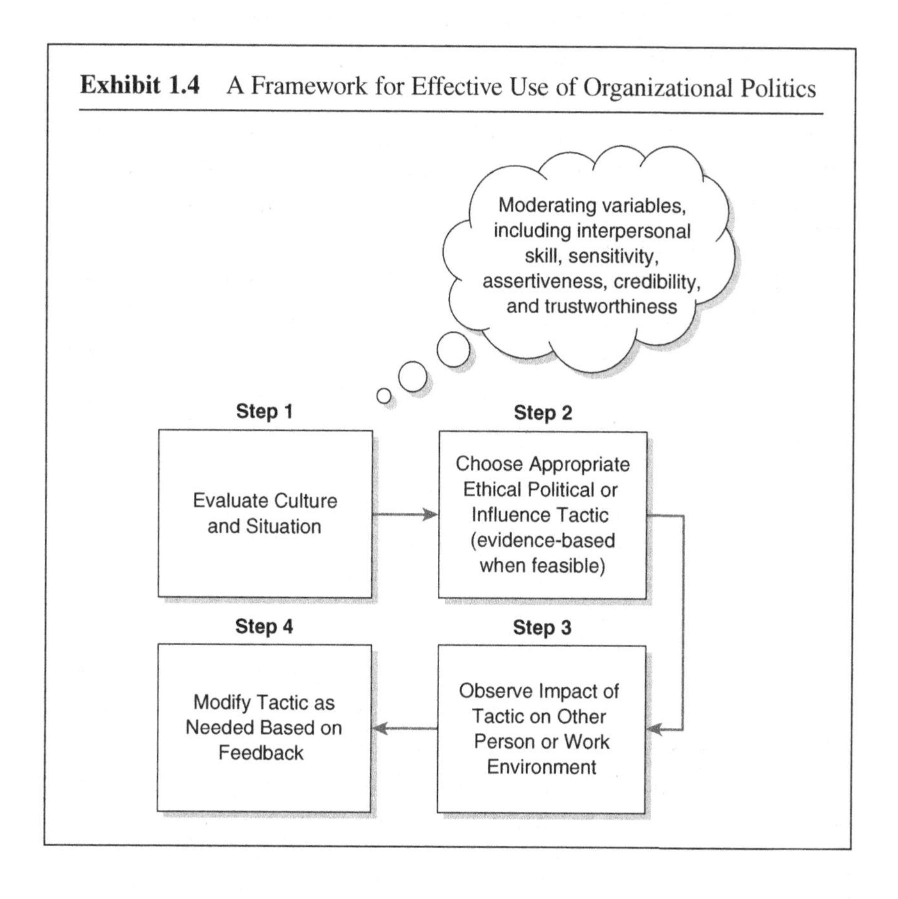

Sizing up the situation focuses more specifically on the target of the political tactic. You might find, for example, that your manager likes to socialize with group members, so inviting him or her to a backyard barbecue at your home might help cultivate a relationship with this particular manager. Another manager might regard fraternizing as a negative. Another example is that it might be politically wise to use fact-filled PowerPoint presentations for one manager, while another might dislike viewing fact-filled screens so it would be better to use more general PowerPoint presentations or avoid them completely.

Step 2 is simply an extension of the first step because, as you size up the environment to determine which tactic will be effective, several tactics may come to mind. However, it is important to think through a number of possibilities, such as by consulting the index to this text or other information about organizational politics. We focus on ethical tactics because unethical tactics are likely to hurt the individual player and the organization in the long run. Suppose you work for a firm heavily focused on building good relationships with customers. A suitable political tactic for you might then be, "Have a satisfied customer contact your boss."

The mention of *evidence-based* in Step 2 refers to the idea that, when possible, it is advisable to use a tactic for which there might be supporting data or other evidence. The study about the importance of ingratiation reported early in the chapter is an example of a political maneuver being supported by data-based research.

The mention of moderating variables in the speech bubble above Step 2 is critical. (A moderating variable influences another variable, such as people with high blood pressure being more likely to develop carpal tunnel syndrome.) People vary substantially in the skills and traits necessary for the successful implementation of certain tactics. Four of these moderating variables are as follows:

1. *Interpersonal skills.* It is easier for a person with well-developed interpersonal skills to rely on building contacts as a political strategy. A strongly task-oriented person might be more effective at displaying expertise as a political tactic.

2. *Sensitivity to people.* With good sensitivity to people (or emotional intelligence), the political actor is likely to be more effective with such political tactics as complimenting people and being politically correct. Intuition is tied in with sensitivity to people because it requires intuition to know when to implement certain tactics, such as when it is a good time to flatter a person in power.

3. *Assertiveness.* For many political tactics, the person engaging in politics has to be assertive or extraverted. Networking is a prime example. To be effective at networking, a person has to reach out to other people—even if the contact is electronic.

4. *Credibility and trustworthiness.* A person with a reputation for credibility and trustworthiness is likely to be a more effective political player. An example would attempts to network with others. If a person has a reputation of manipulating others, it will be more difficult for him or her to acquire network members.

Step 3 is to observe the impact of the tactic on the other person or perhaps the work environment. Returning to the example of remembering to compliment coworkers to get them on your side, you would observe whether people whom you compliment become more positive in their attitudes toward you. You might also observe whether the act of complimenting others leads to your enhanced acceptance in the work environment, such as being granted better assignments or more invitations to join task forces.

Step 4 is to modify your tactic as needed based on the feedback you receive from using the tactic. A research-based case in point is that, when complimenting or praising technically oriented people, it is best to be as specific and work-oriented as possible in the compliment or praise. In contrast, when complimenting or praising a less technically oriented person, more general praise—such as saying "Great job"—is likely to be effective.[33] As with almost all soft and hard skills, we become more skilled when we refine our technique based on feedback.

SUMMARY

Many different meanings of organizational politics have been proposed, often focusing on the idea that the practice of organizational politics is a social influence process designed to maximize self-interest. The definition proposed in this text is that organizational politics embody informal approaches to gaining power and advantage through means other than merit or luck.

Understanding political behavior in organizations is important because managers spend perhaps 20% of their time dealing with internal politics. It is also important to note that being politically astute, such as ingratiating oneself with the boss, can result in career advancement including being selected for membership on a board. When leaders have the power and influence to overcome squabbles, organizational performance may improve. Political skill has been shown to be positively related to job performance, thereby contributing to organizational performance.

Organizational factors contributing to political behavior include (1) the political nature of organizations, (2) a competitive work environment, (3) hierarchical structures and downsizing, (4) built-in conflicts of interest, (5) subjective standards of performance, (6) environmental uncertainty and turbulence, (7) political behavior by senior management, and (8) encouragement of admiration from subordinates.

Individual factors contributing to political behavior in organizations include (1) the political nature of human behavior; (2) predisposing personality factors such as the need for power, Machiavellianism, the self-monitoring trait, and emotional insecurity; and (3) the desire to avoid hard work.

Political behavior can be functional or dysfunctional to the organization, depending on the outcomes. The same behavior can be classified as functional or dysfunctional on the basis of how it affects the organization.

A framework for the effective use of organizational politics proposed here consists of four steps: (1) Evaluate the culture and the situation; (2) choose the appropriate ethical political or influence tactic; (3) observe the impact of the tactic on the other person or the work environment; and (4) modify the tactic as needed based on feedback. The appropriate tactic to choose is subject to moderating variables such as interpersonal skill and sensitivity.

QUESTIONS AND ACTIVITIES

1. Work individually or within a group to identify at least four popular synonyms or terms for organizational politics. Do the terms you have identified tend to be positive? Or are they negative?

2. Would you be willing to place a phase like "skilled at organizational politics" in the skills and accomplishment section of your job résumé. Why or why not?

3. The study about CEOs and nominating people to board membership suggested that ingratiating yourself with a CEO is a powerful technique. Why would intelligent people like CEOs be influenced by ingratiation?

4. In what way might a tax accountant face a conflict of interest that might prompt the accountant to behave politically?

5. In what way do candidates for political office have to be high self-monitors?

6. In what way are organizational politics likely to be present on an athletic team?

7. Some workers, including nurses, say they prefer to work the night shift so they can avoid "all the politics." What is it that they probably are really referring to?

CASE STUDY: THE CURIOUS BEHAVIOR OF CEO STEVE HEYER

The abrupt departure of Steven J. Heyer from Starwood Hotels & Resorts Worldwide, Inc., followed a confrontation with the company's board ignited by an anonymous letter accusing him of personal misconduct. Heyer—who denies engaging in any impropriety—was unexpectedly ousted as chief executive officer in April 2007. In the process, he opted to forfeit an estimated $35 million of severance compensation. A Starwood spokesperson reiterated the company's earlier statement that the board had lost confidence in Heyer's leadership, but added that "his style made some employees uncomfortable."

Heyer, who had been president and chief operating officer of Coca-Cola Co. before taking over at Starwood in 2004, has long been known for brusque, often difficult relations with employees. After investigating claims made in the anonymous letter sent to directors in January 2007, the board pressed Heyer to explain the large number of e-mails and text messages to and from female employees on a variety of topics outside normal working hours. They also questioned him about his hiring and promotion practices.

In an interview, the 54-year-old Heyer characterized the situation as the ugly fallout from extensive strategic and structural changes he had made while "transforming Starwood from a real-estate hotel company to a branding company." He says he doesn't know who wrote or sent the letter, but believes it could have been someone passed over for promotion.

"For an anonymous letter to basically destroy a reputation would be sinful," Heyer said. While acknowledging he could be a difficult boss, he said the chain of events set off by the letter represented the "straw that broke the camel's back" in his increasingly poor relationship with the company. He left without his severance package because "life is too short" to mount a contested defense against the allegations. "I'm burned out," he added. "I wanted to walk away from this job with my head held high."

The letter received by board members in mid-February contained about 10 specific instances that allegedly showed Heyer had created a hostile work environment since arriving at Starwood in October 2004. It alleged, for example, that on at least one occasion Heyer made inappropriate physical contact with a female employee outside a restaurant bathroom. Heyer denied this to the board, and said in an interview that this incident had never occurred.

Starwood's board hired an outside law firm to investigate the letter's allegations. In the course of the ensuing probe, Heyer's e-mails and text messages were scrutinized and found to include an "overwhelming body of evidence" that would have given the board reason to fire him for cause. The investigation uncovered e-mails and text messages between Heyer, who is married, and a young, unmarried female employee that were sent at times outside normal business hours and were of a suggestive nature. "There were several provocative conversations, and there was no question that the conduct was inappropriate for a CEO," a source stated.

The same female employee in question accompanied Heyer and five other employees on the corporate jet to a board meeting in Greece. Heyer said that employee was part of the "Generation Next" program he had created to cultivate younger homegrown managers in what he described as a "generation-skipping exercise" authorized by the company.

Heyer was also questioned by the board about his method of promoting employees, and whether he fostered a culture of favoritism. Heyer noted that all promotions were done through a process and he wasn't on the promotion committee. The board also determined that the women who had exchanged e-mail and text messages with Heyer were essentially "unwilling victims" who felt pressured to curry favor with the CEO.

The Starwood directors were aware of Heyer's reputation for a rough management style, and they had received an extensive briefing about his difficult personality before they chose him as CEO. They learned in detail about the former Coke president's frequent clashes with colleagues there. Coke board members told Starwood recruiters that Heyer didn't get the top job at the beverage giant partly because he was difficult to work with. But Heyer impressed the Starwood board with his marketing background and his plan for the company's hotel brands, which include Westin and Sheraton.

Among the board's biggest gripes with Heyer was that he spent little time at company headquarters in White Plains, instead commuting from his home in Atlanta. Under Heyer's contract, Starwood provided an Atlanta area office. The CEO agreed to spend at least a majority of his workdays over a two-month period either at headquarters or on company business trips.

Case Study Questions

1. What is your evaluation of the political skill of Steve Heyer?
2. What actions should the women in question have taken after they received the provocative e-mail and text messages from CEO Heyer?
3. What was the political significance of Heyer not relocating to the White Plains area?
4. To what extent do you think Steve Heyer was the victim of dirty politics?
5. What advice about organizational politics would you offer Heyer to help him perform better in his next position?

SOURCE: Excerpted from Sanders, P., & Lublin, J. S. (2007). Starwood CEO's ouster followed battle with board over his conduct. *Wall Street Journal,* April 7–8, A1, A2. Permission obtained through Copyright Clearance Center.

POLITICAL SKILL-BUILDING EXERCISE 1

What *Are* Office Politics?

The common-language term for organizational politics is "office politics." Yet, unlike business terms such as "accounting," "inventory," "retail store," and "factory," the term "office politics" has many meanings and connotations. Your job is to conduct three-minute interviews with five different people of any category you choose, to obtain their definitions of "office politics." Conduct your interviews in person, by phone, or via e-mail. Listen attentively to see whether the definitions you receive are positive or negative. After you have collected your interview data, attempt to develop a composite meaning based on your interviews.

1. How do the definitions you collect compare with the definitions presented in this chapter?
2. Do you notice any tendency for experienced business people to have a different definition of office politics than those who are less experienced?

Share your findings with a few classmates to observe how much consensus exists about the meaning of "office politics."

REFERENCES

1. Drakes, S. (2007). All that glitters . . . four fine-jewelry professionals prove they have the mettle for the business. *Black Enterprise, 37,* 99.

2. Beugré, C. D., & Liverpool, P. R. (2006). Politics as determinant of fairness perceptions in organizations. In P. Eran Vigoda-Gadot & Amos Drory (Eds.), *Handbook of organizational politics* [p. 123]. Northampton, MA: Edward Elgar.

3. Pfeffer, J. (1981). *Power in organizations* [p. 8]. Cambridge, MA: Ballinger.

4. Drory, A., & Romm, T. (1990, November). The definition of organizational politics: A review. *Human Relations,* 1133–1155.

5. Bozeman, D. P., Perrewé, P. L., Kacmar, K. M., Hochwarter, W. A., & Brymer, R. A. (1996). *An examination of reactions to perceptions of organizational politics.* Paper presented at the Southern Management Association Meeting, New Orleans, LA.

6. Ferris, G. R., Perrewé, P. L., Anthony, W. P., & Gilmore, D. C. (2000, Spring). Political skill at work. *Organizational Dynamics,* 25–37.

7. Ahearn, K. K., Ferris, G. R., Hockwater, W. A., & Ammeter, A. P. (2004). Leader political skill and team performance. *Journal of Management, 30,* 309.

8. Ferris, G. R., Davidson, S. L., & and Perrewé, P. L. (2005). *Political skill at work* [p. ix]. Mountain View, CA: Davies-Black.

9. Umiker, W. (1990, August). Playing politics fair and square. *Health Care Supervision,* 23–28.

10. Baum, H. S. (1989, Summer). Organizational politics against organizational culture: A psychoanalytic perspective. *Human Resource Management,* 191–207 [p. 193].

11. Bronston, T. M., & Allen, R. W. (1977). Toward a definition of organizational politics. *Academy of Management Review, 2,* 672–678 [p. 675].

12. Kacmar, K. M., & Carlson, D. S. (1997). Further validation of the Perception of Politics Scale (POPS): A multiple sample investigation. *Journal of Management, 23,* 627–658.

13. Ferris, G. R., Russ, G. S., & Fandt, P. M. (1989). Politics in organizations. In R. A. Giacalone & R. Rosenfeld (Eds.), *Impression management in the organization* (pp. 143–170). Hillsdale, NJ: Lawrence Erlbaum.

14. Rue, L. W. & Byars, L. L. (1982). *Supervision: Links to productivity.* Homewood, IL: Irwin.

15. Wieringa, W. R. (2004). Office politics. *Fair practices LLC.* Retrieved 03/07/2007 from www.fairpractices.com.

16. Darr, W., & Johns, G. (2004). Political decision-making climates: Theoretical processes and multi-level antecedents. *Human Relations, 2,* 169–200 [p. 171].

17. One such survey was conducted by AccountTemps.

18. Ferris, G. R., Davidson, S. L., & and Perrewé, P. L. (2005). *Political skill at work* (back cover). Mountain View, CA: Davies-Black.

19. Westphal, J. D., & Stern, I. (2006, June). The other pathway to the boardroom: How interpersonal influence behavior can substitute for elite credential and demographic minority status in gaining access to board appointments. *Administrative Science Quarterly,* 169–204; Hanna, M. (2006, October). Ingratiation: The other pathway to the boardroom. *Wharton Leadership Digest,* 9–10.

20. Taylor, A., III (2006, November 13). Ford's student driver takes the wheel. *Fortune,* 98.

21. Kurchner-Hawkins, R., & Miller, R. (2006). Organizational politics: Building positive political strategies in turbulent times. In P. Eran Vigoda-Gadot & Amos Drory (Eds.), *Handbook of organizational politics* (pp. 328–352) [p. 331]. Northampton, MA: Edward Elgar.

22. Liu, Y., Ferris, G., Perrewé, P., Zinko, R., Weitz, B., & Jun Xu (2007). Dispositional antecedents and outcomes of political skill in organizations: A four study investigation with convergence. *Journal of Vocational Behavior, 71,* 146–165.

23. Pfeffer, J. (1981). *Power in organizations* [p. 28]. Marshfield, MA: Pitman.

24. Survey reported in Parker, C. P., Dipboye, R. L., & Jackson, S. L. (1995, September–October). Perceptions of organizational politics: An investigation of antecedents and consequences. *Journal of Management,* 891–912.

25. Graham, C., & Sagario, D. (2003). "Good fawning" over boss can help in tough times. *Des Moines Register,* syndicated story, n.d.

26. Sawyer, L. B. (1992, February). The political side of internal auditing. *Internal Auditor,* 30.

27. Moore, D. A., Tetlock, P. E., Tanlu, L., & Bazerman, M. H. (2006, January). Conflicts of interest and the case of auditor independence: Moral seduction and strategic issue cycling. *Academy of Management Review,* 10–29.

28. Goldsmith, M. (2003, December). All of us are stuck on suck-ups. *Fast Company,* 117.

29. Boozer, R. W., Forte, M., & Harris, J. R. (2005, January). Psychological type, Machiavellianism, and perceived self-efficacy at playing office politics. *Journal of Psychological Type,* 1–9.

30. Biberman, G. (1985). Personality characteristics and work attitudes of persons with high, moderate, and low political tendencies. *Psychological Reports, 57,* 1303–1310 [p. 1309].

31. Day, D. D., Schleicher, D. J., Unckless, A. L., & Hiller, N. J. (2002, April). Self-monitoring personality at work: A meta-analytic investigation of construct validity. *Journal of Applied Psychology,* 390–401.

32. Cropanzano, R., & Grandey, A. A. (1998). If politics is a game, then what are the rules? Three suggestions for ethical management. In M. Schminke (Ed.), *Managerial ethics: Moral management of people and processes* (pp. 133–152). Mahwah, NJ: Lawrence Erlbaum; Riggio, R. E. (2003). *Introduction to industrial/organizational psychology* (4th ed.) (pp. 389–390). Upper Saddle River, NJ: Prentice Hall.

33. DuBrin, A. J. (2005). Self-perceived technical orientation and attitudes toward being flattered. *Psychological Reports, 95,* 852–854.

TWO

THE ORGANIZATIONAL CONTEXT AND ETHICS OF POLITICAL BEHAVIOR

LEARNING OBJECTIVES

After studying this chapter and doing the exercises, you should be able to do the following:

1. Identify dimensions of organizational culture related to organizational politics.
2. Make a tentative diagnosis of a given organizational culture with respect to its receptivity to political behavior.
3. Size up a situation, including cultural values, in terms of the type of political behavior that might be appropriate.
4. Be aware of ethical considerations in the use of organizational politics, and apply an ethics test.

When James W. McNerney decided that Boeing Co.'s top managers needed a loud wake-up call, the new chief executive chose the obvious place to sound the alarm: the company's annual executive retreat on January 4 and 5, 2006. A year earlier, the event had been held at the posh Mission Hills

Country Club in Palm Springs, California, and nobody apparently had a better time than McNerney's predecessor, Harry Stonecipher. After a day devoted largely to socializing and playing golf, the former CEO, surrounded by Boeing's elite, closed down the bar and then fired up a cigar. It was at the same event that the married Stonecipher began a relationship with a female vice president at Boeing—a misjudgment that ultimately paved the way for his humiliating ousting on March 6, 2005, and for McNerney's appointment as CEO on July 5.

The "Palm Springs Fling," as it became known at Boeing, marked an all-time low for the company. It followed a three-year binge of widely publicized corporate misbehavior, highlighted by the jailing of Boeing's chief financial officer for holding illegal job negotiations with a senior Pentagon official, the indictment of a manager for allegedly stealing some 25,000 pages of proprietary documents from his former employer, Lockheed Martin Corp., and the judicial finding that Boeing had abused attorney–client privilege to help cover up internal studies showing that female employees were paid less than men.

Scandals involving multiple forms of misconduct in geographically scattered locations enveloped nearly every division at Boeing, leaving little doubt that the legendary company, even as it began to enjoy a cyclical boom, was plagued by a poisonous culture.

Given that backdrop, nobody was particularly shocked when the 2006 annual retreat was moved to the more modest Hyatt Regency in Orlando, and pared from three days to one and a half. The real surprises began during a breakfast speech when the normally upbeat McNerney launched into the sharpest critique of the company he had ever aired before such a large audience. Speaking without notes, McNerney said that "management had gotten away with itself," that too many executives had become used to "hiding in the bureaucracy," and that the company had failed to "develop the best leadership."

The next day, McNerney introduced General Counsel Douglas G. Bain, who really lowered the boom, railing against Boeing's "pervasive culture of silence." To grab the group's attention, Bain rattled off the federal prison numbers of two jailed former employees. "These are not zip codes," Bain snapped. With McNerney looking on in clear support, Bain warned the audience that many prosecutors "believe that Boeing is rotten to the core."

McNerney said to a *BusinessWeek* reporter, "I think the culture had morphed in dysfunctional ways in some places. There are elements of our culture that I think we all would like to change."

The new CEO's plans were to unite a Balkanized management team that had been at war ever since Boeing merged with McDonnell Douglas Corp. in 1997. The distinct cultures of the two companies never meshed, and differences calcified into bitter rivalries. McNerney believes that internal rivalry not only is the root of the company's ethical scandals but also has prevented managers from cutting costs and sharing good ideas effectively. His prescription includes exerting more effective central leadership over Boeing's three divisions, changing the way executives are paid, and encouraging managers to exploit the giant manufacturing's cost-cutting leverage. McNerney also plans to encourage managers to talk more openly about Boeing's ethical lapses. "I want to try to make it OK to have that dialogue," says McNerney. The scandals at Boeing aren't something that happened in a separate part of the company for which half of us aren't responsible."[1]

The surprising story about one of the world's best-known—and often prosperous—companies illustrates how a negative culture can breed ethically inappropriate behavior and bickering among warring groups within the organization. Infighting between different divisions with a supposedly united organization represents a dysfunctional form of political behavior. In this chapter, we explore how the context, or setting, of an organization or organizational unit can influence political maneuvering. Toward this end, we first describe aspects of organizational culture most closely associated with political behavior, and suggestions for sizing up the organizational culture in terms of its political nature. We then offer ideas for analyzing a worker's immediate political environment, and for evaluating the ethics of a given political tactic.

DIMENSIONS OF ORGANIZATIONAL CULTURE RELATED TO ORGANIZATIONAL POLITICS

As most readers are aware, **organizational culture** is a system of shared values and beliefs that influence worker behavior. The organizational culture profoundly influences the extent to which political behavior takes place, and also the intensity with which the political tactics are put into play. A highly competitive firm such as a Wall Street investment bank, with loads of people competing for advancement, might be described as a political jungle. Workers throughout the organization will make frequent use of political tactics, such as ingratiating themselves with powerful people at every opportunity. At the same time, they will make intensive use of these tactics, such as giving expensive gifts to people in power. In extreme contrast, workers at a home for assisted living might be much less competitive, and the political tactics used would be implemented in low-key style. For example, a frequent political tactic might be to do small favors for coworkers, such as helping them scrape snow from the windshield of their cars in the parking lot.

Here we look at a number of dimensions, or components, of organizational culture that strongly influence the presence of organizational politics. The more of these dimensions favoring political behavior that are found to be present, the more political the organization is likely to be. Also, organizational culture is said to mediate political behavior in the sense that in some organizational cultures political behavior is more acceptable. The dimensions described here help explain why some cultures breed more political behavior.[2]

1. *Power struggles.* Several organizational theorists, including Jeffrey Pfeffer and Charles Perrow, see organizations as environments in which individuals and groups struggle for limited resources.[3] Given that most organizations are hierarchies, the dimension of struggling for power is likely to be present to some extent in most organizations. The more pronounced the value, the greater the extent to which politics will be present. Although few senior-level managers are likely to admit that struggling for power is a key corporate value, the struggle for power might be recognized by most workers. Some of the past excesses of the corrupt Enron Corporation were attributed to an environment in which the struggle for power prompted managers and financial analysts to seek ever more creative ways of making money.

2. *Fear.* Although most organizational theorists would not classify fear as a value, a culture characterized by fear of being punished, or even of being fired, triggers considerable political activity. A climate of fear fosters such political behaviors as making yourself look good, covering your backside, and blaming others for mistakes. During Carly Fiorina's five-year reign as CEO of Hewlett-Packard, many workers feared either being downgraded for poor performance or losing their jobs. In her first several years in office, 17,900 employees lost their jobs. Fiorina worked 16 hours per day herself, and expected HP employees to work much harder than they had done in the past. A company veteran said, "Employees are now viewed as assets or tools, no different than machines or buildings." As part of the climate of fear, Fiorina instituted the concept of automatically firing the bottom 5% of performers.[4] At one point, workers marched outside a HP facility carrying signs much like pickets. Two of the placards read, "Fire two instead of 15,000," and "Carly's dream is a nightmare for workers."

3. *The importance of human interaction.* Edgar Schein, a pioneer in the scholarly study of organizational culture, observes that organizations make a variety of assumptions about how people interact with each other. Some facilitate interaction among people, while others regard it as a distraction.[5] When interaction among workers is welcome, political behavior is more likely to be positive—such as building networks and creating allies. When interaction is regarded as a distraction, political behavior tends to be more limited in scope, yet also more negative. For example, when interaction is not welcomed, workers are more likely to use e-mail to voice complaints about each other rather than to give compliments.

A related aspect of welcoming interaction is the extent to which the culture is characterized by an *open-door environment.* In such an environment, managers welcome spontaneous visits as well as spontaneous e-mail messages.[6] The open-door environment encourages politicking of a positive nature, such as offering managers compliments about themselves, working conditions, and the company's products and services. Many technology companies have created such an environment, with an emphasis on open work structures in which the management team works in cubicles alongside other workers.

4. *Trust and respect for the individual.* The more an organization values trust and respect for the individual, the less prevalent are negative political behaviors such as blaming others and backstabbing. For many years, the HP Way was the dominant cultural dimension at Hewlett-Packard. It was a code of behavior established by founders Bill Hewlett and Dave Packard. The first sentence of the code states, "We have trust and respect for the individual."[7] Partly as a result of this value, HP was not regarded as a highly political environment. During the reigns of Carly Fiorina and then Mark Hurd, about 30,000 HP workers were downsized, leading to a weakening of the cultural dimension of trust and respect. As HP has returned to high prosperity, including reclaiming its lead in personal computers, trust and respect for individuals is making a comeback at the company. As a consequence, more emphasis in placed on relationship-building approaches to organizational politics.

5. *Organizational stories with underlying meanings.* Stories are circulated in many organizations to reinforce principles that top management thinks are important. An oft-repeated story is how company officials or other workers inconvenienced themselves to satisfy a customer or client need. A positive example is the true story about how the founders of the upscale supermarket

chain Wegmans, Robert Wegman, would bag groceries or help direct traffic in the supermarket parking lot on particularly busy days. Several energy companies circulate stories about how a C-level manager pumped gas for an elderly customer who was experiencing difficulty with the self-service pumps. When these stories are widely repeated, and considered to indicate valued behavior, managers will attempt to be perceived positively by emulating these sterling deeds. The political behavior is positive and winds up helping customers. Sometimes the story might be about employee relations, such as the CEO donating money so a worker can visit a critically ill family member. Here, too, emulating the behavior for political purposes has positive consequences.

6. *Myths.* Myths are dramatic narratives or imagined events about the firm's history. (A myth is generally more exaggerated than an organizational story.) At United Parcel Service (UPS) and FedEx, for example, stories are repeated about drivers—and even company officials—overcoming severe obstacles or reaching inaccessible locations to deliver packages. A story might even be as dramatic as a manager flying in a helicopter to help deliver medical supplies. Political actors who dream up stunts to prove their customer loyalty usually help the organization, so long as company resources are not squandered in the process. An example of such squandering would be to express ship an inexpensive part from Taiwan to New York to satisfy a customer problem.

7. *Organizational heroes and heroines.* Related somewhat to stories and myths, organizations tend to have role models who personify the value systems which demonstrate what the organization defines as success. The heroic figures are often members of upper management, but they could also be other figures such as a sales representative who made a giant sale that saved the company from financial peril or an information technology specialist who rescued the company from a giant virus attack.[8] The positive political consequence of heroes and heroines is that some workers may attempt to engage in behavior and performance that is highly valued in this way. However, the negative side is that some workers may attempt to become heroic figures instead of taking care of more mundane responsibilities, such as responding to inquiries from small customers or assisting others with routine software problems.

8. *Stratification of organizational members.* In a highly stratified organization, people at lower levels are considered to have much less power and status than people at higher levels. Carroll L. Shartle originally identified the stratification dimension as an aspect of group and organizational functioning.[9]

By nature, a steep hierarchy is more stratified than a flatter organization. Nevertheless, in some hierarchical organizations there is a more dramatic difference in status among the various layers. For example, during Bob Nardelli's reign (2000–2006) at Home Depot, he was earning over $12 million per year while many full-time store workers were earning about $20,000 per year. The head of human resources was earning over $6 million during the same time period. A highly stratified organization encourages more political behavior because so many workers feel power deprived. Also, in a highly stratified organization there are more higher-ranking individuals to impress, leading to more political behavior.

9. *Belief in a higher purpose.* A dominant characteristic of the companies judged to be the 100 Best Companies to Work For is that employees have a sense of purpose. Employees derive deep satisfaction from feeling that what they do is good and right. A belief in a higher purpose is easy to understand if one works for an educational institution, hospital, or pharmaceutical company. Yet employees of some financial services firms believe that they are occupying a useful role in society. For example, at Vanguard, the mutual fund giant, helping people pay for retirement is part of the mission.[10] The link between belief in a higher purpose and organizational politics is that the higher purpose will prompt workers toward being less concerned about self-interest and more concerned about the greater good. As a result, political behavior is minimized. Yet some positive political behavior might be useful for the purpose of amassing power, so that more people can be helped.

10. *Rites and rituals.* Part of a firm's culture is made up of its traditions, or its rites and rituals. Few companies think they have rights and rituals, yet an astute observer can identify them. Examples include regular staff meetings, retirement banquets (even for downsized executives), and receptions for visiting dignitaries. The rites-and-rituals dimension makes a small contribution to organization politics because it is considered politically unwise to skip these events or to mock them. Many workers who dread company picnics will attend anyway to avoid being perceived as disloyal.

The general point about the dimensions of culture just described is that the organizational culture, through its various dimensions, can foster both negative and positive political tactics. A strong culture will have a bigger effect than a weak culture, and a strong culture is difficult to change.

DIAGNOSING THE ORGANIZATIONAL CULTURE AND CLIMATE FOR POLITICAL BEHAVIOR

Understanding the dimensions of an organizational culture is a helpful starting point in identifying the types of political behavior that are likely to take place in the organization. It is also helpful to take a careful diagnostic investigation into the extent of political behavior. Exhibit 2.1 presents an instrument to get you thinking in the direction of sizing the political environment. The index contains 25 statements about political behaviors. By reflecting on the extent to which these behaviors are present in an organization familiar to you, it is possible to make a tentative diagnosis of the political nature of the organization. Because political behaviors are unlimited, 25 statements are at best a representative list of symptoms of organizational politics. Yet reflecting on these indicators of political behavior will help sensitize you to other aspects of politics in a given company.

SIZING UP THE SITUATION RELATED TO POLITICAL BEHAVIOR

Understanding the political nature of the organizational culture is important, but not sufficient for understanding the political nature of the workplace. It is also important to size up the given situation, and to examine national cultural factors that influence the appropriate political behavior. As illustrated in Exhibit 2.2, however, the organizational culture influences individual and group behavior. For example, a manager's preferences for appropriate political behavior of group members might be influenced by the organizational culture. In a trustful organization, the manager might expect group members to be open and honest. Also, the organizational culture might be influenced by individual and group factors, as well as by the national culture. An example would be that managers in a company in the United Kingdom might welcome refined and polite behavior.

Our discussion of the situation in relation to choosing the appropriate political behavior includes the preferences of the manager, work group influences, and dimensions of national culture.

Preferences of the Work Unit Manager

A major situational influence in choosing an appropriate or effective political tactic is the preferences of the immediate manager. For example, if the

Exhibit 2.1 The Political Culture Index

Directions: Use the following instrument to size up the political nature of any organization familiar to you, such as a present or past employer of any type. Your answers will be based on subjective impressions, and you may have to stretch your imagination to assign a rating of 1 through 5 to some of the statements. Circle your answers and later add the total.

Observation About the Organization	*Definitely False*	*Somewhat False*	*A Mixture of True and False*	*Somewhat True*	*Definitely True*
1. "Yes-people" are the most likely to be promoted.	1	2	3	4	5
2. You need a mentor or buddy to figure out what is expected of you.	1	2	3	4	5
3. Top-level managers act like they are a private club that is difficult to join.	1	2	3	4	5
4. Laughing at the boss's humor really works.	1	2	3	4	5
5. An effective way to convince people is to say, "This is what the corner office would be like."	1	2	3	4	5
6. What counts around here is not what you know but who you know.	1	2	3	4	5
7. The company talks a lot about welcoming diversity but I don't see much evidence that it is true.	1	2	3	4	5

(Continued)

Exhibit 2.1 (Continued)

Observation About the Organization	*Definitely False*	*Somewhat False*	*A Mixture of True and False*	*Somewhat True*	*Definitely True*
8. There are some people on the payroll who do not appear to have a real job.	1	2	3	4	5
9. Flirting with the boss is a good way to get a bigger than average salary increase.	1	2	3	4	5
10. Some of the different divisions in the company act like warring tribes.	1	2	3	4	5
11. Not attending a company social event can get you out of favor.	1	2	3	4	5
12. Exchanging gossip is a daily activity.	1	2	3	4	5
13. E-mail is often used to explain why somebody is right and somebody else wrong.	1	2	3	4	5
15. The distribution lists on many e-mail messages are used mostly to impress other people.	1	2	3	4	5
16. Top-level management is known to spy on other workers.	1	2	3	4	5
17. I have seen or heard about lots of backstabbing.	1	2	3	4	5
18. You see more cliques around here than you would in a high school.	1	2	3	4	5

Observation About the Organization	*Definitely False*	*Somewhat False*	*A Mixture of True and False*	*Somewhat True*	*Definitely True*
19. It is common practice for managers to steal ideas from subordinates.	1	2	3	4	5
20. Being a kiss-up helps you get ahead in this place.	1	2	3	4	5
21. People in key positions tend to look alike and talk alike.	1	2	3	4	5
22. We have a lot of in-groups and out-groups.	1	2	3	4	5
23. You need a lot of face time with your manager to get on his or her good side.	1	2	3	4	5
24. The messenger of bad news falls into disfavor quickly.	1	2	3	4	5
25. The executives think they should be treated like royalty.	1	2	3	4	5

Total: _____

Interpretation: The higher the score, the more the organizational culture breeds political behavior. However, the individual statements themselves are also useful in helping to understand the type of political behavior that is practiced and acceptable in the organization being evaluated. For example, statement 1 says, "Yes-people are the most likely to get promoted," suggesting that being a "yes-man" or "yes-woman" helps a person advance in the organization.

If possible, compare your diagnosis of the political nature of your organization culture with someone else familiar with the organization. If you agree on about one-half the ratings (especially for ratings of 1 and 5) you have probably accurately sized up the political environment.

Exhibit 2.2 The Reciprocal Influences of Various Factors on Organizational Politics

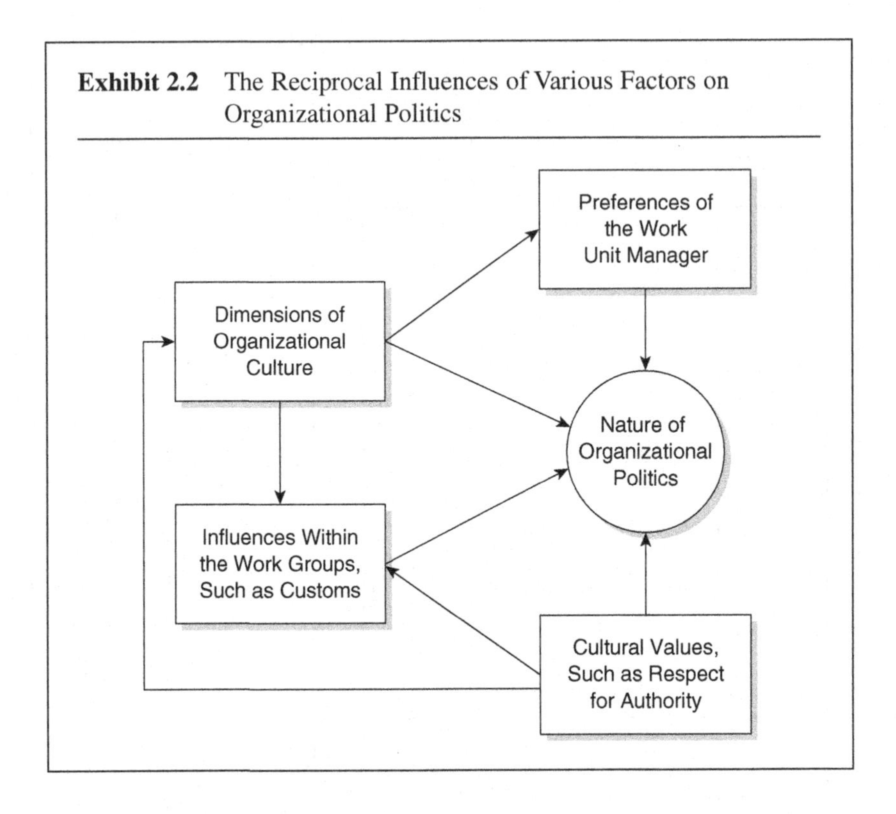

boss welcomes an open and honest work environment, the effective organizational politician offers the boss constructive criticism about work-related issues. In contrast, if the boss prefers deference, the political actor is more muted and less direct in offering criticism. Following is a list of representative questions which can be answered to help decide which political tactics to choose.[11]

1. *What mission is my manager trying to accomplish?* The key to creating a favorable impression on your boss is to help him or her accomplish the most important task facing the organizational unit. The question might be worth asking, in a nonthreatening way, in an individual or group meeting. An example would be, "Are we trying to focus on introducing new services this year? Or is consolidation of what we have and cutting back on costs more important?"

2. *What is the most vexing problem facing my manager?* Give top job priority to those problems of biggest concern to the boss—problems which might ordinarily be linked to the mission. It makes both political and common sense

to tackle these problems. If you find a solution, you will be highly valued by your boss. If you find no solution, you will still be perceived positively for having tried—providing you do not exacerbate the problem. An example of a vexing problem solved by a group member took place at a department store. The manager's most vexing problem was to figure out more sensible ways for the store to be environmentally friendly. The subordinate came in with a playbook from Wal-Mart that included low-maintenance flooring (therefore fewer cleaning chemicals) and more skylighting.

3. *What does my manager regard as superior performance?* In a professionally managed company, performance standards are explicit. However, not all managers are highly professional. An accountant asked her boss, a business owner, what she could do in her job to make a sensational contribution. To her surprise, the business owner answered, "Get our income taxes lower." The accountant then had a new focus on her path toward superior performance.

4. *What practices of group members usually irritate my manager?* Avoid annoying someone you are trying to impress. If your boss dislikes being bombarded with e-mail messages, minimize the number of messages you send. If your boss believes strongly in goal setting, do not complain that goals interfere with your spontaneity.

5. *Does my boss accept compliments graciously?* It is to your political advantage to observe how your manager or team leader receives compliments before praising his or her ordinary actions. A given manager may not think that it is within the role of a group member to compliment him or her, so offering this manager frequent compliments might lead to the manager having a negative perception of you.

6. *What forms of organizational politics does my boss practice?* A cautious guideline is to assume that the type of office politics your manager practices is the type of office politics the boss would consider acceptable to use. Smart politics should include those practices condoned by your manager. For example, if your manager spends considerable time networking to build alliances throughout the company, you might engage in similar behavior and make it known to your boss that you are doing so.

7. *How much does my boss welcome conferring with subordinates?* The modern manager is supposed to consult with group or team members before

making a decision. Nevertheless, managers vary widely in the amount of time they are willing to spend consulting with subordinates. If a manager welcomes input from the group, it is politically sensible to be eager to provide such input, even taking the initiative to maker a contribution. If the manager is not eager to receive group input, wait until asked to contribute to a group decision.

The topic of political tactics for relationships with the manager will be explored at length in Chapter 4.

Work Group Influences on Political Behavior

The immediate work group exerts a major influence on appropriate political behavior. A good starting point for engaging in politically astute behavior is to observe the customs of your work group, especially when you are a new member. If you do not observe the customs, you run the risk of offending colleagues. For six months after starting a new job, a project manager did not check her e-mail over the weekend. "I didn't know," she said. "No one told me." As a result, some group members interpreted her behavior as being indifferent about her work.[12]

Sizing up work group customs and norms is important because few of them are written into the job description. The group will provide clues over such matters as how much to depend on administrative support, particularly because managers and professionals use the Internet and Microsoft Office as their main forms of administrative support. In some companies, office assistants make travel arrangements. In other companies, managers and professionals go online to make their own arrangements and asking for help would violate the company's self-reliant culture.

Breaking the work group's and the company's unwritten culture can have lasting consequences. Ben Dattner, an organizational effectiveness consultant, notes that coworkers may label the newcomer as an outsider who doesn't fit in with the new corporate culture. "You're stuck in your old culture, or you're not going to get it, or you're the new person, so you're not meant to be taken seriously," he says.[13]

To help avoid making political mistakes, such as not answering e-mail over the weekend, it is useful to ask questions about work group customs, and also to make observations. For example, if other workers ask the department assistant for help in making travel arrangements, you might do the same.

Leader–member exchange (LMX) theory provides some insight into deciding upon appropriate political behavior. According to LMX, the quality of the leader–member exchanges determines the nature of certain outcomes for group members. In-group members tend to be more satisfied and productive, and have more open communication with the leader. People become in-group members when their relationship with the leader is generally positive. Neutral to negative relationships result in being part of the out-group. Much of the exchanges between leader and members are political in nature, with in-group members tending to be more political than out-group members.[14]

Membership in the in-group is often based on first impressions by the leader, yet workers may still strive to join the in-group. The behavior of coworkers may provide clues as to what behaviors are necessary to become part of the in-group. Among the possibilities are in-group members disseminating abundant information to the leader, making more effective PowerPoint presentations, supporting the leader more in meetings, or using more of the expressions and clichés used by the leader. One person striving to be part of the in-group in a real-estate development company said, "If I have to repeat that nauseating 'At the end of the day' five times a day, I will do it to get on Larry's good side." Engaging in behaviors that lead to in-group membership would therefore be politically motivated.

Dimensions of National Culture Values Influencing Organizational Politics

Another situational influence on the choice and acceptability of political tactics is the prevailing national culture. If you work at the foreign affiliate of your company, you should take into account cultural values and attitudes which might influence what tactics are acceptable. Here we look at five dimensions of cultural values that could influence what constitutes acceptable political behavior. Recognize that these dimensions are stereotypes, representing a typical value for a person in a given culture.[15] You might find, for example, that most Chinese people are oriented more toward the group than toward seeking individual recognition. However, you might meet some Chinese people who are egotistical and self-centered.

1. *Individualism versus collectivism.* At one end of the continuum is individualism, a mental set in which people see themselves first as individuals and believe that their own interests take priority. Members of a society who value individualism are more concerned with their careers than with the good of the firm. Members of a society who value collectivism, in contrast, are typically

more concerned with the organization or the work group than with themselves. An example of individualistic behavior would be to want to win an Employee of the Month award; an example of collectivistic behavior would be to want to win an award for the team. Highly individualistic cultures include the United States, Canada, and the Netherlands. Japan and Mexico are among the countries that strongly value collectivism. However, with the increasing emphasis on teamwork in American culture, more U.S. workers are becoming collectivistic.

Working in a collectivistic culture, it would be politically sound to emphasize to others how much you enjoy teamwork, and to make frequent use of terms such as "us," "the team," "the group," and "the guys and gals." In an individualistic culture, it would be politically acceptable to showcase your individual accomplishments.

2. *Acceptance of power and authority.* People from some cultures accept the idea that members of an organization have different levels of power and authority. In a culture that believes in concentration of power and authority, the boss makes many decisions simply because he or she is the boss. Group members readily comply because they have a positive orientation toward authority, including a high degree of respect for elders. In a culture with less acceptance of power and authority, employees do not recognize a power hierarchy. They accept directions only when they think the boss is right or when they feel threatened. Cultures that readily accept power and authority include France, China, and India. Countries with much less acceptance of power and authority are the United States and particularly the Scandinavian countries (e.g., Sweden).

Acceptance of power and authority is a major cultural value affecting political behavior. If the culture and the organization highly value power and authority, it behooves the political player to be deferential toward authority. "The boss is always right" has always been a theme song of the office politician, and the theme applies particularly well in a highly stratified firm. It is also important in such a firm to not be openly critical of senior management when discussing the company with colleagues. In a less rank-conscious culture, deference toward authority is a less effective political tactic.

3. *Formality versus informality.* A country that values formality attaches considerable importance to tradition, ceremony, social rules, and rank. At the other extreme, informality refers to a casual attitude toward these same aspects of culture. Workers in Latin American countries highly value formality, such as lavish public receptions and processions. Americans, Canadians, and

Scandinavians are much more informal. Casual observation suggests that most of the industrialized world is becoming more informal through such practices as an emphasis on using the first name only during business introductions.

The same suggestions made in relation to acceptance of power and authority would apply to the value of formality versus informality. In addition, in a formal organization it would be politically astute to dress more formally and not engage in such informal behaviors as talking on a cell phone during group meetings and one-on-one meetings, and reading e-mail while talking to a coworker.

4. *Urgent time orientation versus casual time orientation.* Individuals and nations attach different importance to time. People with an urgent time orientation perceive time as a scarce resource and tend to be impatient. People with a casual time orientation view time as an unlimited and unending resource and tend to be patient. Americans are noted for their urgent time orientation. They frequently impose deadlines and are eager to get started doing business. Asians and Middle Easterners, in contrast, are patient negotiators. Many corporate workers and entrepreneurs engaged in international business recognize the importance of building relationships slowly overseas.

A political consequence of the time orientation value is to show others that time is quite important to you when working in a culture with an urgent time orientation. For example, you might emphasize precise starting and stopping times for meetings, and make statements like, "I will be able to spend 15 minutes with you on this project this morning." In a culture with a casual time orientation, show less concern for time by doing such things as smiling when your manager is late for an appointment with you, and looking at your watch infrequently.

5. *Work orientation versus leisure orientation.* A major cultural difference is the number of hours per week and weeks per year people expect to invest in work versus leisure or other nonwork activities. American corporate professionals typically work about 55 hours per week, take 45-minute lunch breaks, and take two weeks of vacation. Japanese workers share similar values with respect to time invested in work. In contrast, many European countries have steadily reduced the work week in recent years while lengthening vacations.

In a culture with a strong work orientation, talk more about work and less about leisure. Brag about the number of hours you worked last week. In a culture with a strong leisure orientation, be politically astute by talking about leisure activities and the importance of work–life balance.

ETHICAL CONSIDERATIONS IN ORGANIZATIONAL POLITICS

We have already emphasized sizing up the organizational culture and the situation to help determine which political tactics are likely to be appropriate and effective. After identifying suitable tactics, such as those described throughout the book, it is important to evaluate the ethics of a given tactic. Many political tactics are straightforward relationship builders, and require no ethical evaluation. Assume you are jogging in the park, and you pass your boss who is walking his German Shepherd, which you genuinely think is handsome and adorable. So you say to your boss, to gain a grain of political advantage, "What a wonderful-looking dog." You have no need to agonize about the ethics of your decision to behave politically.

The discussion about negative political tactics in Chapter 9 describes many unethical tactics. The two aspects of ethics and political behavior covered here are the intentions of the political actor, and an ethical test.

The Intentions of the Political Actor

When evaluating the ethics of a person engaging in organizational politics, both the means and the ends of political behavior must be considered. In the scenario about the boss and the German Shepherd, you are most likely acting ethically because your end is to establish a better relationship with you manager. To achieve this end, your means is to compliment his or her dog. However, another person complimenting the manager's dog might have an evil end in mind, and therefore be acting unethically. The unethical political actor's intention is to establish rapport with the boss to dig up some negative information that could then be used to discredit the manager or extort a promotion or a large salary increase.

A study of the ethics of organizational politics concluded, "Instead of determining whether human rights or standards of justice are violated, we are often content to judge political behavior according to its outcomes."[16] The authors of the study suggest that, when it comes to the ethics of organizational politics, respect for justice and human rights should prevail for its own sake. According to this perspective on ethics, any time human rights are violated, the political behavior is unethical, even if no one is hurt. Suppose you attempt to trick a coworker by sending him an e-mail with an intentionally incorrect date for a key meeting. His rights have been violated even if he verifies the date of the meeting with another source and just assumes that you made an input error in your e-mail.

Several years ago, World Bank President Paul Wolfowitz was accused of favoritism when his girlfriend, Shaha Riza, was reassigned to a position carrying a tax-free salary of $193,000, about $61,000 more than before she was reassigned. Among the many accusations were that Wolfowitz wrote a memo dictating the salary that Riza, then a communications officer, would earn when she was assigned to a job outside the World Bank, at the expense of the bank. The memo also specified her future salary increases and her status when she returned to the bank after Wolfowitz's term as president expired.[17] The scenario depicted sounded unethical and devious to most people. Wolfowitz, however, claimed he was attempting to create a situation in which a conflict of interest could be avoided by turning responsibility for his girlfriend's transfer to an ethics committee. The point is that the means (favoritism) appeared unethical, but Wolfowitz said his end (attempting to avoid a conflict of interest) was honorable.

A subtle aspect of understanding the intentions of the political actor before concluding that the person is unethical is that we must be clear about the real behavior indicated by a label, such as *favoritism.* If a manager is practicing favoritism by giving an incompetent a good position, that type of favoritism hurts the organization. Yet if favoritism refers to assigning a trusted ally to a good position, that type of favoritism may help the organization. Chris Provis notes that the term "backstabbing" might mean acting contrary to expectations we have induced in someone. Or, thinking more conventionally, backstabbing might refer to going to a third party to complain about someone. In its first meaning, backstabbing would be ethical; in the second meaning, it would be unethical.[18]

A Test of Political Ethics Based on Moral Principles

According to William R. Wieringa, political behavior does not necessarily have to be unethical—which is the same position taken in this text. An act of political behavior is ethical if it satisfies three moral principles:[19]

1. *If the political tactic provides the greatest good for the greatest number of people, it is ethical.* In contrast, if the political tactic mainly benefits the individual, or harms others, then the political behavior is unethical. An example here would be using performance appraisals to assist in downsizing. If the

appraisals are conducted as fairly as possible, and the employees with the lowest appraisals are downsized, then conducting the appraisals would be considered ethical. However, if negative appraisals are purposely assigned to the people management would like to get rid of because they are disliked, then the appraisals are being used in an unethical, political manner.

2. *If the political tactic does not violate anyone else's legal or moral right, it is ethical.* However, if the political behavior threatens another person's privacy, due process, free speech, or other right, then it is inappropriate and unethical even if it benefits the larger group. Assume that Jason receives a compliment by e-mail for a job well done from a manager in another department. Being a political animal, Jason forwards the e-mail to his own boss and his boss's boss. By principle number 2, Jason is behaving ethically. However, if Jason fabricated the e-mail compliment, he would be violating the other manager's privacy and would be acting unethically—and naïvely.

3. *If the political tactic treats all parties fairly, it is ethical.* However, if the tactic benefits those who are better off at the expense of people who are already worse off, it is inappropriate behavior and therefore unethical. Assume vice president Lois believes that she is losing popularity, so she grants larger raises to influential people in her chain of command. She funds the raises by giving very small raises to less influential (and less well-paid) people because her overall budget for raises is fixed. Lois's political act would be unethical by moral principle 3. In contrast, if she found a way to give the same raise to everyone just to build goodwill, she would be acting ethically.

You might apply the moral principles test to political behaviors you are contemplating that are not obviously ethical or unethical. It would also be useful to apply broader ethical screens or tests that you have learned in your study of ethics.

SUMMARY

Ten dimensions of organizational culture related to organizational politics are described here: (1) power struggling, (2) fear, (3) the importance of human interaction, (4) trust and respect for the individual, (5) organizational stories with underlying meanings, (6) myths, (7) organizational heroes and heroines, (8) stratification of organizational members, (9) belief in a higher purpose, and (10) rites and rituals.

A diagnostic investigation into the extent of political behavior is recommended. The Political Culture Index presented in Exhibit 2.1 provides a diagnostic tool. Sizing up the situation related to political behavior, including national cultural dimensions, is also helpful in understanding the political nature of the workplace. In assessing the preferences of the work unit manager, consider (1) the manager's mission, (2) the manager's most vexing problem, (3) the manager's idea of superior performance, (4) practices that irritate the manager, (5) the manager's type of organizational politics, and (6) the manager's preference for conferring with subordinates.

Work group influences on political behavior include understanding the group's customs and norms. Leader–member exchange (LMX) theory provides some clues to sizing up the situation because in-group members have positive relationships with the leader. It may also be helpful to examine the behavior of in-group members.

The prevailing national culture may provide some clues to the choice and acceptability of political tactics within the situation. Five value dimensions of significance are (1) individualism versus collectivism, (2) acceptance of power and authority, (3) formality versus informality, (4) urgent time orientation versus casual time orientation, and (5) work orientation versus leisure orientation.

The ethics of a given political tactic should be evaluated before using the tactic. The intentions of the actor are important with respect to the ends being worthwhile. Respect for justice and human rights is important. A test of political ethics based on moral principles focuses on three issues concerning the political tactics: (1) the greatest good for the greatest number of people, (2) violation of legal and moral rights, and (3) fair treatment for all.

QUESTIONS AND ACTIVITIES

1. If the Boeing Co. had as much infighting and scandalous behavior as described at the start of this chapter, how did the company ever get airplanes out the door?
2. Why would working in a culture of fear prompt some people to behave politically?
3. Create a story or myth that might inspire Microsoft employees. Do the same for Wal-Mart.

4. How might being part of your manager's in-group help you advance in your career?

5. Assume that you are on a one-year assignment in Sweden, and you know that Swedish people emphasize equality rather than being rank conscious. Describe a political tactic you might use to get on the good side of your Swedish boss.

6. Suppose you are on a one-year assignment in India, and you know that Indian people emphasize rank rather than equality in work relationships. Describe a political tactic you might use to get on the good side of your Indian boss.

7. What is your opinion of the ethics of falsely telling people they look wonderful just to enhance your relationship with them?

CASE STUDY: PAY-FOR-PLAY AT THE NORTH CAROLINA TREASURER'S OFFICE

Richard Moore is an appealing politician—so appealing that, although he won reelection as North Carolina's state treasurer in 2004, last year he landed a $4,000 contribution from a self-employed interior designer who lives on the Upper West Side of Manhattan. His benefactor, Julie Marshall, has no real need to fund Moore's likely run for the North Carolina governorship in 2008. "My husband went to a fundraiser in New York and afterward was all excited," she says. Her husband, Gerald Marshall, also gave Moore $4,000; Marshall runs the investment firm Amerimar Enterprises.

As state treasurer, Moore, a Democrat, is the sole fiduciary for the North Carolina Retirement System, with $73 billion in assets. He holds sway over which money managers are entrusted to invest funds from the state pension plans. At stake are millions of dollars in fees. He has parlayed this clout into one of the biggest fundraising machines in the state by eagerly accepting contributions from dozens of financial firms that benefit (or could benefit) from his largesse.

Moore, since winning reelection, has raised more than half a million dollars from the financiers far outside the Tar Heel State, from Massachusetts to California. His campaign fund got $381,000 in this way, 11% of the total take; a fiscal education foundation run from Moore's private office got $163,000. Of 90 firms that invest in North Carolina funds, 40 have employees who funded his campaign.

Employees of another 40 investment firms not working for the state also donated. The campaign donations Moore receives are entirely legal in North Carolina, as they are in most of the United States.

Moore has built his career crusading against conflicts of interest on Wall Street. He calls himself "North Carolina's elected guardian of the state treasury" and advises the New York Stock Exchange on good governance. He forces investment banks that work for the state to swear off conflicts. In 2002, amid a raft of corporate scandals, he grandstanded before a U.S. Senate commerce committee: "We are demanding that broker/dealers and money managers eliminate actual and potential conflict of interest from the way they pay analysts and conduct their affairs."

Moore applies no such prohibitions to himself, and he is unrepentant about it. "I didn't set up the rules, but I play by the rules," he says. "We do not have a culture of pay-to-play in the treasurer's office in the state of North Carolina."

Moore has been feted at out-of-state fundraisers, two of them in the New York home of Donaldson, Lufkin & Jenrette cofounder Richard Jenrette. His contributors include billionaire financiers Steven Schwarzman, Nelson Peltz, and Paul Tudor (none of whom landed state funds). "I don't know what they think they're going to get," says Moore. "I like to think they respect somebody who runs a good business."

Moore duns money managers for dollars: the fees the treasurer's office pays out to them have jumped sixfold under his reign to $116 million in a recent year. North Carolina paid $15 million in incentives to a Deutsche Bank/RREFF real estate fund in a recent fiscal year in which its closing balance was only $29 million. All told, over half the state's fees, or $63 million, went to firms that manage just 6.3% of its assets: hedge, private equity, and real estate funds. These same firms were disproportionately large contributors to Moore's campaign.

Moore's office in each of his last six years as treasurer has failed to provide the state legislature with a state-mandated annual report detailing his managers' results. Moore's state Web site posts sparse details, most of them from past years; it does not disclose the names of the money managers he hires or their fees. When asked for state-mandated reports, Moore said they were unavailable. He handed over data on payments to fund managers after *Forbes* magazine prepared to take him to court. To handle *Forbes*'s inquiries, Moore's office retains the Durham, NC, law firm of Womble Carlyle Sandridge & Rice, and lawyers from that firm kicked in $34,560 to Moore's campaigns. "There's a huge difference between asking for contributions to my campaign and things that go in my own pocket," Moore insists.

Shortly after he was elected treasurer in 2000, Moore won headlines demanding that Wall Street clean up its act. He also persuaded the state legislature to increase the portion of the pension fund in hedge funds and private equity funds—from 0.1% to 5%. Supporting that effort was Eugene McDonald, former manager of Duke University's endowment, who wrote a paper on it. McDonald was a member of Moore's five-person investment committee. After Moore won wide latitude, he quickly handed $400 million to Quellos Asset Management, a private equity firm in Seattle. Quellos's investment chief is Eugene McDonald. Moore stuck with Quellos after it was slammed in 2005 for flogging tax shelters that the U.S. Senate declared "a bowl of spaghetti." The cost to U.S. taxpayers was $300 million.

Asked about this, Moore said McDonald joined Quellos only after the firm got state pension money—a fact that proved to be untrue. Informed on his misstatement, Moore was undaunted, saying that even "if I had known about it, I don't think it would have made any difference." Quellos says it has returned "superior results," but in fact it has earned about half as much as the S&P 500 during a five-year period. In a recent year, Quellos received $6.1 million from Moore's office. Quellos executives, including McDonald, have contributed $16,000 to Moore's campaign.

Billionaire Robert Johnson of BET and seven employees of his RLJ Development kicked $23,000 into Moore's fund. Moore agreed in 2005 to lend $50 million to RLJ for investing. Fourteen executives at Bank of New York gave $22,757 to Moore. His office uses the bank for securities custody.

Tracking Moore's results has been difficult. The state auditor found in 2005 that 40% of his high-risk fund managers ran 6 to 18 months late supplying returns data. One data set, though, shows they are trailing behind industry benchmarks. In five years, hedge and private equity funds returned 2.3% annually for the state against a benchmark of 7.7%, real-estate funds returned 10.5% versus the benchmark 11.9%. Moore hit up 28 of these lavishly paid managers for $211,700.

Case Study Questions

1. In what ways is Richard Moore engaged in organizational politics?
2. What is your evaluation of the ethics of Moore accepting campaign fund contributions from outside investment managers?

3. If the outside investment managers turned in results much superior to those of the benchmarks, would Moore's accepting campaign fund contributions be more acceptable? Explain your reasoning.
4. What recommendations might you offer Moore so he can escape receiving so much outside criticism?
5. How ethical is it for the outside money managers to be making contributions to Moore's campaign fund?

SOURCE: Weinberg, N. (2007). Pensions, polls, payola. *Forbes,* March 12, 42–44.

POLITICAL SKILL-BUILDING EXERCISE 2

Creating an Organizational Story With an Underlying Meaning

This exercise about organizational stories to communicate an underlying meaning proceeds in two stages, and involves a group role-play.

Stage 1: Visualize one of your favorite companies, with you being a highly placed manager in that company. Your job is to create a story that tells an important message about the company and its values. An example is that Microsoft circulates the story about how the heroic Bill Gates would sleep under his desk during the early years at Microsoft so he could spend as much time as possible writing the software that propelled the company to greatness. The story has helped communicate a strong work ethic at the company. Your story can be just one or two minutes in length, but it should communicate a strong message.

Stage 2: Each manager/storyteller meets with about five other classmates who play the role of new employees during a company orientation. All five members of the group will have their chance at being (a) a storyteller and (b) an employee going through the orientation. When you are the storyteller, communicate your story with passion and commitment. The four other employees can be as cooperative (gullible) or as skeptical as they would like. However, being politically astute, several of the employees will most likely express appreciation for the message sent by the manager.

After the role-plays are completed, think through whether if the stories were true they might have had an impact on how the people who heard the story might behave in the organization.

REFERENCES

1. Excerpted from Holmes, S. (2006, March 13). Cleaning up Boeing. *Business Week,* 62–68.

2. Kurchner-Hawkins, R., & Miller, R. (2006). Organizational politics: Building positive political strategies in turbulent times. In E. Vigoda-Gadot & A. Drory (Eds.), *Handbook of organizational politics* (pp. 328–352) [p. 343]. Northampton, MA: Edward Elgar.

3. Cited in Seo, M. G. (2003, March). Overcoming emotional barriers, political obstacles, and control imperatives in the action-science approach to individual and organizational learning. *Academy of Management Learning and Education,* 11.

4. Caudron, S. (2003, July). Don't mess with Carly. *Workforce Management,* 28–33 [p. 30].

5. Schein, E. (2002). Organizational culture and leadership. In Perseus Publishing, *Business: The ultimate resource* (p. 937). Cambridge, MA: Perseus.

6. Perseus Publishing. (2002). Virtual jobs: Staying connected and visible while telecommuting. In *Business: The ultimate resource* (pp. 796–797). Cambridge, MA: Perseus.

7. Colvin, G. (2006, October 16). A growth plan for HP's CEO. *Fortune,* 70.

8. Bowditch, J. L., & Buono, A. F. (2001). *A primer on organizational behavior* (5th ed.) [p. 291]. New York: Wiley.

9. Shartle, C. L. (1956). *Executive performance and leadership* (pp. 63–65). Englewood Cliffs, NJ: Prentice-Hall.

10. Colvin, G. (2006, January 23). The 100 best companies to work for. *Fortune,* 74.

11. DuBrin, A. J. (1990). *Winning office politics: DuBrin's guide for the 90s* (pp. 42–47). Englewood Cliffs, NJ: Prentice Hall.

12. White, E. (2006, November 28). Culture shock: Learning customs of a new office. *Wall Street Journal,* B6.

13. Cited in White, E. (2006, November 28). Culture shock.

14. Graen, G. B., & Uhl-Bien, M. (1995). Relationship-based approach to leadership: Development of leader–member exchange (LMX) theory of leadership over 25 years—applying a multi-level domain perspective. *Leadership Quarterly, 6,* 219–247; James, K. (2006). Antecedents, processes, and outcomes of collective (group-level) politics in organizations. In E. Vigoda-Gadot & A. Drory (Eds.), *Handbook of organizational politics* (pp. 59–60). Northampton, MA: Edward Elgar.

15. Hofstede, G. (1980). *Culture's consequences: International differences in work-related values.* Beverly Hills, CA: Sage; updated and expanded in Hofstede, G. (1993, Spring). A conversation with Geert Hofstede. *Organizational Dynamics,* 53–61; Triandis, H. (2004, February). The many dimensions of culture. *Academy of Management Executive,* 88–93.

16. Cavanagh, G. F., Moberg, D. J., & Valesquez, M. (1981, July). The ethics of organizational politics. *Academy of Management Review,* 363–374 [p. 372].

17. Hitt, G. (2007, April 14–15). Wolfowitz memo, dictating raises given to friend, now haunts him. *Wall Street Journal,* A1, A5.

18. Provis, C. (2006). Organizational politics, definitions and ethics. In E. Vigoda-Gadot & A. Drory (Eds.), *Handbook of organizational politics* (pp. 89–106) [p. 102]. Northampton, MA: Edward Elgar.

19. Wieringa, W. R. (2004). Office politics. *Fair practices, LLC.* Retrieved 03/07/2007 from www.fairpractices.com.

PART II

STRATEGIES AND TACTICS OF POSITIVE ORGANIZATIONAL POLITICS

THREE

MAJOR INITIATIVES FOR ACQUIRING POWER

LEARNING OBJECTIVES

After studying this chapter and doing the exercises, you should be able to do the following:

1. Identify 10 sources and types of power.
2. Be prepared to perform a power analysis before attempting to acquire power within an organization.
3. Describe a variety of strategies and tactics for acquiring power.
4. Understand how power can be abused within organizations.

Kimberly Davis, age 47, is senior vice president, global philanthropy at JPMorganChase and president of the JP Morgan Chase Foundation in New York. She has survived—and thrived—after eight banking industry mergers. Part of the story she explained to a business reporter is presented next:

> In 1995, Chase and Chemical Bank merged. Chemical and Manufacturer's Hanover had just merged, and those two organizations hadn't really integrated when Chase and Chemical merged, so it was really three mergers: Manufacturer's Hanover, Chemical, and Chase. That was very ugly and the

cultures were very different. There was a lot of infighting. But I met the head of human resources at an event a year before the merger. When the merger happened, I got a call from him saying he was impressed with me, and I took the initiative to build a relationship with him. He later had a big opportunity in human resources and asked me if I'd be willing to do a two-year stint. People thought I was crazy to leave a P&L [profit and loss] position and move to human resources, but strategically it was a wonderful way for me to learn the new organization from the top. Being in that staff role in corporate, I was able to see all of the business as opposed to being in a narrow business premerger.

Once a merger is on the horizon, a professional has to be prepared. You have to identify where the growth opportunities are, and what the new business model is going to be. Who's in power, who's out of power? Align yourself with those who are in power and show your ability to deliver results very quickly. Don't be afraid to take the risk of knocking on doors, getting to know people, letting people know your intentions about your career. Many times after a merger we lay low and want to let the dust settle. All of the good opportunities are being divvied up while we're lying low. It takes a long time even after a merger is announced for things to become integrated—almost two years. There's a lot that you can deliver and produce during that period of time.[1]

Kimberly Davis tells us a lot about holding on to and gaining power in a complex organization. Among her strategies and tactics were to form an alliance with a powerful person, conduct a power analysis of the organization, and deliver some good results in a hurry. **Power** has several definitions, but not as many as organizational politics. A representative meaning of the term is the ability or potential to influence. An entrepreneur who has launched several successful businesses is powerful because he or she influenced many people in the past to invest in those enterprises. The same entrepreneur is powerful because he or she has the potential to attract investors into other enterprises in the future.[2]

The meaning of power, as formulated by Max Weber over 60 years ago, provides additional insight: power is the probability that a person can carry out his or her own will despite resistance.[3] For example, a retailing CEO might decide to close a bunch of underperforming stores despite many home-office managers and store managers objecting to the plan.

Both meanings of power point to the idea of other people's perception in determining whether a person is powerful. If others think you are powerful, you will often get what you want. Another point to consider in understanding power is that it is often a positive force, such as Wal-Mart executives using their power to influence consumers to purchase fluorescent rather than incandescent light bulbs.

In this chapter, we focus on major approaches to acquiring power, including understanding where power stems from, identifying who holds power in the organization, and offering a description of power-gaining methods; we also mention the abuse of power.

THE SOURCES AND TYPES OF POWER

The s*ources and types of power refer* to where power stems from. Because you may already be familiar with this information, these power sources and types are listed briefly here.[4] Some of the sources and types of power stem from the position one occupies, and others from personal characteristics.

Position Power

Sources of power stemming from the organization are listed below. To some extent, society grants some of the power because public organizations (those owned by stockholders) are chartered by the state.

1. *Legitimate power.* The lawful right to make a decision and expect compliance is referred to as *legitimate power.* **Legitimate power** usually varies directly with the organizational level of the position. A study about executives getting their stock options repriced in a way favorable to them illustrates the workings of legitimate power. When the CEO also occupied the position of chairman of the board, the favorable repricing was more likely.[5] In recent years, business executives at numerous firms have exerted their legitimate power to have the timing of their strike price (the price when the option is granted) changed to create wealth for themselves—a tactic of questionable legality.

2. *Reward power.* The authority to give employees rewards for compliance and good performance is referred to as **reward power.** The person who authorizes your pay and evaluates your performance has some power over you.

3. *Coercive power.* The power to punish for noncompliance or poor performance is referred to as **coercive power.** This type of power is based on fear, and therefore is primarily effective when people perceive themselves to have limited options, such as finding another job.

4. *Information power.* The power stemming from formal control over the information people need to do their work is **information power.** A minor example would be the authority to issue passwords that enable workers to access company databases or the intranet. A bigger example would be a real estate developer giving brokers leads on potential purchasers of residences or buildings.

5. *Dependence.* According to the **dependence perspective,** one person accrues power through others being dependent on that person for the things they value. Because the things valued could be physical resources or a personal relationship, dependence power can be positional or personal. Richard M. Emerson noted that the power resides implicitly in the other's dependence.[6] A modern example is that the healthcare system in the United States is becoming more dependent on information technology to help streamline the system. Healthcare information technology specialists therefore have more power. In the words of Lee Scott, the CEO of Wal-Mart, whose company is developing in-store clinics, "Health IT is perhaps the single largest opportunity to drive cost out of the healthcare system."[7]

6. *Providing resources.* An extension of the dependency model is the **resource dependence perspective.** It states that the organization requires a continuing flow of human resources, money, customers, technological inputs, and material to continue to function. Subunits or individuals within the organizations who can provide these resources derive power from this ability.[8] The example of the health IT specialist fits here also.

7. *Centrality.* Power stemming from being close to power is referred to as **centrality.** When others perceive you to be "in the loop" because your position places you in contact with powerful people, you are considered to be influential. An administrative assistant to a major executive or a person occupying a position such as assistant to the CEO therefore acquires some power. For example, many organization members believe that people occupying these two positions can be instrumental in getting a proposal listened to or approved by the CEO.

Personal Power

The characteristics or behaviors of the power actor create several sources of types of power. All are classified as **personal power** because they are derived from the person rather than the organization.

1. *Expert power.* The ability to influence others through specialized skills, knowledge, and ability is referred to as **expert power.** The vast majority of successful careers are based on expert power, such as being an outstanding sales representative, information systems specialist, or contract negotiator. A current example is Edward (Eddie) S. Lampert, whose knowledge of exotic investments called hedge funds provided the base for his becoming a highly influential businessperson. He is featured in the case study to this chapter.

According to the research of D. J. Hickson and colleagues, expert power makes others dependent on you to the extent that another person with your expertise cannot readily be found.[9] For example, if you are the only person available in your company who knows how to prepare documentation for an ISO (International Standards Organization) certification, you will have power at least temporarily.

2. *Referent power.* The ability to influence others through desirable traits and characteristics is referred to as **referent power.** Being perceived as charismatic is often a combination of referent power and expert power because attaining good results contributes to a person's aura. Part of the referent power comes from the unconscious tendency of many workers to relate to their leader as some important person from the past, such as a parent, a sibling, close friend, or even a nanny. If the person from the past was liked, the leader will have stronger referent power.[10] For example, a manager at Avon Products who had a great relationship with her mother might attempt to please Avon CEO Andrea Jung.

3. *Prestige power.* The power stemming from one's status and reputation is referred to as **prestige power.**[11] A manager who has accumulated major business successes acquires prestige power. Developing a good reputation within your specialty in your industry is therefore a major career-building tactic. An example would be developing a good reputation as a municipal bond trader within the state of New Jersey.

4. *Connection power.* The use of people in your network who can influence the person you are dealing with is **connection power.**[12] The importance of being connected and developing allies is stressed throughout this book, particularly in Chapter 8 about social networks.

An understanding of where power stems from helps a person perform a power analysis as presented next. Before delving further into a study of power, it could prove illuminating to reflect on your own desire for power as provided for in Exhibit 3.1.

Exhibit 3.1 My Power Orientation

Directions: Rate each statement on a 1-to-5 scale: (1) disagree strongly; (2) disagree; (3) neutral; (4) agree; (5) agree strongly.

Statement	*Rating*
1. A major purpose of my career is to gain power for myself.	
2. Power is beautiful.	
3. I would like to be as rich and famous as Warren Buffett or Oprah Winfrey.	
4. I would like to have an important building such as a college, high school, or hospital named after me.	
5. I look forward to the day when I have my own charitable foundation.	
6. It would make me happy to own a professional sports team.	
7. I would hope that someday a Google search of my name would find at least a million entries.	
8. I enjoy controlling other people in terms of having them do what I want them to do.	
9. My hope is to own a private jet rather than relying on commercial airplanes.	
10. I hope that some people will fear doing me wrong or irritating me.	
11. I like to have lots of people dependent on me.	
12. I would like to develop rare expertise that would make me important and well-known.	
13. It would make me happy to be perceived as charismatic by many people.	
14. I like the idea of my name being a trademark, just like that of Donald Trump™.	
15. It would be fabulous for me to be on the *Forbes* list of the 400 richest people in the world.	
16. I aspire to become a member of top management.	

Statement	*Rating*
17. I aspire to serve on the board of at least one major corporation.	
18. I would enjoy having residence in at least three homes, with one of them being in another country.	
19. I would like to be included in *Time* magazine's annual list of the 100 most influential people in the world.	
20. Analyzing my power orientation in this quiz is getting me excited about the possibilities of my becoming extremely powerful.	

Scoring and Interpretation: Add the numbers you have circled to attain your total score.

90–100 You have an unusually strong drive for power, fame, and wealth. With this much of a power drive, you might have to guard against being ruthless, manipulative, and cruel. However, please invite your professor and your author for a ride on the 100-foot yacht you will most likely own in the future.

71–89 You have a strong drive for power, fame, and wealth. Many people in prominent positions have similar strivings for and attitude toward power.

41–70 You have a moderate drive for power, fame, and wealth. You are likely to achieve many of your career goals without obsessing over accomplishment.

20–40 You have an unusually low drive for power, fame, and fortune. You may need to increase your level of self-motivation from time to time. Guard against the perception of being too laid back.

PERFORMING A POWER ANALYSIS

An axiom of applying strategies and tactics for acquiring power is to first figure out where the power lies in the organization and who the power players are. Before you can ally yourself with powerful people, you first have to know who they are. A power analysis is also useful when attempting to identify who would make a strong mentor for you. A practical approach to analyzing where power lies in an organization is to find answers to a handful of diagnostic questions.

The political actor would have to ask others for help in answering these questions. Because of their sensitive nature, many of the questions would be better asked in person, by text messaging, or by telephone rather than e-mail. Some of the questions can also be answered through careful observation. The power analysis questions are presented next.[13]

1. *Is the hierarchy of authority the primary clue to holding the true power here?* The organization chart is the obvious starting point for identifying powerful people. If you studied the organization chart of Starbucks, you would see that the chairman holds more power than a barista. However, you might find that some of the store owners and a few of the managers with lesser titles are able to influence chairman and CEO Howard Schultz. You might find in your analysis that other players besides the people in obvious positions of power are also in a strong position of power or influence.

2. *What drives the top people in positions of power?* What do they really value? Is it profits, sales volume, dividends, expansion, shareholders, customer satisfaction, or high quality? You will impress key people by delivering what they value.

3. *What positions and roles are most valued?* Why? Who is getting developed, mentored, or promoted? What skills, experiences, and behaviors count the most? Who is emulating whom? For example, your digging might indicate that the people who get developed, mentored, and promoted frequently explain how their work adds value for customers.

4. *What other factors seem to be tied to power and influence here?* Being outspoken? Nonchallenging? Well liked? Loyal? Long service? Social or community connections?

5. *Where do you fall in the organizational and power hierarchy?* How does your standing compare with that of others? Do you have any power currency? If so, what is it? If not, why not?

Responses to the above questions will help you understand who the powerful people are and what is valued by the organization. It is also important to redo your analysis from time to time because the powerful payers may change and so might the things the organization values. For example, a subtle shift might take place away from investing in new ideas and toward stabilizing a product line and cost cutting.

After identifying the powerful people in an organization, a refined step would be to analyze how much power or clout the players of most interest to you really have. Finding answers to the following questions should prove helpful in conducting your power analysis.[14]

1. *To whom does this person report? What is that person's position?* The higher a person reports in the hierarchy, the more power he or she possesses. With so many elaborate impressive titles given to managers today, it is helpful to find out to whom a manager actually reports. For example, a manager with the title of "President, North American Operations," might be down several layers in the hierarchy.

2. *How many people report to the person and what kind of work do they perform?* Organizations have flattened considerably in recent years, so the number of direct and indirect reports is an even stronger measure of position power. When organizations were taller, many managers had many direct reports. Another important consideration is the job level of employees in their chain of command. An operations manager with 250 support workers reporting to him might be less influential than a manager of research and development with 35 researchers reporting to her.

3. *Who reviews this person's decisions, and are these decisions often vetoed?* A powerful manager can make many decisions without having to confer with a superior. If the power player you have identified has many decisions vetoed by the next level of management, that individual may not really be so powerful.

4. *How much impact do these persons' decisions have on the organization?* The more impact the person's decisions have on the organization, the more powerful the person is. For example, Marissa Mayer is a member of the Google Management Group, which is one layer below the executive group. She leads a group called Vice President Search Products and User Experiences, and is therefore responsible for product management on Google Search products. As a result, Mayer's decisions have an enormous impact on the livelihood of Google—and she is therefore a powerful person.

5. *How many people of equal rank consult with this person on their decisions?* An unequivocal sign of power is the person who is consulted by coworkers for advice. This is true because such advice is not required and carries no penalty for noncompliance.

6. *How liked or disliked is this person?* A person who is widely liked has a better chance of remaining powerful than one who is widely disliked. Jeffrey Skilling, the former Enron CEO later convicted of securities fraud, was intensely disliked during the later phases of his career—partly because of his abrasiveness. Several of the enemies he had cultivated eagerly testified against him. It is also politically unwise to be closely linked to a despised executive, because you might lose your position when the disliked executive is overthrown.

SOCIAL EXCHANGE THEORY AND THE ACQUISITION OF POWER

Three of the sources of power described above help provide a theoretical explanation of power. Both the dependence and the resource dependence perspectives emphasize that when others need you urgently, you have more power. Expertise as a source of power points to a similar idea—the more people need your knowledge and skill, the more power you have. Another theoretical underpinning to explain power acquisition in organizations is **social exchange theory**, the idea that the most fundamental form of social interaction is an exchange of benefits or favors between two parties. The benefits can be material, such as money, or psychological, such as recognition and appreciation.[15]

Social exchange theory has been used to explain aspects of motivation and leadership, as well as personal relationships. Our concern is with those aspects of the theory that relate most directly to power. The amount of power granted to a person is proportionate to the group's evaluation of what he or she can contribute to the group's benefit. The contribution may focus on matters such as control over scarce resources, access to vital information, or expertise in dealing with key problems. A leader who offered promise of helping an organization find funding for growth would therefore be perceived as powerful. Another way for a leader or a group member to acquire power is to suggest innovative ideas that prove to be successful. For example, Tony Fadell, the person within Apple Corp. who developed the iPod, enhanced his power considerably. The leader or group member who suggests ideas that flop will soon lose power.

Social exchange theory also takes into account position power. The fact of occupying a high-level position gives one the authority to assist others by such means as giving them a job or purchasing their product or service. When the person loses position power, his or her ability to receive worthwhile exchanges from others rapidly diminishes. Unfortunately, many executives who are downsized find that their pool of friends dissipates quickly.

STRATEGIES AND TACTICS FOR ACQUIRING POWER

A major purpose of organizational politics is to acquire power, so an understanding of strategies and tactics aimed directly at acquiring power is an essential part of understanding political behavior in organizations. Several of the tactics listed here would also fit the topics of influence tactics as described in Chapter 7, and networking as described in Chapter 8. Also, many of the techniques for acquiring power stem from the sources and types of power described earlier. More important than attempting to place strategies and tactics into clear-cut categories is to understand their nature and potential application. As outlined in Exhibit 3.2, 10 different methods of acquiring power are presented next.

When studying strategies and tactics for acquiring power, it is helpful to recognize that being powerful helps the power actor acquire what he or she wants, while at the same time avoiding what he or she does not want. Imagine that a company is planning to relocate its headquarters from New York to Raleigh, North Carolina. The marketing executive lives in a penthouse condominium overlooking Central Park, and is quite involved in the social life of New York. Furthermore, her husband and children love living in New York. With enough power, the executive can say, "I'm staying here. I will commute from New York, and maintain a studio apartment in Raleigh. But I am not relocating." If the executive were less powerful, she might be fired for refusing to relocate.

Perform Well and Establish a Good Reputation

As implied from expert power, the development of a power base often stems from using expertise to perform in an outstanding manner. Expertise combined with almost total devotion to work helps make good performance visible to people in power. An extreme example of devotion to performance by a major business executive is Carlos Ghosn, who for several years was the chief executive of both Renault and Nissan. A sample of his work schedule is that during the month of October 2006 he traveled 18,300 miles on business

Exhibit 3.2 Strategies and Tactics for Acquiring Power

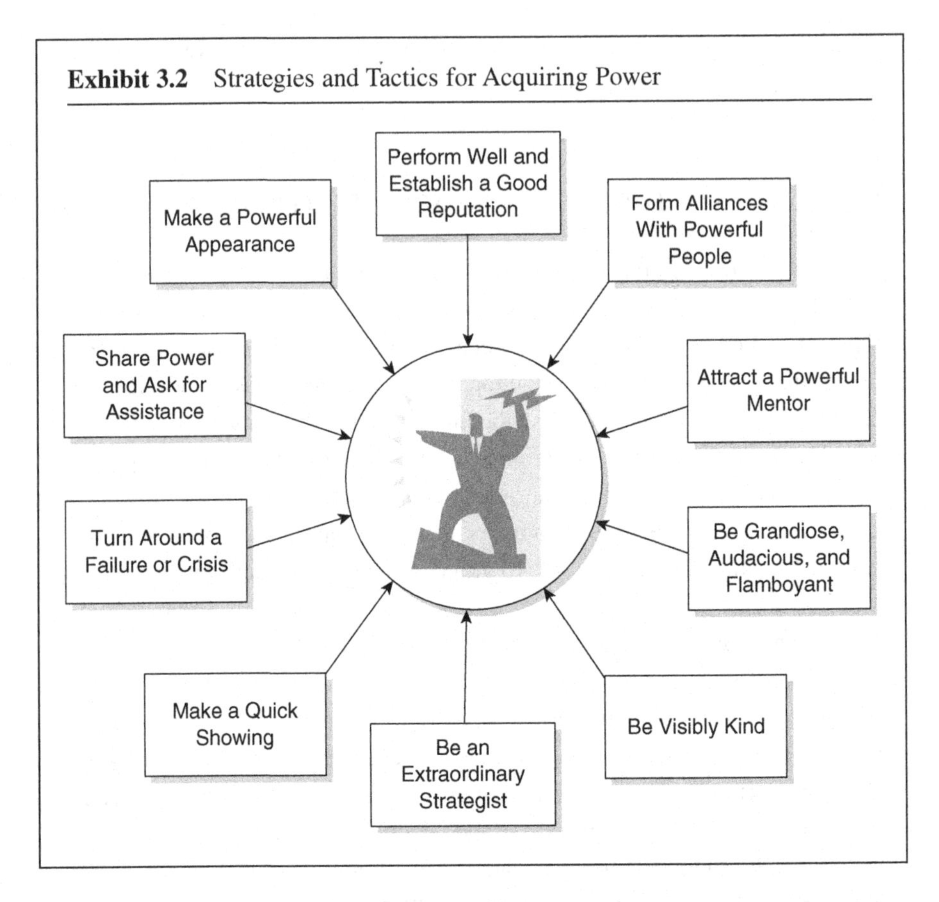

trips, and took care of business problems in five countries on two continents. Many of his work days are 12 hours long.[16] In addition to achieving most of his goals set for the company, Ghosn became the world's best-known automotive executive.

As noted in *The 48 Laws of Power,* reputation is the cornerstone of power, so power seekers must guard their reputation carefully.[17] One of the many contributors to performing well, and therefore contributing to a good reputation, is to place yourself in an environment best suited to your strengths. Fitting into an organizational culture suited to your personality is part of this strategy. An example would be an innovative person joining an innovative company. Steven Bennett, the CEO of Intuit, and a former GE executive, was asked why some former GE executives prosper at their next employer, and others perform poorly. In referring to a Harvard paper he once read, Bennett said that to succeed, the former GE executive had to be placed in a company in which his or her skills and experience were needed. For example, if there was a GE manager who was a finance-driven cost cutter, and that person was placed in a company wanting growth, the results would be poor. Bennett said he succeeded at Intuit because the company wanted growth, and he had a background at GE of growing a large division.[18]

A person's reputation stems from the major factors of attaining good results and trustworthiness. Companies are digging into a person's background more than ever for both hiring and promotion, to help certify whether the person is trustworthy. One of hundreds of possible examples of visible executives with a good reputation is Aylwin B. Lewis, the CEO at Sears Holdings Corp. When first hired as the Kmart CEO in 2004, he had established a strong reputation for brand expansion and team building. The hiring executive, Eddie Lampert, said at the time, "I did not know him previously, but I certainly knew his reputation."[19] Lewis lasted several years at Sears Holdings until the company was reorganized to help cope with the diminishing market share of Sears and Kmart.

Form Alliances With Powerful People

The theme of enhancing power by forming alliances with powerful people presents itself at several places in the study of organizational politics. Chapter 8, about developing networks, delves further into this theme. The executive described at the outset of the chapter relied in part on power contacts to enhance her own power. Having friends in the right places has always been a success strategy. Many corporate managers and professionals, as well as business owners, play golf at private clubs in the hope of forming relationships with powerful people.

A specific way in which alliances with powerful people enhance a person's power is by providing support for an individual's proposals and programs. In one company, the director of human resources wanted to initiate a weight loss program in which workers would receive cash incentives for losing weight, provided their BMI (body mass index) indicated a need for improvement. Many managers objected to what they thought was an unnecessary use of corporate resources. The human resource director had an ally in the chairperson of the board, and spoke to the latter about the resistance she was encountering. The chairperson soon distributed an e-mail to all managers supporting the new health program, thereby leading to its implementation.

Attract a Powerful Mentor

An extension of forming alliances with powerful people is to have one or more of them serve as your mentor. At times, the mentor will seek out a talented person to mentor, yet a combination of talent and taking the initiative for form an alliance will help attract a mentor. The powerful mentor can teach valuable skills and impart wisdom to the person mentored. In addition, being associated with the powerful mentor gives you additional clout. Several examples of powerful people having had powerful mentors follow.

- From the start of his career, Eddie Lampert has sought out powerful mentors. At various stages of his career, he worked with former Goldman Sachs & Co. head Robert E. Rubin, Nobel-Prize-winning economist James Tobin, and investor Richard Rainwater (who is a true rainmaker).[20]

- Donald Trump says he learned a lot from his father (who was also a real estate developer). Trump says, "He was the best possible mentor anyone could have."[21]

- A number of famous business executives were mentored by Jack Welch, the former CEO and chairman of General Electric. Among these stars are Jeff Immelt, Welch's replacement; James McNerney, now the CEO and chairman of Boeing; and Robert Nardelli, the former Home Depot top executive. Nardelli was considered too abrasive and vastly overpaid, yet as a chief executive he was powerful and highly publicized. Nardelli was appointed as the CEO of Chrysler Corp. in 2007, after a private equity firm purchased the company.

Be Grandiose, Audacious, and Flamboyant

Many, though not all, powerful people are grandiose, audacious, and flamboyant. We do not know with certainty whether these qualities help the person become powerful, or whether being powerful encourages a person to be grandiose, audacious, and flamboyant. Are these characteristics antecedents or a consequence of being powerful? For example, powerful businesspeople and celebrities might wear outrageously expensive clothing. We do not always know whether the powerful garb helped them become powerful, or whether being powerful enabled them to purchase the expensive clothing.

A specific example of flamboyant living by a business executive is Lakshmi Mittal, the founder and chief executive of steel giant Arcelor Mittal.

His preferred transportation is a Maybach limousine, and his home is a 12-bedroom, $100 million mansion in London. His 31-year-old son, the company's chief financial officer, is also flamboyant. He prefers to take a helicopter to the airport, and then board a private plane.[22] Exhibit 3.3 presents a few details about the grandiosity and flamboyance of Donald Trump in terms of his symbols of power, not his behavior as it relates to interactions with people.

Exhibit 3.3 A Sampling of the Symbols of Power and Wealth Displayed by Donald Trump

- The Donald Trump Organization is a major developer of luxury office and residential buildings throughout the world, including the famous 40 Wall Street and the Trump Tower. Trump's name is prominently displayed on most of his buildings. The privately held Trump Organization has annual sales of about $11 billion. In the last several years, the Trump Organization has built towers in Dubai, United Arab Emirates; Istanbul, Turkey; and Seoul, South Korea.
- He operates casinos in Atlantic City and Las Vegas.
- Trump was listed 314th on the *Forbes* list of 557 U.S. billionaires in 2007.
- He stars in his own reality TV show, *The Apprentice*, and is a part-owner of the Miss Universe, Miss USA, and Miss Teen USA pageants. He also has a production company called Trump Productions.[23]
- The Trump Organization's products and services include mortgages, golf clubs, and restaurants. His name is on a line of men's clothing (the Donald J. Trump Signature Collection) as well as a travel agency and a line of home furnishings. He opened the Trump Exchange in the Trump Taj Mahal Casino & Resort to sell consumer products carrying his name including the 12-inch talking doll from *The Apprentice.* The Trump name is used to signify luxurious lifestyle elements rather than ordinary products.[24]
- He is a best-selling author of several business books, including *How to Get Rich.*
- His firm has established Trump University (www.trumpuniversity.com), an e-learning venture about career and business success. The university operates despite New York State education law forbidding an enterprise to transact business under the name "university" or "college" without approval by the state Board of Regents.[25]
- He owns a private Boeing 727, which resembles a luxury hotel room inside.

Grandiosity, audacity, and flamboyance are not confined to conspicuous displays of material possessions and wealth. Flamboyant thinking and speaking also contribute to power, as exemplified by Scott McNealy, the chairman and cofounder of Sun Microsystems CEO and major figure in the growth of the Internet. In the example that follows, he was talking about what he meant by the "participation age."[26]

> If you are not on the Internet, you aren't participating in the greatest accumulation of creativity on the planet ever—look at Wikipedia, instant messaging, blogging, podcasting, home shopping, telemedicine, home banking, distance learning, voice over IP. The problem is that three in four folks on earth aren't there yet. There's a huge digital divide. Our mission is to provide the infrastructure that powers the participation age. But our cause is to eliminate the digital divide. That's personal.

Observe the flamboyance in the statement about the mission to provide the infrastructure that powers the information age. McNealy has been successfully flamboyant since the beginning of his career.

Be Visibly Kind

An altruistic way of attaining and holding on to power is to be exceptionally nice and kind. By being tender and kind, a manager acquires even more power as he or she gains the support of more people. In the process of being visibly kind, the manager shares power and glory. An outstanding example of *tender power* is Margaret (Meg) Whitman, the former eBay chief executive. She was known for sharing decision making with others, using the team approach, and being outright kind. Whitman was ranked as one of the most powerful women in business by both *Fortune* and *Forbes,* and was also considered to be one of the most powerful players in high technology. A story about Whitman's kindness circulates through the company, as follows:

> She was on a flight to India with three other eBay employees when one of them developed a dangerous gastrointestinal problem somewhere over Tehran. Whitman pulled out an atlas and decided Istanbul was the nearest, safest city in which they could land. She called an air emergency service and arranged for an ambulance to be waiting on the tarmac when the plane landed. Whitman rode in the ambulance with the ill executive and stayed with

> him for hours in the hospital, talking to his wife on the phone. Once the executive was stabilized, Whitman took him to a hospital in London in the corporate jet. She and the other eBay employees flew commercial to India, leaving the jet for the patient to fly to California.

The power and influence of behaviors like this on the part of Whitman are summed up by Rajiv Dutta, head of eBay's PayPal division: "She will exert herself personally, far and above the call of duty. She makes you want to do the right thing."[27]

Warren Buffett, who is frequently ranked as the world's richest man, is also an example of a person whose kindness appears to have contributed to his power. At the height of his career, he donated $31 billion to the Bill & Melinda Gates Foundation, which helps such causes as fighting poverty, low educational opportunity, and AIDS. Yet along the way Buffett has always reached out to college students. Melinda Gates says that Buffett is a fantastic teacher: "Over the years, Warren has talked to thousands of college students—usually in informal sessions in which his sense of humor and high ethical standards shine through."[28]

Be an Extraordinary Strategist

Many powerful people are strategic thinkers, and thinking strategically can help a person be granted position of power in the form of a big promotion. To be perceived as a *strategic thinker* is an asset for most careers, both in and outside of business. A case in point is Indra Nooyi, now president and chief executive of PepsiCo, who was awarded this position in large part because of her successful strategic thinking. In her previous position, Nooyi was a key force behind the strategy that transformed the company into a convenience-food powerhouse, from one with mediocre financial results struggling to compete with Coca-Cola Co. Another aspect of her successful strategic thinking was to point PepsiCo in the direction of healthier drinks and snacks.[29]

An example of high-level thinking that has helped someone retain power is Richard Harvey, the group chief executive at Aviva PLC, one of the world's largest insurance companies. His strategic contribution was to identify the financial risks associated with living too long that face many baby boomers. So his company has pioneered *longevity insurance* in the form of guaranteed lifetime income annuities.[30] (Is Harvey also being grandiose?)

Make a Quick Showing

A display of dramatic results in a hurry can help gain acceptance and some power for one's efforts or those of the group. After a person has impressed management with his or her ability to solve that first problem, the person can look forward to problems that will bring greater power. Making a quick showing has become increasingly important for new CEOs to hang on to their job and its associated power. A rule of thumb is that the CEO has to show promising results in about 90 days because quarterly results are due by then. Michael Watkins says, "Boards are willing to toss people out and giving CEOs a much shorter leash. Many senior executives feel they have a much shorter time frame to prove themselves."[31]

One recommended way for the new CEO to make a quick showing is to come up early with a few important but easy-to-attain goals that can be shown to the board, Wall Street analysts, or employees as examples of what the organization can achieve. An activity such as immediately reducing carbon dioxide emissions, as well as heating and cooling costs, is a step in the right direction.

Turn Around a Failure or a Crisis

An effective way of making a good showing at any point in your career is to reverse a failing situation or crisis. At the same time, the person who can reverse a negative situation quickly builds his or her reputation. "Getting involved in a high-risk, high-failure situation is a way to make a name for yourself," says Laurence J. Stybel, the head of a leadership consultancy.[32]

A senior project manager at a grocery chain provides a useful example of turning around a project that seemed doomed. The purpose of the project was to automate the store-shelf tagging system. The new manager faced the challenge of rolling out the new system at the chain's 120 stores within six months. She identified 45 stores that would gain the most from the improved tagging and installed the system there six months later. The electronic tags saved about $500,000 in staff costs, thereby enhancing the project manager's reputation.[33]

Share Power and Ask for Assistance

A standard strategy for modern managers to multiply their power is to share power with subordinates. By empowering subordinates, they are able to accomplish more, and their accomplishments become part of the manager's accomplishments. In turn, the more accomplished manager becomes more powerful. In contrast, the more the manager hogs power, the less the subordinates—and the unit—can accomplish. In turn, the less the unit accomplishes, the less powerful the manager becomes.

A subtle way of empowering group members is to ask for their assistance, thereby implying that their input is valuable and that they are important contributors to your decision making. When Anne Mulcahy was appointed CEO of Xerox Corp. in 2000, she stepped into a near-bankrupt company, and she had no background in finance. She asked executives in the treasurer's office to tutor her, and also sought the advice of sales people. Mulcahy's consensus leadership style ultimately made her a powerful and admired executive, and she helped pilot Xerox back to prosperity and glory.[34]

Make a Powerful Appearance

Appearing powerful is a superficial, yet sometimes effective, approach to gaining power. If you look powerful, some people will be willing to grant you power or defer to you. Attire that makes you look powerful is also important for dealing with some customers and clients, particularly in the field of investment banking. Richard S. Fuld, the CEO of investment banker Lehman Brothers, presided over the forced move of the firm after the World Trade Center attack of 9/11. He used the occasion for the professional staff to become more powerful looking by ending casual dress. "We were moving into a new building, and we were going to have a ton of clients there, and although I had allowed casual dress, I was dead-set against it," says Fuld. "If you dress sloppy, you think sloppy. Actually, I was even more violently opposed to it than that." The look at Lehman includes women conservatively dressed and the men in white or blue shirts and ties.[35] (Again, the organizational culture counts. A white shirt and a tie might look goofy and nonpowerful at Google or Yahoo!)

The décor of your cubicle or office is an extension of your appearance that can also contribute to a power look. Powerful business people tend to have uncluttered work areas with a minimum of personal memorabilia. In contrast, powerful professors, scientists, and information technology specialists tend to have more clutter and personal memorabilia.

Being charming and charismatic also contributes to a powerful appearance, and at the same time is an influence tactic. Many—though certainly not all—powerful people are charming. The lack of charm, as described in the case study about Steve Heyer in Chapter 2, can facilitate a powerful person's demise. Charm and charisma as influence tactics will be described in Chapter 7.

THE ABUSE OF POWER WITHIN ORGANIZATIONS

A major concern about powerful people is that they might abuse the power they attain, even if they behaved ethically on the way to power. The Machiavellianism described in Chapter 1 contributes to both the presence of organizational politics and power abuse. Another contributing factor to power abuse is when a person's psychological need for power is excessively strong. The power need has long been cited as a contributor to managerial and leadership success;[36] however, when this need becomes too intense it can lead to a quest for power beyond healthy limits.

Occupying a position of immense power triggers the motives of greed, gluttony, and avarice in many business executives, as well as executives in the nonprofit sector including political office holders. Former Federal Reserve chairman Alan Greenspan said that "an infectious greed" had contaminated the business community in the late 1990s, as one executive after another manipulated earnings or resorted to fraudulent accounting to capitalize on soaring stock prices.[37] Although well-publicized financial scandals in large business firms decreased in the 2000s, many prominent business executives in a variety of industries were accused of changing dates on stock options. The purpose was to guarantee large profits for themselves, even though the purpose of the options was to reward good performance.

A commonly cited form of power abuse is gigantic compensation for some business executives. (The executives and their boards retort that executive talent is rare, and the large compensation is deserved.) The public outcry about executive compensation prompted the Securities & Exchange Commission to create tougher new rules on pay disclosures. Exhibit 3.4 presents ten examples of total executive compensation (salary, bonus, and stock gains including options) in 2007. You will observe that employers like Walt Disney and Ralph Lauren have many employees not making much more than the minimum wage. Another perspective on power abuse is that John A. Thain is paid 2,617 times the $30,000 earnings of a clerical support person in his company who is responsible for sending monthly statements to clients.

Other forms of power abuse of a financial nature are executives charging the company for private living accommodations, lavish parties, and family travel on the corporate jet. One former high-technology executive was known to have her athletic equipment flown around the world so she could exercise properly on business trips.

Another form of power abuse is sexually harassing people under one's command. The harassed individual might feel the need to consent to harassment due

Exhibit 3.4 Examples of Business Executive Compensation in 2007

Industry	*Highest-Paid Chief Executive in Industry*	*Total Compensation*
Basic materials	Celanese, Daniel N. Weidman	$21,232,800
Consumer goods	Coca-Cola Co., E. Neville Isdell	$27,658,800
Consumer services	Walt Disney, Robert A. Iger	$29,734,600
Financials	Merrill Lynch, John A. Thain	$78,521,500
Healthcare	Abbott Labs, Miles D. White	$22,793,400
Industrials	Honeywell International, David M. Cote	$28,867,900
Oil and gas	Occidental, Ray R. Irani	$63,459,100
Technology	Hewlett-Packard, Mark V. Hurd	$23,665,400
Telecommunications	AT&T, Randall L. Stephenson	$25,031,300
Utilities	Entergy, J. Wayne Leonard	$14,187,300

SOURCE: Compiled from data presented in The WSJ/Jay Group 2007 CEO Compensation Survey, *Wall Street Journal,* April 14, 2008, pp. R5–R7.

to the fear of potential job loss. Another concern the harassment victim might have is that she (and sometimes he) would be discredited with a charge of harassment because the powerful executive is more respected.

The percentage of powerful people who abuse their position is probably small, yet the impact can be great. An example of this would be a CEO being angry with the labor union leadership, and therefore closing a plant because of this anger.

SUMMARY

Power refers to the ability or potential to influence. The sources and types of position power include (1) legitimate power, (2) reward power, (3) coercive power, (4) information power, (5) dependence, and (6) centrality. The sources and types of personal power include (1) expert power, (2) referent power, (3) prestige power, and (4) connection power.

Before applying strategies and tactics for acquiring power, it is helpful to perform a power analysis. Questions to ask for the analysis might be asked about (1) how revealing the hierarchy of authority is, (2) what drives the people in power, (3) which positions and roles are the most important, (4) what other factors are tied to power and influence, and (5) what is your place in the power hierarchy.

To learn how much power and clout a powerful people has, ask questions about (1) to whom the person reports, (2) the number of direct reports and their type of work, (3) who reviews his or her decisions, (4) the impact of the person's decisions, (5) how people of equal rank consult the person, and (6) how much the person is liked or disliked.

Social exchange theory presents several ideas for understanding power in organizations, particularly from the standpoint that the person with resources is able to engage the cooperation of others. The more benefits the person brings to the group, the more power that person accrues.

Strategies and tactics for acquiring power described here are: (1) Perform well and establish a good reputation; (2) form alliances with powerful people; (3) attract a powerful mentor; (4) be grandiose, audacious, and flamboyant; (5) be visibly kind; (6) be an extraordinary strategist; (7) make a quick showing; (8) turn around a failure or crisis; (9) share power and ask for assistance; and (10) make a powerful appearance.

A major concern about powerful people is that they might abuse the power they attain, even if they behaved ethically on the way to power. Being in a powerful position can trigger greed, gluttony, and avarice. Financial scandals might be considered a form of power abuse, as well as excessive compensation packages paid to business executives, company payment for personal luxuries, and sexual harassment of subordinates.

QUESTIONS AND ACTIVITIES

1. What can you do this week to start enhancing your power base?
2. Get into a huddle with a few classmates to identify at least three powerful people who do not earn a lot of money.

3. Which of the other strategies and tactics for acquiring power would be helpful in implementing the tactic of "attract a powerful mentor"?
4. How might a tax accountant or a business consultant "make a quick showing"?
5. What might be the downside to the tactic of "asking for assistance"?
6. To what extent do you think Dick Fuld was abusing his power by abolishing casual dress for the professional staff at Lehman Brothers?
7. Former U.S. president Bill Clinton charges about $150,000 for a talk, even at colleges and universities. Explain whether you think he is abusing his power and, if so, why.

CASE STUDY: BIG EDDIE LAMPERT LIKES TO DEAL

The mood was tense at a luxury hotel in West Hollywood, California, one day several years ago. The top two dozen executives of Sears Roebuck & Co. were gathering for a strategy session with Eddie Lampert, age 42 at the time. The billionaire hedge fund manager had just worked out a difficult-to-believe takeover of their struggling company. A major source of anxiety was that Kmart was being used as leverage for the acquisition. Another problem was that Lampert began challenging virtually every idea submitted. "What's the benefit of that?" he asked repeatedly. "What's the value?" He rejected a modest $2 million proposal to enhance lighting in the stores. "Why invest in that?"

Expressions of bewilderment could be seen in the room. All present knew that Lampert was an alluring character. He had worked himself into one of the richest men in America, and somehow supercharged the listless stock of Kmart. He wears tailored suits rather than choosing off-the-rack clothing from Kmart or Sears.

Lampert was able to escape a kidnapping that threatened his life. On January 10, 2003, as he walked in the underground garage of his headquarters, four masked men grabbed him. An hour later, Lampert was locked in a motel bathroom. His abductors told him they had been hired to kill him. One of the kidnappers used a credit card he took from Lampert to order pizza, giving Lampert a wedge to convince the four men that police were on their trail so they would be better off letting him go. Another version of the story is that Lampert convinced his captors to let him go by promising to leave $40,000 in a Dumpster behind a Wendy's. The young kidnappers were later caught because they had used the Internet to track down facts about Lampert.

Lampert's hedge fund, ESL Investments, has delivered average annual returns of approximately 30% after fees since its launch in 1988. Lampert's clients include Dell founder Michael Dell and media giant David Geffen. Lampert's key investment strategy is to buy undervalued stocks and hold them for a long time. Lampert's hedge fund owns 40% of Sears Holdings—the firm consisting of Kmart, Sears, and perhaps other future acquisitions.

ESL is located in small offices in Greenwich, Connecticut. Lampert manages his $54 billon a year, 333,000-employee giant by phone, e-mail, and videoconference. Lampert makes many of the big marketing and merchandising decisions, claiming that although he does not have a heavy retailing background, he is a big shopper. He frequently tells his executives to be willing to sacrifice sales for profitability, and question everything. Lampert is a heavy user of computer-based tools to analyze sales, profit margins, and inventories by store, by region, and by merchandise group. Lampert is considered a BlackBerry addict who expects Sears managers to drop everything and respond when they receive a message from him.

One of his retailing strategies is to remove unprofitable items from the store. His strategy for reviving Kmart was to cut spending, reduce inventories, and stop money-losing promotions. An example of cost cutting is that travel budgets are tightly limited, with employees being reimbursed a maximum of $25 a day for three meals. Before Kmart bought out Sears, Lampert had sold 70 Kmart stores to Sears and Home Depot for more than $900 million.

Lampert continues to find ways to extract cash from company money not strictly tied to retail. For example, in 2006 when Sears was losing money on some of its complicated investments, it earned a pretax profit of $20 million on property sales after deducting the investment losses. Also, Kmart and Sears continue to generate cash surpluses.

Critics of Lampert's retailing strategies warn that his willingness to give up market share to fatter profit margins is shortsighted and self-defeating. A retailing consultant said that Sears Holding had handed customers to J. C. Penney, Kohl's, Target, and others. Some of these problems were surfacing in 2008 as profits declined and cash flow decreased enough to worry some investors.

Lampert proclaims he wants to be known as a great businessman.

Case Study Questions

1. Identify, with examples, several sources or types of power that Eddie Lampert uses.
2. What suggestions might you offer Lampert to help him guard against an erosion of power?
3. In what ways does Lampert display a high level of strategic thinking?
4. What evidence, if any, do you find that Lampert abuses power?
5. What would you say to Lampert and his management team if they asked you whether the company should attempt to purchase Wal-Mart and/or Gap?

SOURCE: Covert, J. (2007). Sears outlook solid, somehow. *Wall Street Journal,* January 11, C8; Chandler, S. (2006). "Good life" is elusive for Lampert's Sears. www.chicagotribune.com/business, March 20; Sellers, P. (2006). Eddie Lampert: The best investor of his generation. *Fortune,* February 6; Berner, R. (2004). Eddie's master stroke. *BusinessWeek,* November 29, 34–36; Eavis, P. (2008). Sears' till stirs concern. *Wall Street Journal,* February 8, C1.

POLITICAL SKILL-BUILDING EXERCISE 3

Creating an Impression of Power

One way of being powerful is to look and act powerful. Groups of about six people are invited to participate in this role-play, with one person being the power actor and the other five people playing the role of the top-management team who the power actor will meet today. If time permits, everyone in the group has an opportunity to play the role of the power actor once, and a member of the top-management team five times.

Visualize yourself as a middle manager, perhaps in charge of a large organizational unit or a company division. Today you will meet with the top-management team of your company to ask for a 25% increase in your budget in order to expand your unit of the company. Think of any scenario you want that would justify an expansion. Your specific role involves creating a power presence. Use

(Continued)

(Continued)

any of the strategies and tactics outline in Exhibit 3.2 to create your power presence and image. If you are given advance notice for this exercise, you might consider dressing to look powerful.

After you have made your presentation of about 10 minutes to the top-management team, each executive will rate you on a 1-to-10 scale (10 is high) in terms of the impression of power you created. Each executive will also give you about a brief explanation—even one or two sentences—to justify that rating. The feedback you receive can be via paper, e-mail, text messaging, or given orally right after your presentation.

If this exercise is a total success, you will receive some useful ideas about the power impression you create, and how you can create an even stronger power presence.

REFERENCES

1. Adapted and excerpted from Egodigwe, L. (2007, March). Survivor instinct: How a strategic executive read all the corporate signs—and played her vantage points. *Black Enterprise,* 63.

2. Synthesized from other researchers in Fiol, C. M., O'Connor, E. J., & Aguinis, H. (2001, April). All for one and one for all? The development and transfer of power across organizational levels. *Academy of Management Review,* 224.

3. Cited in Kim, P. H., Pinkley, R. L., & Fragale, A. R. (2005, October). Power dynamics in negotiation. *Academy of Management Review,* 800.

4. The original source of power sources and types is French, J. B., & Raven, B. (1962). The basis of social power. In D. Cartwright & A. Zander (Eds.), *Group dynamics: Research and theory* (pp. 607–623). Evanston, IL: Row, Peterson and Company.

5. Pollock, T. G., Fisher, H. M., & Wade, J. B. (2002, December). The role of power and politics in the repricing of executive options. *Academy of Management Journal,* 1172–1182.

6. Emerson, R. M. (1962). Power–dependence relations. *American Sociological Review, 27,* 31–41 [p. 32].

7. Quoted in Smerd, J. (2007, May 7). Wal-Mart betting on tech, clinics. *Workforce Management,* 3.

8. Pfeffer, J. (1990). *Managing with power* [pp. 100–101]. Boston: Harvard Business Review Publications.

9. Hickson, D. J., Hinings, C. R., Lees, C. A., Schneck, R. S., & Pennings, J. M. (1971). A strategic contingencies theory of intra-organizational power. *Administrative Science Quarterly, 16,* 216–229.

10. Maccoby, M. (2004, September). Why people follow the leader: The power of transference. *Harvard Business Review,* 76–85.

11. Finkelstein, S. (1992, August). Power in top management teams: Dimensions, measurement, and validation. *Academy of Management Journal,* 505–538 [p. 510].

12. Lussier, R. N. (2008). *Human relations in organizations: Applications and skill building* (7th ed.) [p. 359]. New York: McGraw-Hill.

13. Marshall, J. L. (2004, Summer). *Power and office politics: Rumor and reality.* Newspaper Association of America. Retrieved 04/14/2007 from www.naa.org.

14. Kennedy, M. M. (1980). *Office politics: Seizing power, wielding clout* [p. 67]. New York: Warner Books.

15. Yukl, G. (2002). *Leadership in organizations* (5th ed.) [p. 154]. Upper Saddle River, NJ: Prentice Hall; Blau, P. M. (1974). *Exchange and power in social life.* New York: John Wiley.

16. Taylor, A., III (2006, December 11). The world according to Ghosn. *Fortune,* 114–121.

17. Greene, R. (1998). *The 48 laws of power: A Joost Elffers production.* New York: Viking.

18. Vara, V. (2007, April 16). After GE. *Wall Street Journal,* R3.

19. Alleyne, S. (2004, December). Kmart makes branding pro its new chief. *Black Enterprise,* 33.

20. Berner, R. (2004, November 22). The next Warren Buffett? *BusinessWeek,* cover story.

21. Timberlake, J. (2007, March 19). Questions for The Donald, *Fortune,* 70.

22. Reed, S. (2007, April 16). Mittal & Son. *BusinessWeek,* 47–48.

23. Timberlake, J. (2007, March 19). Questions for The Donald, *Fortune,* 70–72.

24. Parmley, S. (2006, August 4). *Retailing Trump.* Retrieved 04/25/2007 from www.philly.com.

25. Hindo, B. (2005, June 20). Call it Trump trade school? *BusinessWeek,* 13.

26. Kirkpatrick, D. (2005, October 31). Still feisty after all these years. *Fortune,* 42.

27. Both quotes are from Brown, E. (2007, May 21). What would Meg do? *Forbes,* 94.

28. Gates, M. (2007, May 14). Warren Buffett: A plainspoken business wizard makes philanthropic history. *Time,* 82.

29. McKay, B. (2006, November 20). The 50 women to watch: Indra Noovi. *Wall Street Journal,* R3.

30. McDonald, I. (2007, January 22). Here's to a long life. *Wall Street Journal,* R6.

31. McGregor, J. (2007, February 5). How to take the reins at top speed. *Business Week,* 55–56.

32. Lublin, J. S. (2007, May 1). Assigned a flop? You could wind up looking like a winner. *Wall Street Journal,* B1.

33. Lublin, J. S. (2007, May 1). Assigned a flop?

34. *Fortune* magazine (2007, March 19).The list of industry stars: Ask for help: Anne Mulcahy. *Fortune,* 128–129.

35. Serwer, A. (2006, April 17). The improbable power broker. *Fortune,* 146.

36. McClelland, D. C., & Burnam, D. H. (2003, January). Power is the great motivator. *Harvard Business Review,* 117–126, 142 (reprint of 1976 article plus *HBR* editor update).

37. Gannett News Service. (2002, July 17). *Fed chief points to cautious recovery.*

FOUR

UPWARD RELATIONS

LEARNING OBJECTIVES

After studying this chapter and doing the exercises, you should be able to do the following:

1. Understand how several facets of organizational citizenship behavior contribute to positive upward relations.
2. Be aware of the positive and constructive aspects of impression management, and how to avoid the negative aspects.
3. Be prepared to choose from a variety of relationship builders with superiors for purposes of present or future implementation.
4. Understand several tactics for dealing with a difficult boss.

Todd Averett is director of the Learning and Development Team at Payless ShoeSource, the largest family footwear dealer in the Western Hemisphere. He wrote the following about the importance of organizational citizenship behavior at his company:

> Most organizational leaders, when asked, would say they prefer to staff their organizations with individuals who are good "organizational citizens"—individuals who go above and beyond the call of duty. Over the

past few years, Payless ShoeSource has strived to develop a culture that focuses on principles and values related to organizational citizenship. At Payless, this focus began with the realization at the executive level that to reach our full potential as an organization, the hearts and minds of our Associates had to be fully engaged in achieving common goals. For Payless, a retailer in a competitive market, this meant moving from a culture of "results at all costs" to a culture driven by "Guiding Values." These Guiding Values are: personal accountability, risk taking and innovation, teamwork, change, and open communication. To change the culture, Payless had to convince employees to let go of longstanding norms and accept, on faith, that living the Guiding Values would bring greater success for both the company and themselves.

Similar to Payless's Guiding Values, the essence of organizational citizenship is employee behavior that goes above and beyond the call of duty. Perhaps more importantly, these behaviors represent, or are the manifestations of, beliefs that individuals have about their roles at work.[1]

The comments by the learning and development director at Payless ShoeSource emphasize one of the major themes of this chapter: that organizational citizenship behavior not only helps the company; it is also good organizational politics because such behavior helps you develop a solid relationship with superiors. Other key topics concerning upward relations included in this chapter are impression management, a variety of strategies and tactics for building upward relations, and suggestions for coping with a boss who you consider to be difficult.

A strong relationship with superiors has been described as the best kind of organizational politics.[2] Furthermore, a synthesis of opinion suggests that one of the greatest determinants of career success is **managing up**: the ability to influence your boss to invest in your ideas and advancement.[3] At the same time, managing up is building constructive relationships with superiors.

ORGANIZATIONAL CITIZENSHIP BEHAVIOR AS ORGANIZATIONAL POLITICS

A meritorious strategy for developing positive upward relationships is to go beyond the call of duty. Instead of saying, "It's not my job," the good organizational citizen and political player says, "What can I do to help even if it is not part of my job, and no reward is guaranteed?" **Organizational citizenship behavior (OCB)** is discretionary individual behavior not directly or explicitly recognized by the formal reward system, and in the aggregate promotes the efficient and effective functioning of the organization.[4] Simply stated, OCB is the willingness to work for the good of the organization without the promise of a specific reward. Five important components of organizational citizenship behavior are conscientiousness, altruism, civic virtue, courtesy, and sportsmanship. A good organizational citizen would engage in behaviors such as assisting a person with a computer problem outside his or her own team, assisting someone outside the group to move a desk within his or her cubicle, or picking up a bottle on the company lawn.

If you engage in good citizenship behavior with the intent of enhancing your relationship with superiors, you are behaving politically. However, an oxymoron is built into this last sentence. The true organizational citizen is not concerned with receiving a reward. Four specific aspects of organizational citizenship behavior linked to developing upward relations are presented next.

1. *Organizational citizenship behavior creates social capital.* **Social capital** is a resource derived from the relationships among individuals, organizations, communities, and societies. This type of capital in organizations is reflected by the existence of close interpersonal relationships between and among employees.[5] If, as a good organizational citizen, you do good deeds for many people, they will be predisposed to support you in such ways as recommending you for higher salary increases, promotions, and exciting project assignments. The relational dimension of social capital links directly to organizational politics because it focuses on the quality of the connections you make with others. Achieving good social capital with a superior is similar to having good chemistry with that person.

2. *Altruistic citizenship behavior might lead to higher performance evaluations and stronger recommendations for rewards.* Madeline E. Heilman and Julie J. Chen conducted three experimental studies about the effect of altruistic organizational behavior on two important outcomes: performance evaluations and recommendations for the rewards of salary increase, promotion, involvement in a high-profile project, and bonus pay. Altruism in this context involves assisting others with work-related tasks. Participants in the study were 135 male and female undergraduate students enrolled in an introductory psychology class, with two thirds being female. The basic study materials were

360-degree feedback forms (multiple raters of the fictitious workers), along with photos of the workers. Based on these materials, the participants evaluated the workers and made recommendations for rewards.

A general finding was that the same altruistic behavior can result in different performance evaluations and reward recommendations for men and women. The first two studies indicated that providing work-related help resulted in more favorable reactions to men, but a negligible effect on reactions to women. The withholding of altruistic behavior resulted in unfavorable reactions to women but had a negligible effect on reactions to men. The third study demonstrated that altruism is perceived to be less discretionary and more required for women than men.[6] These studies support the gender stereotype that women are expected to be more altruistic. An implication of these studies is that men can obtain more political advantage by being altruistic in the workplace.

3. *When tasks are interdependent, organizational citizenship behavior is likely to be perceived as more important.* A set of two studies involving 348 undergraduate and MBA students investigated the influence of task interdependence on the perceived importance of organizational citizenship behavior. A third study of 130 managers investigated the same relationship. A general finding was that when tasks are interdependent (requiring cooperation among people), OCB is perceived as more important by people evaluating performance. The study also found that high unit-level performance was more likely to be attributed to cooperative behavior when task interdependence was also high.[7] The implication of this set of studies for upward relations is that when faced with an interdependent task (such as providing a joint report), it is helpful to display high organizational citizenship behavior to attain a high performance evaluation.

4. *Deliver beyond your expectations.* A basic way of displaying organizational citizenship behavior is to accomplish more than people expect, thereby cementing your relationships with superiors. As advised by Jack and Suzy Welch, the best way to get back on your boss's radar if you have been overlooked is to overdeliver: "Whatever you are doing, do it better and faster. Expand your job's horizons to include bold new activities. Come up with a new concept or process that doesn't just improve your results, but your unit's results and the company's overall performance. Surprise everyone."[8] (A display of organizational citizenship behavior of this magnitude would require considerable talent, imagination, and planning.)

IMPRESSION MANAGEMENT

Another broad set of behaviors for building upward relations is to manage the impression you create. **Impression management** is a specific form of social influence behavior directed at enhancing one's image by drawing attention to oneself. Often the attention is directed toward superficial aspects of behavior, such as clothing and appearance. Impression management also includes deeper aspects of behavior, such as telling people about your accomplishments, speaking well, and appearing self-confident. As explained by Amos Drory and Nurit Zaidman, the power of the individual in the organization stems not only from the person's formal position and control of resources, but also from how the person is perceived by other members in the organization. Creating the right image is the practice of impression management.[9]

Although impression management can be used in a wide variety of relationships, it is most commonly found in the attempt of a subordinate to please a superior. For example, impression management is frequently used during performance evaluation in order to impress the superior with the subordinate's results.

Contextual Variables Influencing Impression Management

The context or setting is important in understanding why people are likely to engage in impression management, with the five contextual variables presented next being particularly important.[10]

1. *Power relations in the organization.* The more power managers have over workers in the organization, the more likely workers will be to engage in impression management. Greater power also implies more dependency on the power figures, so impression management seems all the more important. Similarly, in an organization that endorses the cultural value of power distance (more respect for authority), workers will think it is more legitimate to impress their superiors.

2. *Limited economic and political opportunities of subgroups.* Impression management may be more common in societies with limited economic and political opportunities. In an organization, this could mean that minorities might engage in more impression management because they are relatively less powerful.

3. *Culture-specific codes.* A national culture that emphasizes harmonious interpersonal relationships may encourage members of that culture to manage their impressions. An example is that impression management among Hispanics may be attributed to a culture-specific Hispanic script know as *sympatia* (the need for behaviors that encourage smooth interpersonal relations).

4. *Occupational status.* Individuals in low-status jobs are more likely to use impression management toward their superiors in order to improve their conditions. Although this generalization may be true, many people in relatively high-status positions, such as corporate professionals and middle managers, regularly use impression management to gain an advantage. The use of glitzy PowerPoint presentations to impress the boss or members of higher management illustrates this point.

5. *Individualistic versus collective culture.* In an individualistic culture, more people may attempt to generate the impression of an independent and self-reliant individual. In contrast, in a collectivistic culture, more political actors will work toward generating an image of a person who displays politeness and harmony.

Specific Tactics of Impression Management

Understanding the nature of impression management and some of its contextual variables is a good starting point in managing your impression. In addition, it is helpful to be aware of several specific tactics among the many possibilities.

Build Trust and Confidence

A key strategy for creating a positive impression with your immediate superior and higher-ranking managers is to build trust and confidence. Project the authentic impression of a person who can be trusted to carry out responsibilities faithfully and ethically. Rather than take action without permission (e.g., spending beyond budget), know the bounds of your authority and work within those bounds. Be aware that your boss has other responsibilities, so do not take up more than your fair share of his or her time. You will generate an impression of confidence if you suggest alternative solutions to the problems you bring to your manager.[11]

A rapid way to lose your boss's trust and confidence is to bypass (go over the boss's head) when you disagree with the boss, such as complaining about your performance evaluation to the manager of your manager. The *boss bypass* is such a career retardant that it will be reintroduced in the discussion of political blunders in Chapter 9.

Be Visible and Create a Strong Presence

An essential part of impression management is to be perceived as a valuable contributor on the job. Visibility is attained in many ways, such as regular attendance at meetings and company social events, being assigned to important projects, and doing volunteer work in the community. Helping in the launch of a new product or redesigning work methods are other ways of attaining visibility and creating a strong presence. Face-to-face visibility is perhaps the best, but electronic visibility can also be effective. This includes making intelligent contributions to company intranets and blogs, and sending e-mail messages of substance to the right people. Terry Bragg observes that many employees are shocked to learn that they lost their jobs during a downsizing because upper management did not know that they were valuable contributors.[12]

Being visible creates a positive impression, and being *invisible* can create an extremely negative impression. Kevin P. Coyne and Edward J. Coyne, Sr. investigated how some managers survived a new CEO, and others were fired or demoted. A surprising portion of the CEOs studied reported cases of executives who displayed a dismaying lack of political skill during the critical "honeymoon" weeks. One leader described a subordinate who took a two-week vacation during the CEO's first month on the job. "The vacation had been scheduled for a long time, and I didn't stop him, but I still never forgave him," the CEO said. "It was the dumbest thing he could do."[13]

Admit Mistakes

Many people believe that, to create a good impression, it is best to deny or cover up mistakes. In this way you will not appear vulnerable. More astute political behavior is to admit mistakes, thereby appearing more forthright and trustworthy. The simple statement "I goofed" will often gain you sympathy and support whereas an attempted cover up will decrease your social capital.

At the managerial level, a mistake often involves making a major decision that proved to have expensive negative consequences such as a change in organization structure that resulted in poor customer service. Honesty is recommended when changing a plan of action. Career coach Rhoda Smackum suggests you say something like: "This is what I thought at the time, this is why I made the decision that I did, and how based on current information, I think we should have done X, Y, and Z." Smackum also says that when you lay things out and communicate openly with people, they may become upset when you do change course. However, they at least know that you are going to try to make decisions based on honesty and your best available information.[14]

For purposes of impression management, the bottom line of being wrong is to (a) admit the error, (b) request guidance, (c) step up and repair, and (d) learn from it.[15] Requesting guidance is important because it conveys the impression that you have humility and that you trust the advice and counsel of others.

Minimize Being a Yes-Person

A conventional view of organizational politics suggests that being a yes-person is an excellent way of developing a good relationship with those higher up, generating the impression of a loyal and supportive subordinate. The yes-person operates by the principle "the boss is always right." Often the boss cultivates yes-person behavior among subordinates by being intimidating and unapproachable.[16] When working for an emotionally secure and competent manager, you are likely to create a better impression by not agreeing with all the boss's ideas and plans. Instead, express constructive disagreement by explaining how the boss's plan might be enhanced, or an error avoided.

Assume that you work in the marketing department of Jitterbug, a simplified cell phone that focuses on the senior market. Your boss suggests an advertising theme suggesting that even people with arthritis and those who are technically challenged can easily operate a Jitterbug. Your intuition tells you this theme would be a humiliating insult to seniors. So you respond to your boss, "I know that Jitterbug targets seniors, but I suggest that we tone down the terms 'arthritis' and 'technically challenged.'" Why not be positive and state that the keys are easy to manipulate, and that the Jitterbug is as easy to operate as a landline phone?

Although expressing constructive disagreement generally creates a better impression than being a yes-person, some yes-people advance far in their careers. Particularly when the recipient of all the agreement is insecure, the yes-person might receive favorable performance evaluations and be recommended for promotion. An example is that many people who receive political appointments were yes-people for their sponsor during the latter's campaign for office.

Create a Healthy Image

A superficial yet important part of impression management is to project a healthy, physically fit appearance. Appearing physically fit in the workplace has gained in importance as many business firms offer workers rewards for being physically fit and avoiding smoking and obesity. Among the rewards offered by employers are electronic gadgets, discounted health insurance, and cash bonuses. At IBM Corp., employees get as much as $300 annually for exercising regularly, quitting smoking, or logging on to the company's preventive care Web site.[17] Microsoft has a wellness program directed specifically at combating obesity, with such features as a personal trainer, a custom nutritional plan, and health spa facilities.[18] From an impression management perspective, being obese at a health-conscious company would be a negative.

Projecting an image of emotional fitness also contributes to a healthy image. *Emotional fitness* would include such behaviors as appearing relaxed, appropriate laughter and smiling, and a minimum of nervous mannerisms and gestures. Being physically fit helps project emotional fitness.

Display Appropriate Etiquette

A major component of managing your impression is practicing good etiquette. **Business etiquette** is a special code of behavior required in work situations. Business etiquette is much more than knowing how to use the correct utensil, not speaking with food in your mouth, or knowing how to dress in a given situation. Businesspeople today must know how to be at ease with strangers and groups, be able to offer congratulations smoothly, know how to make introductions, and know how to conduct themselves at company functions.[19]

Electronic devices, including e-mail, cell phones, and personal digital assistants (such as a BlackBerry), have created new etiquette demands. An industrial sales representative was playing golf with his potential customer, a CEO. The sales rep checked his BlackBerry after every stroke. His insensitivity and poor etiquette so infuriated the CEO that the latter cancelled his plans for a $300,000 order.

Another challenging area for practicing good etiquette, and thereby creating a good impression, is the use of profanity. Some people believe that you should follow the lead of the highest-ranking manager in your unit. If that person is profane, you should use profanity frequently in his or her presence. One manager said he likes the members of his group to use profanity because it shows passion.[20] In contrast, if the highest-ranking manager avoids profanity, so should you. Also, some companies frown on profanity because it could lead to charges of sexual harassment.

In general, the corporate culture and subculture dictate whether profanity is acceptable, and which particular profane words create a good impression. In an organizational culture that encourages profanity, using less profanity than other workers would probably create a good impression. Or the political actor might try out "soft profanity," like "Great Balls of Fire," and gauge the reaction of others.

Basking in Reflected Glory

A slightly devious, yet widely used, tactic of impression management is to claim association with prestige figures or prestigious institutions.[21] The association with prestige figures and institutions in used in many ways, including the following:

- A human resource manager wanting to be regarded more positively by his manager might say, "At lunch today with Ursula (the CEO), she said my ideas for a healthy lifestyle training program were really exciting."
- Wanting to impress superiors in the company, a financial analyst adds to her credentials in the company database, "Studied at the Fuqua School, Duke University." Her "studying" consisted of taking a weekend seminar in a management development program.
- A consultant attempting to build a good relationship with the unit manager to which he is assigned says, "Both your chief operations officer and many others at Fortune 500 companies think that this program can save a manufacturing division tons of money."

Engage in Strategic Self-Presentation

A theory of impression management tactics has been developed that fits well the tactics mentioned in this chapter, as well as several of those to be introduced as influence tactics in Chapter 7. Collectively, the categories of impression management behavior developed by E. E. Jones and T. S. Pitman are referred to as **strategic self-presentation.**[22] If one does not create a strong enough impression, you move on to the next. The categories of impression management are as follows:

1. *Ingratiation*—the attempt to appear likeable, perhaps through such means as smiling and being agreeable.
2. *Exemplification*—the attempt to appear dedicated such as working late in the office or sending work-related e-mail messages to your boss at 3:00 a.m.
3. *Intimidation*—the attempt to appear threatening, perhaps through such means as grimacing or dressing in unusually expensive clothing.
4. *Self-promotion*—the attempt to appear competent through such means as making an informed and graphically exciting PowerPoint presentation to management.
5. *Supplication*—the attempt to appear in need of assistance, such as asking how to make sense of the quarterly financial statement released by the company.

We have presented a sampling of impression management tactics. To reflect on the type of impression management tactics you use, or might use, take the self-quiz presented in Exhibit 4.1.

A VARIETY OF RELATIONSHIP BUILDERS WITH SUPERIORS

Being a good organizational citizen and managing your impression are effective strategies for building relationships with superiors. In this section, we focus on seven representative tactics for enhancing relationships with the immediate superior, and quite often higher-ups at the same time.

Understand Your Manager's Style and Work Preferences

A logical way to build a strong relationship with your manager is to understand his or her management and leadership style and work preferences.

Exhibit 4.1 The Positive Impression Survey

Directions: Please indicate how often you use the following ways of impressing work associates, including customers. Use the following ratings: 1 = very infrequently (VI); 2 = infrequently (I); 3 = sometimes (S); 4 = frequently (F); 5 = very frequently (VF). Circle the most accurate answer.

Tactic or Method	*VI*	*I*	*S*	*F*	*VF*
1. Dressing well	1	2	3	4	5
2. Making a favorable appearance other than through dress	1	2	3	4	5
3. Using colorful speech	1	2	3	4	5
4. Being cheerful	1	2	3	4	5
5. Appearing self-confident	1	2	3	4	5
6. Being neat and orderly	1	2	3	4	5
7. Pretending to others that I am in demand	1	2	3	4	5
8. Talking about quality as it relates to the job	1	2	3	4	5
9. Talking about own accomplishments	1	2	3	4	5
10. Being knowledgeable about the topic at hand	1	2	3	4	5
11. Achieving high job performance	1	2	3	4	5
12. Creating a problem and then solving it to look good	1	2	3	4	5
13. Talking about team play	1	2	3	4	5
14. Being diplomatic	1	2	3	4	5
15. Sharing expertise with others	1	2	3	4	5
16. Sharing credit with others	1	2	3	4	5
17. Giving warmth and support	1	2	3	4	5
18. Following through on promises	1	2	3	4	5
19. Exaggerating my accomplishments	1	2	3	4	5
20. Saying what the other person wants to hear	1	2	3	4	5

Tactic or Method	*VI*	*I*	*S*	*F*	*VF*
21. Listening carefully	1	2	3	4	5
22. Making small talk	1	2	3	4	5
23. Talking about work	1	2	3	4	5
24. Showing good ethics	1	2	3	4	5
25. Sending greeting cards to work associates	1	2	3	4	5
26. Avoiding a direct "No" in dealing with others	1	2	3	4	5
27. Being calm under pressure	1	2	3	4	5
28. Flattering others	1	2	3	4	5

Interpretation: This questionnaire is not designed to provide a score. Instead, compare your frequency ratings with those of a group of 300 men and women holding a variety of managerial, sales, and professional jobs. The following mean scores refer to ratings on the 1-to-5 scale.

Tactic or Method	*Mean Score*
1. Dressing well	4.1
2. Favorable appearance	4.3
3. Colorful speech	3.6
4. Cheerfulness	4.3
5. Self-confident appearance	4.5
6. Neatness	4.2
7. Pretending to be in demand	2.0
8. Talk of quality	4.2
9. Talk of accomplishments	2.6
10. Knowledge of topic	4.2
11. High performance	4.7
12. Creating problems	1.8

(Continued)

Exhibit 4.1 (Continued)

Tactic or Method	*Mean Score*
13. Team player talk	3.6
14. Diplomacy	4.0
15. Share expertise	4.2
16. Share credit	3.9
17. Warmth and support	4.1
18. Following through	4.4
19. Exaggeration	2.0
20. Saying what people want to hear	2.7
21. Listening	4.1
22. Small talk	3.0
23. Work talk	3.3
24. Ethics display	4.4
25. Greeting cards	2.6
26. Avoiding direct "No"	3.1
27. Pressure handling	4.1
28. Flattery	0.9

Your rating of the impression-management tactics may provide useful clues to skill development. If you use a given tactic much less frequently than others, you might consider evaluating whether you are using this tactic enough. For example, if you make very infrequent use of warmth and support to impress others, you might increase the frequency of such behavior to the norm (4.1 = frequently). In other instances, you might decide that you are overusing a tactic (such as exaggerating).

SOURCE: DuBrin, A. J. (1994). Sex differences in the use and effectiveness of tactics of impression management. *Psychological Reports, 74,* 531–544.

NOTE: In the comparison groups, only one statistically significant difference was found between men and women in the use of these impression tactics. Women gave a mean frequency rating of 2.9 for the use of greeting cards, while men gave a frequency rating of 2.3.

Without sacrificing your ability to work well, you make slight adaptations. A starting point would be to observe your manager's leadership style. If he or she is a consensus manager, be prepared to provide loads of input even on such matters as the choice of setting for the annual party. If the manager has a more autocratic style, you provide input only for major decisions, and only when asked. The study about surviving a new CEO mentioned earlier found that the new CEOs want their direct reports to be sensitive to their working style and then match it. One CEO in the study was impressed when one of his managers asked about how he should express disagreement, such as only in private. The direct report also asked how persistent he should be if turned down once. The executive in question survived throughout the CEO's 12-year tenure.[23]

A major consideration in understanding your manager's style and work preferences rests in communication, with digital communication adding complexity. Among the choices are the following: (1) almost all communication through e-mail, and the occasional face-to-face meeting; (2) mostly e-mail supplemented by instant messaging (IM) for urgent items; (3) mostly IM, with e-mail only for the most routine items; (4) loads of telephone and face-to-face communication, with e-mail used only for documentation; and (5) getting back to the manager immediately with a text message in nonworking hours—during the week, weekends, vacations, and holidays included. An extreme example of demanding instant communication with direct reports was Charles Potruck, the former CEO of Charles Schwabb. He had a cell phone built into his ski helmet so he could communicate with direct reports while racing downhill.

Help Your Manager Succeed

As obvious as this advice sounds, many workers sometimes forget that one of their major responsibilities is to help their manager succeed. Most likely the person who hired you into his or her business unit thought you could contribute directly or indirectly to the unit's success. Even if the manager did not hire you, your assistance is needed. A new CEO pointed out that so many managers do not recognize how much the CEO is looking for teammates on day one. He was amazed at how few people come through the door and say, "I want to help. I may not be perfect, but I buy into your vision."[24]

One of many ways of helping your boss succeed is to identify your manager's most pressing problems, and put extra effort into responding to those problems. In 2007, Dell Computer was struggling to recapture some of its past glory because Hewlett-Packard Co. had taken over as the number one seller of personal computers. In response to this major problem facing Michael Dell, a manager in the marketing department developed a program to sell two desktop models through 3,000 Wal-Mart stores. Whether or not the Wal-Mart affiliation propels Dell to the number one position, the marketing manager's plan was aimed directly at helping his manager succeed.

Another deft approach to helping your manager succeed is to emphasize bringing solutions rather than problems to him or her. The rationale is that dealing with loads of additional problems is not perceived by the boss as a path to success, yet solutions to problems are welcome. Returning to the Dell marketing manager above, bringing problems to the boss would take this approach: "The latest industry data have arrived. It looks like HP is gaining further ground on us. This is a monster problem." The solutions approach would be, "The latest data . . . don't look good for us. Although we have built our reputation on the direct seller model, I see a way for us to gain back market share. Why not join the competition and sell through Wal-Mart?"

Be Dependable and Honest

A classic article by John J. Gabarro and John P. Kotter describes a variety of positive tactics for managing your boss.[25] Most of their ideas support the relationship builders described in this chapter. Among the many positive suggestions Gabarro and Kotter make are to be dependable and honest. Part of the rationale is that few things are more disabling to a boss than a subordinate who cannot be depended upon or trusted.

Many managers become undependable simply because they are uncertain about their boss's priorities, and therefore might not be delivering the right project on time—but instead working on a project of lesser priority. One of the surest ways of being perceived as undependable is to be late with an important deliverable. As one CEO said in describing a subordinate, "I'd rather he be more consistent even if he delivered fewer peak successes—at least I could rely on him."

A person might appear dishonest to a boss simply because he or she frequently plays down the truth or plays down issues. With good use of information technology, many managers get information directly without relying on subordinates. Yet some subordinates still have a tendency to hide nasty data from the boss, such as not explaining that a couple of major accounts appear to be in jeopardy.

Make Good Use of Time and Resources

Another suggestion Gabarro and Kotter make is to recognize that your boss has only so much time, energy, and influence to give.[26] Every request you make represents a drain on these resources. An example would be sending 15 e-mail messages to your boss in one day asking for clarification about minor items. If all the other subordinates wrote the same number of messages, the boss would be overwhelmed taking care of e-mail. Another way of making poor use of your manager's resources is to frequently ask for his or her involvement in problems and opportunities you might better manage yourself. An example would be asking your boss to help you deal with an irate customer, with some exceptions depending on the size of the customer. To repeat, if you understand your manager's style and priorities, you will probably know what problems require his or her intervention.

Engage in Favorable Interactions With Your Manager

Favorable interactions with another person help build a relationship with him or her. The leader–member exchange theory described in Chapter 2 explains that a high-quality relationship with the manager includes favorable interactions. A study of interactions between bank employees and their supervisors showed that purposely trying to create a positive impression on a supervisor through favorable interactions led to better performance ratings. Among the favorable interactions were (1) praising your supervisor on his or her accomplishments, (2) volunteering to help your supervisor on a task, and (3) agreeing with you supervisor's major ideas.[27]

A subtle approach to having favorable interactions with the manager is to ask for counsel, yet avoiding the trap of being perceived as bringing too many problems to higher-ups. A welcome form of counsel relates to career matters because more experienced people frequently like to share their experience with less experienced people. It is best to ask sincere questions about issues and topics that could serve the organization well, along with you. Here are three examples:

- Based on your knowledge of where the company's global efforts are headed, in which foreign language do you think I should built competency?
- What would the company regard as really outstanding performance for a person at my level in the organization?
- What new skills and competencies will the company need in the next few years?

The advice sought by the above questions is political in the sense that you are making a conscious effort to build a good relationship with a superior. In the process, you are emphasizing a positive approach.

Minimizing complaints is another useful aspect of having favorable interactions with superiors. In the interest of honest communication, some complaining may be warranted. However, dealing with chronic complainers is time consuming and emotionally draining for many managers. During a downsizing, top-level managers often take the opportunity to get rid of troublesome employees, complainers included.

One possibility for minimizing the need for complaints is to attempt to look at decisions from the manager's perspective. Company management might decide to prohibit workers from using e-mail for personal reasons during working hours. Instead of complaining that the prohibition on e-mail is unjust, the worker might try to understand why company management thinks that using e-mail for personal reasons lowers productivity.

Favorable interactions with the manager will sometimes include socializing during nonworking hours. Socializing with the boss must be done prudently because of the possible role confusion. The worker must avoid confusing the role of subordinate with the role as a friend. Being a friend of the boss outside of work should not lead to favored treatment on the job in terms of salary increases, bonuses, and performance evaluations. Too much socializing with the boss can lead to charges of favoritism. Many companies discourage close friendships off the job to minimize charges of sexual harassment by subordinates. Socializing with the boss in the context of group activities might be an effective way of having favorable interactions with the boss yet avoiding conflicts of interest.

Be Loyal in a Variety of Ways

The traditional virtue of loyalty to the immediate superior and the organization remains a successful strategy for building upward relations. As loyalty to one's career rather than to the organization has gained momentum as a value, being a loyal subordinate helps a person stand out even more. Supporting the boss's position or vision is a major approach to being loyal. Loyalty is expressed in many ways, including defending the boss when he or she is under attack during a meeting, and not participating in a group mocking of the manager when he or she is not present.

An important form of loyalty is avoiding disloyalty in forms such as buying the competitor's brand of product instead of your employer's, not participating in an after-hours gathering to celebrate the boss's birthday or special accomplishment, and at least tolerating your boss's personal interests.[28] For example, if you detest professional hockey and your boss is a rabid hockey fan, think of something positive to say about hockey. Stretch your imagination by saying, "I like the way the NHL is taking a stronger stand against players intentionally injuring other players."

Bob Iger, president and CEO of the Disney Company, represents a high-level example of how loyalty to the boss can pay enormous dividends. He was widely known as a lackey to the pompous Disney CEO Michael Eisner, and even referred to as "Michael's concierge" by a few detractors. Yet, with Eisner's backing, Iger soon won the top job at Disney over strong outside candidates.[29] One might think that being perceived as a lackey means the person is unethical, yet from Iger's standpoint, he was being a supportive and faithful number two player.

Flatter Your Manager With Sincerity

A powerful technique for ingratiating yourself with higher-ups, as well as others, is to flatter them with sincerity. Although one meaning of the term "flattery" is insincere praise, another meaning refers to a legitimate compliment. Charismatic people use flattery regularly. You may recall the research study cited in Chapter 1 about the effectiveness of political behavior in receiving board appointments. An extension of the study showed that ingratiation toward peer directors increased the chances of receiving a board appointment at another company. Flattery was a key ingratiating technique. Although flattery was important in receiving a nomination to additional boards, another contributing factor was providing useful advice and information to CEOs.[30]

Effective flattery has at least a spoonful of credibility, implying that you say something positive about the target person that is plausible. Credibility is also increased when you point to a person's tangible accomplishments. An example would be saying to your boss, "I was really impressed that the energy-reduction plan you developed actually reduced the company carbon dioxide emissions by 8%. I was proud to have worked on the project." Technical people in particular expect flattery to be specific and aimed at genuine accomplishment.[31]

Strive for Ample and Open Communication

A general-purpose approach for building a positive relationship with an immediate superior is to communicate well with him or her. Although this tactic is widely recognized as the key to most personal and business relationships, it is not easy to attain. A major part of open communication is to inform the manager quickly of trouble spots. If an angry customer is a potential source of trouble, alert the boss. Inform the boss and offer assistance if a project is flawed or behind schedule.[32] As explained earlier, when critical problems are brought to the boss's attention, it is best to offer proposed solutions. An example might be, "Our supplier in Taiwan is down because of a typhoon, but I have already spoken with our supplier in Malaysia. They can pick up the slack within 10 days."

Asking for feedback can also facilitate open communication. Assume your manager asks you to compile data on accidents in the office that have taken place in the last five years. After submitting the data, you hear nothing from your boss. You might gently ask, "How useful were the accident data I submitted last week?" If your boss were an excellent communicator, you would have received the feedback—but not every boss has the time or the inclination to be an excellent communicator.

Career coach Donna Schwarz advises that being out of touch with the boss can lead to job loss because the relationship with the boss weakens considerably. If the manager appears inaccessible, find ways to accomplish small updates—perhaps by e-mail or telephone. Also, find a good time for the brief update. Some managers, for example, reserve Saturday mornings to catch up on e-mails related to internal matters.[33]

DEALING WITH A DIFFICULT BOSS

A highly challenging aspect of building a good relationship with the boss occurs when faced with a problem manager—one who makes it difficult for the subordinate to get the job done. The problem could lie in the boss's personality or incompetence. At other times, differences in values or goals could be creating the problem. Another consideration is that the subordinate might be misperceiving the situation. For example, a manager might be perceived as making outrageous demands on group members, yet the manager is simply responding to pressures from upper-level management to boost productivity and lower costs. A few suggestions for dealing with a difficult boss are described next.

1. *First, look at your own attitude.* You might be the reason for the problem. A person who complains and gripes about work, who bad-mouths the manager, and who attempts to get out of assignments creates a situation that makes the boss appear difficult.[34]

2. *Confront your manager constructively.* A general-purpose way of dealing with a difficult boss is to confront the problem in a tactful way then look for a solution. A beginning point is to gently ask for an explanation of the problem. If it appears that your manager dislikes you, try this confrontation: "I want to improve my performance. What might I be doing wrong that is creating a problem between us?" Confrontation can also be helpful with a micromanaging boss. You might say, for example, "I notice that you check almost everything I do. Are you concerned that I am not as capable as I need to be for the job?"

3. *Take the initiative to get credit for your ideas.* A commonly cited behavior of a difficult boss is using your ideas without sharing the credit. Because you report to a manager, your ideas belong to him or her, yet credit sharing is expected. Doug White of Robert Half International recommends that you maintain a written record of the ideas you contribute to your boss. Documentation establishes a paper or electronic trail that can be referenced later in a performance review, or when discussing your contribution with others in the organization. You might also ask your boss for guidance on how to receive recognition for your efforts because you want to advance in the company.[35]

4. *Send gentle reminders for taking action on unfinished tasks.* Many bosses are perceived as difficult because they are slow in getting back to subordinates with approval for taking action, or providing information that is needed to complete a project.[36] For example, you might need the boss's authorization to pay a large bill to a supplier. The supplier is putting the pressure on you, and you need the supplier in order to accomplish your work. A series of gentle reminders may be necessary that include a brief statement of why action must be taken soon. The urgent-message flag on e-mail sometimes works, but many of these flags go unnoticed. You might begin your urgent message with, "What I need to complete my project will only take about three minutes of your time."

5. *Report outrageous behavior to higher management.* It is conceivable that during a person's career he or she will be supervised by a manager whose outrageous behavior suggests mental illness. Robert Hare defines the *corporate psychopath* as the nonviolent person prone to "selfish, callous, and remorseless use of others." Such behavior might include enlisting the assistance of subordinates to create inflated expense accounts, firing subordinates who criticize the manager's plans, and sexually abusing group members. One of most infamous executives who might have been classified as a corporate psychopath was "Chainsaw" Al Dunlap. At one point, he fired half the labor force at Sunbeam and almost destroyed the company's ability to provide good customer service. He hurled a chair at his human resources director, who was the same person who had approved Dunlap's handgun and bulletproof vest on his expense report.[37] (Dunlap is an exception—a corporate psychopath who is violent.)

A recommended approach to dealing with a boss who exhibits outrageous behavior repeatedly is to report the incident to a higher manager, preferably as a group in order to minimize the threat of retaliation. In most cases, the next level of management probably has some awareness that a severe problem exists and the additional documentation will help resolve the problem.

SUMMARY

One of the greatest determinants of career success is managing upward relations. Organizational citizenship behavior can be regarded as organizational politics geared toward upward relations. Four specific aspects of organizational citizenship behavior linked to developing upward relations are (1) the creation of social capital; (2) altruistic citizenship behavior, which can lead to higher performance evaluations and recommendations for rewards; (3) organizational citizenship behavior, which is more important for interdependent tasks; and (4) delivering beyond expectations.

Impression management is directed at enhancing one's image, and can relate to both superficial and deeper aspects of behavior. Contextual variables influencing impression management include (1) power relations in the firm, (2) limited economic and political opportunities of subgroups, (3) culture-specific codes, (4) occupational status, and (5) individualistic versus collective culture.

The specific tactics of impression management presented here are (1) build trust and confidence, (2) be visible and create a strong presence, (3) admit mistakes, (4) minimize being a yes-person, (5) create a healthy image, (6) display appropriate etiquette, and (7) basking in reflected glory.

Relationship builders with superiors presented here are (1) understanding your manager's style and work preferences; (2) helping your manager succeed; (3) being dependable and honest; (4) making good use of time and resources; (5) engaging in favorable interactions with your manager, including minimizing complaints; (6) being loyal in a variety of ways; (7) flattering your manager with sincerity; and (8) striving for ample and open communication.

A few suggestions for dealing with a difficult manager include (1) first looking at your own attitude, (2) confronting your manager constructively, (3) taking the initiative to get credit for your ideas, (4) sending gentle reminders for taking action on unfinished tasks, and (5) reporting outrageous behavior to higher management.

QUESTIONS AND ACTIVITIES

1. Describe a research project that could be undertaken to provide evidence that being a good organizational citizen really improves a person's upward relations.
2. Among the strategies and tactics described for establishing effective upward relations, identify the three that you are most likely to use. Explain your reasoning.
3. Among the strategies and tactics described for establishing upward relations, identify one that you think clashes with your values and ethics. Explain your reasoning.
4. What do you perceive to be the negative consequences of making no effort to establish good upward relations?
5. Assume that you urgently need input from your boss to complete a project. What is your evaluation of the effectiveness of using smiley faces and unhappy faces to capture your boss's attention on e-mail messages?
6. Develop a sincere statement of flattery for (a) any manager you have ever worked for, (b) the CEO of Ford Motor Company, and (c) your professor for this course.
7. Ask two experienced businesspeople what they think is the best method of getting along with the boss. Compare your findings with those of other class members.

CASE STUDY: THE IMAGE DOCTOR WILL SEE YOU NOW

"You are being Googled, maybe even right now," William Arruda says to 150 people who have tuned in to a Career Coach Institute teleconference. He pauses for effect, then continues, "If you don't show up in Google, you don't exist."

Arruda, a former IBM marketing executive and the 45-year-old founder of Reach Communication Consulting in New York, pulled in $1 million in a recent year milking the latest consulting gimmick, "personal branding." That means showing you how, among other things, to pretty up the picture of yourself that shows up on search sites, YouTube, and blogs. Arruda says you need a presence as distinctive as a Nike swoosh—"What makes you unique makes you successful." Think of this work as something like repositioning a tired toothpaste brand.

Fee: up to $15,000. To find out what is promotable or problematic about the executives who hire him, Arruda interviews them, polls friends and colleagues—typical question: If this person were a car, what kind would he or she be?—and then tells them how to stand out by writing blogs, giving speeches, and changing they way they talk or dress.

Pierre Van Beneden, 53, says Arruda helped him develop an expertise in how technology affects education. Since then, at Arruda's urging, he has delivered speeches on the topic and created a slick Web site. He credits Arruda with helping him get noticed and recruited. Now he is vice president of Adobe's business in Europe, Africa, and the Middle East.

Sometimes an executive just needs a personality correction. Laura Tessinari, a senior partner at Ogilvy & Mather in New York, learned from Arruda that colleagues considered her too brash. Arruda told her to tone down her act. Tessinari now has candles, a couch, and tea in her office at the advertising agency to make it more welcoming. She credits Arruda's coaching with helping her get a teaching gig at Fordham. She says, "You can't understand business unless you understand yourself."

Big companies tap Arruda to lead charisma-boosting workshops. Starwood Hotels & Resorts recently hired him to speak to 300 execs. He has gotten business from American Express, JPMorgan Chase, and Microsoft.

Some executives are uneasy self-promoters. Jane Swift, a program director at British Telecom in London, followed Arruda's advice to network with higher-ups—she hosted a lunch for women executives at the company—but she isn't convinced she needs her own Web site. "I don't want a 'Who does she think she is?' response," she frets.

That's not the kind of thing that troubles Arruda. When he isn't dolling out doses of oomph, he is busy recruiting coaches to help him build his own brand. Currently there are 150 Arrudaites around the world preaching his gospel of personal branding; they pay him $3,200 for 60 hours of training plus a 5% cut of their consulting gigs. A top earner after Arruda is Paul Copcutt, a former executive recruiter in Toronto, who pulled in less that $100,000 last year. Arruda hoped to sign on 200 more acolytes in the following year. If you want to reach him, just Google "reach" with "Arruda."

Three of Arruda's suggestions for selling yourself are as follows:

- Build a powerful online identity and make sure you have stellar Google results (volume and relevance).
- Seek out speaking engagements at industry events to boost your visibility to leaders and potential employers.
- Color is an important element of your brand identity. Pick a signature hue and buy clothes and luggage in that color.

Case Study Questions

1. How important do you think it is for your career for your name to have a large number of entries in Google or another search engine? And how could one attain good volume and relevance?

2. How does this case study about the "image doctor" relate to upward relations?

3. Which aspects of impression management does Arruda appear to be emphasizing?

4. What is your opinion of the declaration that color is an important element of your brand identity?

5. What is your opinion of Arruda's qualifications to give people a "personality correction"?

SOURCE: Excerpted from Hoppough, S. (2007). Image doctor. *Forbes*, February 26, 60.

POLITICAL SKILL-BUILDING EXERCISE 4

Engaging in Effective Flattery

As described in the chapter, effective use of flattery is useful in building upward relationships. Flattery is generally most effective when it is sincere and focuses on legitimate accomplishment of the flattery target. In each of the following scenarios, one person plays the role of the flatterer, and one person is the flattery target. The latter will be either the immediate manager of the flatterer, or another higher-ranking individual. Carry out the flattery episode for about four minutes.

Scenario A: You are riding alone in the elevator with your manager, who has played a key role in your company purchasing a smaller company that fits nicely into your company's product line. You probably only have a couple of minutes to accomplish your flattery, so act fast.

Scenario B: By coincidence, you and the vice president of finance are standing on the same line at the airport, waiting to check in. You are headed to different cities so you will not be seated next to the vice president during the flight. You have heard that the vice president was instrumental in getting the company some new funding, so you see a wedge for some flattery.

Scenario C: Your boss is just back from vacation, looks vibrant, and appears to have lost about 10 pounds. You are a little concerned about making personal compliments in a job setting, but this looks like an opportunity worth exploring.

Students observing the flattery incidents will comment on the most likely effectiveness of the flattery episodes, and might also offer some constructive criticism. Also comment on how well the flattery targets received the flattery attempts.

REFERENCES

1. Averett, T. (2003, August). Executive commentary by Todd Averett in response to Mark C. Bolino and William H. Turnley, "Going the Extra Mile: Cultivating and Managing Employee Citizenship Behavior." *Academy of Management Executive,* 60–71 [pp. 72–73].

2. Umiker, W. (1990, July). Playing politics fair and square. *Health Care Supervisor,* 27.

3. Sandberg, J. (2006, May 16). Working for a boss who only manages up can be a real downer. *Wall Street Journal,* B1.

4. Organ, D. W., Podaskoff, P. M., & MacKenzie, S. B. (2006). *Organizational citizenship behavior: Its nature, antecedents, and consequences.* Thousand Oaks, CA: Sage.

5. Bolino, M. C., Turnley, W. H., & Bloodgood, J. M. (2002, October). Citizenship behavior and the creation of social capital in organizations. *Academy of Management Review,* 505–506.

6. Heilman, M. E., & Chen, J. J. (2005, May). Same behavior, different consequences: Reactions to men's and women's altruistic citizenship behavior. *Journal of Applied Psychology,* 431–441.

7. Bachrach, D. G., Powell, B. C., Bendoly, E., & Richey, R. G. (2006, January). Organizational citizenship behavior and performance evaluations: Exploring the impact of task interdependence. *Journal of Applied Psychology,* 193–201.

8. Welch, J., & Welch, S. (2006, December 18). Getting back on the radar. *BusinessWeek,* 160.

9. Drory, A., & Zaidman, N. (2006). The politics of impression management in organizations: Contextual effects. In E. Vigoda-Gadot & A. Drory (Eds.), *Handbook of organizational politics* (pp. 75–88). Northampton, MA: Edward Elgar.

10. Synthesized from the literature in Drory, A., & Zaidman, N. (2006). The politics of impression management in organizations: Contextual effects. In E. Vigoda-Gadot & A. Drory (Eds.), *Handbook of organizational politics* (pp. 75–88). Northampton, MA: Edward Elgar.

11. *Career article 103: Getting along with your boss (2002–2006).* Retrieved 05/05/2007 from www.seekingsuccess.com.

12. Bragg, T. (2005). *Nine strategies for successfully playing office politics.* Retrieved 05/26/2007 from www.tbragg.addr.com.

13. Coyne, K. P., & Coyne, E. J. Sr. (2007, May). Surviving your new CEO. *Harvard Business Review,* 68.

14. Holmes, T. E. (2007, May). Admitting when you're wrong. *Black Enterprise,* 124.

15. Holmes, T. E. (2007, May). Admitting when you're wrong.

16. *Manager's Edge* (2006, Spring). Get rid of "yes men." *Manager's Edge,* Special Bulletin, 2.

17. Yi, D. (2007, March 12). For many employees, fitness has its prize. *Los Angeles Times.* Retrieved 05/30/2007 from latimes.com.

18. *Nu-Living Weight Management-Microsoft Program* (2007, May 24). Retrieved 06/02/2007 from www.nu-living.com/microsoft.

19. Rucker, J., & Sellers, J. A. (1998, February). Changes in business etiquette. *Business Education Forum,* 43.

20. Sandberg, J. (2006, March 21). In the workplace, every bleeping word can show your rank. *Wall Street Journal,* B1.

21. McFarland, L. A. (2005, Winter). An examination of impression management use and effectiveness across assessment center exercises: The role of competency demands. *Personnel Psychology,* 953.

22. Jones, E. E., & Pitman, T. S. (1982). Toward a general theory of strategic self-presentation. In J. Suls (Ed.), *Psychological perspectives of the self* (pp. 231–262). Hillsdale, NJ: Lawrence Erlbaum.

23. Coyne, K. P., & Coyne, E. J., Sr. (2007, May). Surviving your new CEO. *Harvard Business Review,* 61–66.

24. Coyne, K. P., & Coyne, E. J., Sr. (2007, May). Surviving your new CEO.

25. Gabarro, J. J., & Kotter, J. P. (2005, January). Managing your boss. *Harvard Business Review,* 99. (Reprint of article first published in 1980.)

26. Gabarro, J. J., & Kotter, J. P. (2005, January). Managing your boss.

27. Wayne, S. J., & Ferris, G. R. (1990, October). Influence tactics, affect, and exchange quality in supervisor–subordinate interactions: A laboratory experiment and field study. *Journal of Applied Psychology,* 487–490.

28. Bruzzese, A. (2006, May 15). Reading your boss is a valuable skill. Gannett News Service.

29. Sellers, P. (2005 March 7). The two faces of Bob Iger. *Fortune,* n.p.

30. Westphal, J. D., & Stern, I. (2007, April). Flattery will get you everywhere (especially if you are a male Caucasian): How ingratiation, boardroom behavior, and demographic minority status affect additional board appointments at U.S. companies. *Academy of Management Journal,* 267–288.

31. DuBrin, A. J. (2005). Self-perceived technical orientation and attitudes toward being flattered. *Psychological Reports, 96,* 852–854.

32. Bruzzese, A. (2006, May 15). Reading your boss is a valuable skill. Gannett News Service.

33. Lublin, J. S. (2006, September 5). How to work around your boss's habit of not being available. *Wall Street Journal,* A15.

34. Owens, M. B. (2004, October 18). Pleasing your boss may be possible. *Detroit News.* Retrieved 06/16/2007 from www.detnews.com.

35. White, D. (2007). Credit problems: When your boss won't share the spotlight. *Yahoo! hotjobs.* Retrieved 06/28/2007 from www.yahoo.com.

36. Mintz, J. (2005, August 30). The jungle: Focus on recruitment, pay and getting ahead. *Wall Street Journal,* B6.

37. Hare cited in Deutschman, A. (2005, July). Is your boss a psychopath? *Fast Company,* 47.

FIVE

LATERAL RELATIONS

LEARNING OBJECTIVES

After studying this chapter and doing the exercises, you should be able to do the following:

1. Explain why positive lateral relations are important for the individual and the organization.
2. Identify and describe political tactics for enhancing coworker relationships.
3. Identify and describe political tactics for enhancing team play.
4. Describe how to attain individual recognition while at the same time having positive lateral relations, including being a good team player.

The French business school HEC is located on a hilltop campus in the Paris suburb of Joyy-en-Josas. The MBA program has undergone a striking transformation. As recently as 1997, the majority of its students were French and the program was little known overseas. Today, thanks to aggressive international recruiting, only about 15% of the students are

French, while roughly a third are from Asia and another third from the Americas.

Along with greater diversity has come global recognition. "We are a symbol of France's openness to the world," says Associated Dean Valérie Gauthier, who oversees the MBA program. HEC isn't the only European B-school with a strong international flavor. But its small size—just 200 students—and relatively long 16-month program (compared with only 10 months at France's INSEAD and Switzerland's IMD) allow students to forge close relationships with others from different backgrounds. Indeed, an emphasis on interpersonal skills is one of HEC's selling points. During the first eight months, each student is assigned to a group of five or six students who work intensively together on projects. Disagreements arise more often from differences in professional training—engineers versus financial types, for example—than from culture clashes, says Nicolas Hobeliah, a student from Syria. "If you're here to adapt and open your eyes, it's a great place to be," he says.

For most students, HEC is merely the latest stop in an impressive global itinerary. Hobeliah graduated from the American University of Beirut and worked for a French company in Dubai; another student, Jennifer Miller, spent six years on development projects in Africa. Students are required to speak one foreign language besides English, and 80% speak at least three languages.

The school held an India Week celebration that hardly seems necessary for such a cosmopolitan crowd. But participants say that such student-organized activities reinforce the esprit de corps. Every spring, HEC hosts a sports tournament for students from 10 European MBA programs who compete in events ranging from basketball to mountain biking.[1]

(*Note to reader:* "HEC," "INSEAD," and "IMD" are no longer acronyms, but the true names of the schools mentioned.)

The story about the MBA program at the French university is yet another illustration of how interpersonal skills and working well with other people are important qualifications for working effectively in an organization. Getting along with coworkers, or having effective lateral relations, is a major component of organizational politics. In this chapter we look at the importance of lateral relations, followed by political tactics for developing coworker relationships and being a team player. A final section describes how to have good lateral relations yet also receive the individual recognition needed for advancement.

THE POSITIVE CONSEQUENCES OF GOOD LATERAL RELATIONS

The most obvious reason why good lateral relations are important in the workplace is that an organization, by definition, is a collection of people engaged in a collaborative venture. Collaboration is essential for the organization to survive, and when people work smoothly together, collaboration is easier to attain. According to research involving 8 million interviews directed by Tom Rath at the Gallup Organization, good lateral relations in the form of personal friendships provide substantial benefits to the individual and the organization.

Rath and his researchers found that although workplace friendships cause some problems such as jealousy, cliques, and people angry about broken romances, the positive consequences of employees being friends far outweigh the negatives. Approximately 30% of employees who reported having a best friend at work were seven times more likely to be engaged on the job. The same employees were also significantly more likely to engage customers, be more productive, experience higher job satisfaction, have fewer accidents, innovate and share ideas, and have the opportunity to focus on their strengths each day. Rath concluded that if you want to be happier and more engaged at work, consider developing a few strong friendships at the office.

One reason offered for the contribution of friendships on the job is that close relationships and friendships satisfy key needs and motives. The recommendation in terms of lateral relationships is to have clear expectations of which workers can assist in what ways. Figure out who can help you with a specific type of problem. It is also important to reach out to newcomers because they might be a source of friendship.[2]

The team member exchange (TMX) theory developed by Anson Seers provides additional confirmation of the positive consequences of good lateral relations. In one study, 429 individual workers' relationships were tested in work settings in three organizations in the United States and Canada. The major finding of relevance here was that high-quality peer relationships were positively associated with five outcomes: job satisfaction, emotional commitment to the organization, perceived group performance and effectiveness, and group cohesiveness.[3] We do not know for sure whether the outcomes might lead to positive exchanges, such as whether being part of a high-performing group triggers someone to have high-quality coworker relationships. Nevertheless, positive TMX is making at least a partial contribution to successful team outcomes.

Positive lateral relations also contribute to career advancement because workers who do not get along well with coworkers frequently receive lower performance evaluations or are passed over for promotion. A person who does not get along well with coworkers might be regarded as a poor team player and communicator.[4] Furthermore, good human relations skills are considered to be a requirement for a supervisory position.

POLITICAL TACTICS FOR COWORKER RELATIONSHIPS

In this section, we present a representative group of political tactics for establishing and maintaining good coworker relationships. The following section describes tactics more sharply focused on achieving good teamwork. The topics of coworker relationships and teamwork overlap and are mutually supportive.

Engage in Interpersonal Citizenship Behavior

We have already discussed organizational citizenship behavior (OCB) as part of organizational politics in several contexts. The aspect of OCB most relevant for lateral relations concerns the citizenship behavior directed toward coworkers and immediate others—referred to as **interpersonal citizenship behavior.** In contrast, *task-focused citizenship behavior* involves activities such as helping coworkers with difficult assignments and heavy workloads. Interpersonal citizenship behavior has been found to be an outcome of high-quality relationships that promote mutual concern and increased sensitivity to the needs of others.[5] Yet the cause and effect (or antecedents and consequences) can also be reversed. If you go out of your way to help coworkers, the result can be high-quality relationships. Workers who engage in interpersonal citizenship behaviors have a positive influence on the attitudes and behaviors of coworkers, leading to a harmonious environment.[6]

The most relevant parts of two research findings dealing with the intricate relationship between interpersonal citizenship behavior and upward relations are presented next.

1. *Interpersonal citizenship behavior and its influence on other aspects of employee interpersonal relationships.* A total of 234 workers were studied in a university and in hospital service units, with the work being complex enough that communication and coordination among employees were required. Data were collected through employees' self-reports, supervisors, and coworkers.

As hypothesized, coworker support, trust, perspective taking, and empathy for others were all positively correlated with interpersonal citizenship behavior. Some support was found for the premise that in high-quality lateral relations, individuals are not prone to help others for the purpose of directly obligating coworkers to reciprocate for a good deed. A secondary finding was that showing empathy is important for building trust with another individual.[7]

2. *The impact of interpersonal citizenship behavior as a function of the amount of abusive supervision.* The moderating effect of abusive supervision on the impact of organizational citizenship behavior was examined in two related studies. In one study, 173 workers from a wide variety of work settings were surveyed about the extent of abusive supervision they received, as well as coworkers' organizational citizenship behavior, job satisfaction, and organizational commitment. The interpersonal aspect of citizenship behavior was defined by statements such as "go out of their way to help coworkers with work-related problems." A finding related to lateral relations was that the relationship between coworkers' organizational citizenship behavior and job satisfaction was positive when abusive supervision was low.

In a related study, 95 municipal workers were studied using measures of coworkers' citizenship behavior and job satisfaction, among other variables. When abusive supervision was low, coworkers' citizenship behavior was positively related to job satisfaction. In contrast, when abusive supervision was high, coworkers' organizational citizenship behavior was negatively related to job satisfaction. A tentative explanation is that citizenship behavior may not be helpful in elevating the job satisfaction of coworkers if they are burdened with an abusive supervisor. Part of the problem is that an abusive supervisor contributes to a climate of distrust. Another finding was that employees were more satisfied with their jobs when they perceived their coworkers' citizenship behavior to be altruistic rather than self-serving. Authenticity and being trustful influence the effectiveness of citizenship behavior as a method of enhancing lateral relations.[8]

Engage in Positive Coworker Exchanges

Leader–member exchanges (LMXs) are important for understanding the behavior and performance of subordinates. Coworker exchanges (CWXs) have also been studied to provide insight into the quality of lateral relations, and they represent the same idea as the TMXs mentioned above. **Coworker exchanges** refer to exchanges or interactions between and among people who report to the same supervisor. A high-quality exchange is characterized by mutual respect, trust, and obligation.[9] Assume that Jason and Wanda report to the same manager of e-commerce. Jason prefers to rely on intuition in solving problems, and Wanda has a preference for relying on hard data. Jason and Wanda both respect each other's decision style, which contributes to positive exchanges between the two.

Positive coworker exchanges are only political in the sense that the initiator of the exchange recognizes that engaging in these exchanges will enhance lateral relations. The political actor here is behaving ethically and practicing good human relations, yet still has political motivation. Here we look at three specific methods of bringing about positive coworker exchanges: be positive, make others feel important, and be diplomatic.

Be Positive

A straightforward tactic for engaging in positive coworker exchanges is to be positive. A coworker who is frequently negative and constantly complaining about something annoys other people. It is preferable to be discreet about your complaints, rather than voicing them to all the other group members. Another detractor from effective lateral relations is to become the sounding board for others who seek to complain about work-related topics. Workers who seek to hear the negativity of others risk being perceived as negative themselves.[10]

Make Other People Feel Important

A fundamental principle of fostering good relationships with coworkers and others is to make them feel important. Although the leader has the primary responsibility for satisfying this recognition need, coworkers play a key role. One approach to making a coworker feel important would be to bring a notable accomplishment of his or hers to the attention of the group.

Another constructive approach to making others feel important is to express an interest in their work and personal life. The rationale for this tactic is that everyone is self-centered to some extent. As a result, favored topics are those closely related to themselves—such as their children, friends, hobbies, work, or possessions. Sales representatives rely heavily on this fact in sustaining relationships with established customers. Closely related to expressing an interest in others is to investigate what you have in common with coworkers, both professionally and personally. You might identify common interests such as a focus on the company's market share, or a personal interest such as bicycling.[11]

The quiz in Exhibit 5.1 gives you an opportunity to think through your tendencies to make other people feel important.

Exhibit 5.1 How Important Do I Make People Feel?

Directions: Indicate on a 1-to-5 scale how frequently you act (or would act if the situation presented itself) in the ways indicated below: very infrequently (VI); infrequently (I); sometimes (S); frequently (F); very frequently (VF). Circle the number underneath the column that best fits your answer.

Tactic or Method	*VI*	*I*	*S*	*F*	*VF*
1. I do my best to correctly pronounce a coworker's name.	1	2	3	4	5
2. I avoid letting other people's egos get too big.	5	4	3	2	1
3. I brag to others about the accomplishments of my coworkers.	1	2	3	4	5
4. I recognize the birthdays of friends in a tangible way.	1	2	3	4	5
5. It makes me anxious to listen to others brag about their accomplishments.	5	4	3	2	1
6. After hearing that a friend has done something outstanding, I shake his or her hand.	1	2	3	4	5
7. If a friend or coworker recently received a degree or certificate, I would offer my congratulations.	1	2	3	4	5
8. If a friend or coworker finished second in a contest, I would inquire why he or she did not finish first.	5	4	3	2	1
9. If a coworker showed me how to do something, I would compliment that person's skill.	1	2	3	4	5
10. When a coworker starts bragging about a family member's accomplishments, I do not respond.	5	4	3	2	1

Total: _____

Scoring and Interpretation: Total the numbers corresponding to your answers. Scoring 40–50 points suggests that you typically make people feel important; 16–39 points suggests that you have a moderate tendency toward making others feel important; 10–15 points suggests that you need to develop skill in making others feel important.

Be Diplomatic

Despite all that has been said about the importance of openness and honesty in building relationships, this principle cannot be pushed to the point of hurting the feelings of others. The egos of coworkers are too tender to accept the raw truth when faced with disapproval of their thoughts or actions. To foster smooth working relationships with coworkers, it is necessary to be diplomatic in expressing disagreement. Suppose a coworker shows you a new Web site homepage design for your organizational division. Your visceral reaction is that it looks as cluttered and confusing as the Yahoo! homepage. Your impulse is to say "horrid looking," but instead you communicate your displeasure more diplomatically in this manner: "I like the assortment of bold colors, and most of the elements, yet I think the homepage might be a little more focused and less busy."

Participate in Positive Gossip and Small Talk

The ability to engage in positive small talk and gossip has long been practiced as a way of coworkers establishing mutual rapport. Gossip in the context used here refers to talk about people known to the parties in exchange that is based on fact. In recent years, gossip in particular has been studied as an important form of communication for enhancing lateral relations. Social psychologists have conducted research showing that gossip can be the glue that binds social groups together. A more striking finding is that our desire to chatter about one another may be the evolutionary spur that prompted humanity to develop language.[12]

Gossiping helps create bonds among people by demonstrating to others that we trust them enough to share information. To enhance lateral relations, the political actor should contribute as well as listen to positive gossip, otherwise the coworker relationship will be unbalanced.

Small talk is trivial almost by definition, yet it can convey warmth. As others engage in small talk, throw in a question or comment to show that you are involved. If two coworkers are conversing about how warm it is today, you might comment, "Did you know that today it is hotter in Phoenix than in Saudi Arabia?" (Interesting facts often perk up small talk.) A danger in small talk is that, if it goes on for too long, it can be dysfunctional to your work and that of the organization. To end the conversation, small-talk researcher Don Gabor recommends a closure such as, "Well, got to get back to work, but it was really fun hearing about . . ." Restating what the person said shows you were really listening, further strengthening the bond.[13]

Supplement E-Mail With More Personal Contact

E-mail, including instant messaging and text messaging, has become the default method of communicating with coworkers. The potential downside in terms of developing lateral relations is that the human touch might be so diminished that a personal relationship between the sender and receiver fails to develop. One major problem with brief e-mail messages is that the underlying message may be misinterpreted. Another problem is the degree to which e-mail often substitutes for the nuanced conversations that are so helpful in developing lateral relations.

Current research suggests that the problems of e-mail are substantial. Justin Kruger has found that as few as 50% of users catch on to the tone or intent of an e-mail, and that most people greatly overestimate their ability to send and receive messages accurately. Smiley faces and exclamation points add to the confusion.[14] Scott A. Doktor, the CEO of PBD Worldwide Fulfillment Services, launched "no e-mail Fridays." He was concerned that e-mail usage was lowering productivity and sales. E-mail usage has dropped 80%, leading to improved communication and more one-on-one interaction among coworkers. (Now the company has to deal more with the problem of telephone tag.)

The research of Janice Nadler reinforces the importance of voice communication in building personal relationships. Students paired up to negotiate a commercial transaction. Half of the students used e-mail exclusively, and half conducted a brief phone conversation before beginning the negotiation via e-mail. The students who first interacted by phone were four times more likely to reach an agreement than those who relied only on e-mail. The experiment highlighted the problem that there are no visual or audio cues (such as facial expressions or voice tone) to establish rapport when using e-mail.[15]

Repair Damage Quickly

In a competitive work environment, and given the naturally poor chemistry between some workers, conflicts and problems inevitably arise. Part of the same problem is that a good relationship with a coworker becomes strained.[16] In the interests of maintaining harmony within the group, and to avoid the distractions of continuing conflict with a coworker, it is best to repair the damage quickly.

An example of the need for damage control might be when a coworker is reprimanded for a flawed project. The coworker proceeds to cite your input for the problems with the project. Word gets back to you through third parties about your being blamed. Unless the issue is resolved between the two of you, your dislike of your coworker and your discomfort in working with him or her is likely to grow. A potentially useful approach is to confront the coworker in a constructive way to talk about the problem. In this case you might say, "I've been told that you are attributing much of the blame to me for a troubled project of yours. What went wrong? I would like to know. I don't want to lose the good working relationship we had in the past."

Not every coworker problem will be resolved with one polite confrontation. However, it is a starting point in working out differences and conflicts. Keep in mind one of the most fundamental principles of organizational politics: have as many allies and as few enemies as possible in your place of work.

POLITICAL TACTICS FOR ENHANCING TEAM PLAY

Almost any strategy or tactic for cultivating lateral relations will have some impact on team play within the work group. Nevertheless, as outlined in Exhibit 5.2, we concentrate in this section on political tactics that help a person become a good team player, thereby enhancing teamwork. The tactics described here are aimed toward helping a person gain the support of other team members. Exhibit 5.3 provides you with an opportunity to reflect on your present tendencies toward practicing team politics.

Contribute to the Team Culture

A starting point in enhancing team play is for the individual to contribute to a culture of teamwork—one in which cooperation, trust, and coordinated effort are part of the value system. Among the specific behaviors contributing to a culture of teamwork would be frequent use of the words "we," "us," and "the team." Most forms of organizational citizenship behavior would also contribute to a culture of teamwork, as would being eager to socialize with the group during and after standard working hours. When Jim McNerney was revamping Boeing, one of his major goals was to shift from a culture characterized by internal rivalries to a team culture. Part of the approach was to place top executives in charge of teams responsible for standardizing production lines or redundant and costly research and development centers.[17]

Contributing to a team culture also takes the form of following group norms, or standards of conduct. Norms become a standard of what each

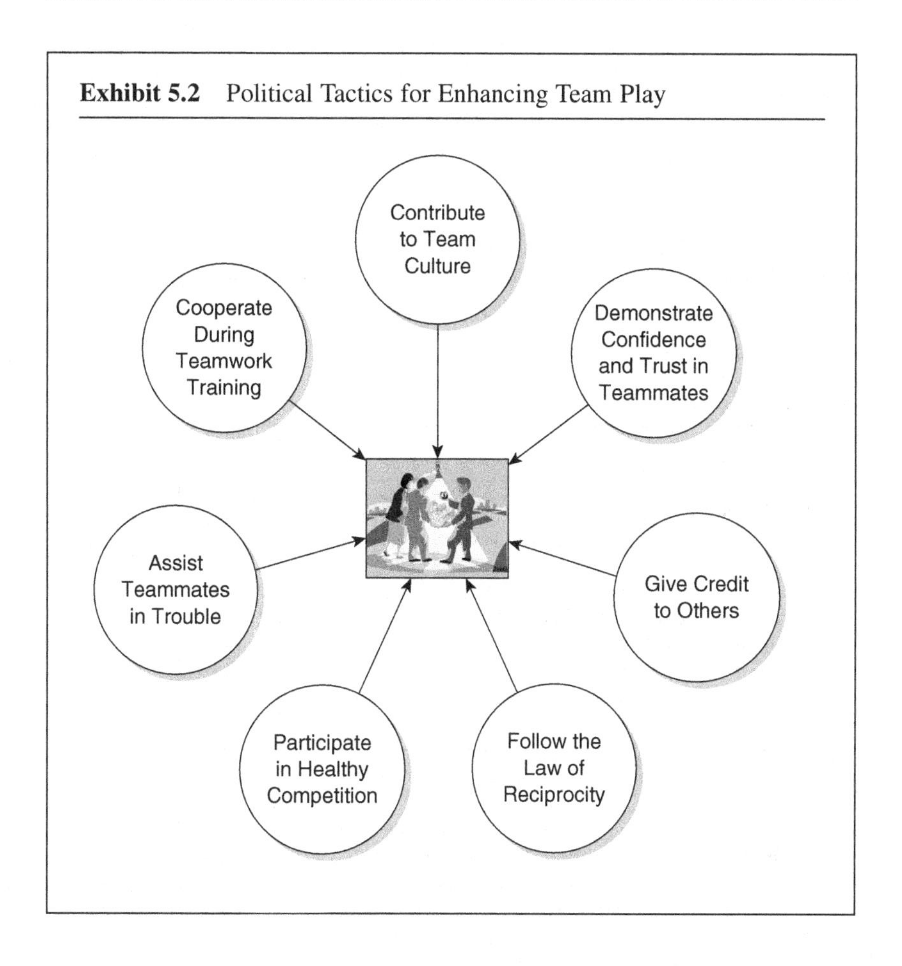

Exhibit 5.2 Political Tactics for Enhancing Team Play

person should do or not do within the group. The norms develop through interaction among group members, and are informally agreed upon by work group members. Norms also provide general guidelines for reacting constructively to the behavior of others. When Alan R. Mulally was in the process of revamping the Ford Motor Company, new group norms emerged. Among them were not to use BlackBerrys during meetings and not have side conversations even if the presenter was speaking through video conferencing. So the norm shifted from the multitasking that had been prevalent in the past to complete attention focused on the issue at hand.[18] (Note that violating group norms can be a political blunder which might place a person in disfavor.)

Mark G. Ehrhart and Stefanie E. Naumann propose that when a certain number of work group members engage in organizational citizenship behavior,

Exhibit 5.3 The Team Politics Questionnaire

Directions: Respond to the following statements as they relate to your team experience. If you have never been a member of a team either on the job, in school, or off the job, imagine how you would act or think if you were a team member. Indicate the extent to which you agree or disagree with each of the following statements: strongly agree (SA); agree (A); neutral (N); disagree (D); strongly disagree (SD). Circle the number under the most accurate answer for each question.

Thought or Action	*SA*	*A*	*N*	*D*	*SD*
1. I would ask a team member's opinion on personal matters even if I didn't need the advice, just to show that I respect his or her judgment.	5	4	3	2	1
2. I would help a team member with a household chore on a Sunday afternoon.	5	4	3	2	1
3. I would invite a teammate to a party in my home even if I didn't like him or her.	5	4	3	2	1
4. I would compliment teammates only when it was truly deserved.	1	2	3	4	5
5. When not in a team meeting, I would make no special effort to interact with teammates.	1	2	3	4	5
6. I would be willing to start negative rumors about a rival teammate.	5	4	3	2	1
7. Given a choice, I would only take on assignments within the team that would make me look good.	5	4	3	2	1
8. I would never tell a teammate anything that he or she could conceivably use against me in the future.	5	4	3	2	1
9. On occasion, I would surprise the team by bringing refreshments to a meeting.	5	4	3	2	1
10. I would not try to impress my teammates. It is better to let my good work speak for itself.	1	2	3	4	5

Thought or Action	*SA*	*A*	*N*	*D*	*SD*
11. I would try to be as nice as possible to all my teammates, even if I didn't like a particular person.	5	4	3	2	1
12. I would attend a team picnic just to be seen, even if I had something more important to do that day.	5	4	3	2	1
13. The best way to impress people would be to tell them what they want to hear.	5	4	3	2	1
14. I would attempt to give each team member a sincere compliment at least once a month.	5	4	3	2	1
15. I would not kiss up to the team leader.	1	2	3	4	5
16. I would work late in the office just to impress my teammates.	5	4	3	2	1
17. I would share my experience with teammates, even though it might mean that I no longer had a technical edge over them.	1	2	3	4	5
18. I would readily adapt to the jargon of the team, just so I fit right into the group.	5	4	3	2	1
19. When time was at a premium, I would put aside politeness toward team members.	1	2	3	4	5
20. I would recommend a highly competent person for membership on our team even if I thought that person would outperform me.	1	2	3	4	5
21. I would ask other team members' advice even if I didn't intend to use their input.	5	4	3	2	1
22. I would specifically let my teammates know that I was available for them when they needed my help.	5	4	3	2	1
23. Whenever I could do it tactfully, I would let other members of the team know of my accomplishments.	5	4	3	2	1

(Continued)

Exhibit 5.3 (Continued)

Thought or Action	*SA*	*A*	*N*	*D*	*SD*
24. It would not be unusual for me to do a favor for a teammate, even if I was not concerned about getting the favor returned in the future.	1	2	3	4	5
25. I think that flattering teammates is a waste of time.	1	2	3	4	5

Total: ____

Scoring and Interpretation: Calculate your total score by adding the numbers that you circled. Your score provides an approximate guide to your tendencies toward playing team politics (organizational politics directed specifically at winning favor as a team member).

100–125 You are going too far in playing team politics. Being this political could lead to the perception that you are insincere and much too concerned about self-advancement at the expense of the team. Some might even describe you as ruthless or Machiavellian. Study this chapter carefully to gain insight into how to practice team politics without appearing to be, or in fact being, insincere or ruthless.

75–99 You are politically astute without being or appearing insincere or ruthless. Most likely you have enough political sensitivity to facilitate your becoming a first-rate team player.

25–74 Most likely you are highly sincere, idealistic, and politically naïve. You could be too self-sacrificing to gain political advantage. Study carefully the tactics in this chapter and elsewhere in the text to acquire political skill. Also, invest time observing skilled organizational politicians to discover how they conduct themselves.

the behavior comes to be regarded as a group norm. Among the propositions developed in their analysis that relate to lateral relations and group norms are the following:

- The greater the degree of work group cohesiveness, the more likely it is that group norms for organizational citizenship behavior will develop.

- The greater the task interdependence among group members, the more likely it is that group norms of OCB will develop.
- The higher the descriptive norms for OCB in a group, the higher the performance of OCB by individual group members.[19] (Descriptive norms develop from watching what other group members do in certain situations.)

A general point to consider here is that group norms exert a powerful force on lateral relations, including the likelihood that norms dictate organizational citizenship behavior by group members. Following group norms then becomes a sensible and positive form of organizational politics.

Demonstrate Confidence and Trust in Teammates

Teamwork is based on confidence and trust, so it is essential to demonstrate confidence and trust in other team members. Trusting team members includes believing that their ideas are technically sound until proven otherwise. Another manifestation of trust is taking risks with others. You can take risks by trying out one of their unproved ideas. You can also take a risk by submitting an unproved idea and not worrying about being ridiculed.

As with most dimensions of interpersonal relationships, too much confidence and trust in teammates can be dysfunctional. A study by Claus W. Langfred conducted with 71 self-managing teams of MBA students, found that a high level of trust can make team members reluctant to monitor one another. The task was competing on the analysis of cases. When low monitoring of others was combined with high individual autonomy (working alone), team performance suffered.[20]

Give Credit to Others

You have probably heard or read many times about a business executive or athlete receiving an award, who then says something like, "I'm not the one who deserves the credit. It's really the team that made all this possible." Cliché or not, the sentiment still contributes to effective team play. Given that most performances in a team are the result of a joint contribution, sharing credit with others is an important part of being a team player. An example would be a sales representative who closes a big sale, and then explains what other members of the group did to facilitate the sale.

Brian Roberts, the CEO of Comcast, was explaining how his father Ralph Roberts was a great influence on his career. In describing what he learned from his father, Brian Roberts said, "Just by listening and asking questions, he lets you get to the heart of the issue that you are chewing on. He's not looking to take credit for anybody's work. In fact the single best piece of advice Ralph ever gave me was to let others take the credit. He said that you don't need all the glory. If you let others take the credit, it makes them feel like they're part of something special."[21]

Follow the Law of Reciprocity

According to organizational behavior scholar Allan Cohen, the *law of reciprocity* governs relationships in organizations. He says, "The secret of the universe lies in six words: Everyone expects to be paid back."[22] The payback to teammates can take many forms, such as thanking people for helping you on a project, helping them on a future project, or making positive statements about their helpfulness during a meeting. If you fail to pay a teammate back for assistance, you might be perceived as uncooperative and therefore a poor team player.

Sharing credit also fits under the law of reciprocity because giving teammates some credit for your accomplishments is a form of payback, particularly in an organization that values imagination.

Participate in Healthy Competition

Although team members cooperate and share, they also participate in constructive or healthy competition. Healthy competition is used in some companies to create enthusiasm and camaraderie among coworkers, as well as a sense of pride after a victory. The internal competition might take the form of submitting the best idea for a quality improvement or cost reduction. Domino's Pizza LLC holds an international pizza-making contest annually among its employees. The goal in the competition is to make as many pizzas good enough to serve to customers as possible in 60 seconds.[23]

The pizza-making competition, as well as other forms of competition, links to team play in several ways. First, the contestants demonstrate being a good sport, which is a form of teamwork. Competitors practice regularly, looking for every opportunity to strengthen their skills and sharpen their pizza-making ability. Second, widespread participation in the contest helps build team spirit.

Assist Teammates in Trouble

One of the kindest acts of being a good team player is to help poor performers improve their performance and regain self-confidence with respect to the troubled task. Such assistance could be regarded as yet another form of organizational citizenship behavior. Jeffrey A. Lepine and Linn Van Dyne have developed a model of how coworkers help a poor performer, depending on the coworkers' *attributions* about the problem. An attribution refers to what we think is the cause of the problem, such as attributing a coworker's problem to lack of skill or poor equipment.

Attributional theory is quite complex, yet a few of the key ideas of the theory will set the stage for understanding why coworkers will reach out to help a team member in trouble. An attributional process is triggered after there is an unexpected, important, or negative goal-related outcome. An example would be a manufacturing group not getting a prototype of a medical device ready on time for a trade show. Group members want to understand such outcomes so they can anticipate or influence them in the future, and avoid a repeat of poor group performance.

Because group members work interdependently, the performance of every member counts. The group members recognize this linkage, so when the group members want to attain the group goal, poor performance by a coworker will prompt the attributional process. The three steps in the attributional process are (1) attributions, (2) emotional and cognitive reactions, and (3) behavioral responses. The foundation of the attribution model includes three attributional dimensions: locus of causality (internal or external to the person), controllability (how well the person might have controlled the outcome), and stability (the extent to which the behavior persists).

Four propositions of this attributional model are particularly relevant for understanding the helping process within the group.[24]

> *Proposition 1:* Coworker low performance attributed to external causes will result in peers performing some of the low performer's work, referred to as *compensation.*

> *Proposition 2:* Coworker low performance attributed to causes that are internal, difficult to control, and high in stability will result in coworkers performing some of the low performer's work (*compensation* again). Stability refers to a problem of relatively long duration.

Proposition 3: Coworker low performance attributed to causes that are internal, low in controllability, and low in stability will result in coworkers *training* the low performer.

Proposition 4: Coworker low performance attributed to causes that are internal, high in controllability, and low in stability will result in peers attempting to *motivate* the low performer. (Here, the coworker is perceived to not be trying hard enough and the causes of poor performance are seen to be under his or her control.)

The aspects of the model mentioned all reflect a degree of teamwork because coworkers are attempting to restore the poor performer back to good performance. Another aspect of the model deals with rejecting a coworker who could perform better if he or she wanted, but we do not consider rejection to be part of good teamwork.

Cooperate During Teamwork Training

Most readers of this book have participated in some form of teamwork training, such as the trust fall, cliff climbing, or swinging from tree to tree. Such offsite training continues to expand into such forms as preparing gourmet meals, rehabilitating homes for poor people, go-carting, and simulated sumo wrestling. An extreme team-building exercise is waterboarding, in which teammates hold a person down while the boss pours water on his or her face, placed downhill. One sales representative who was subjected to waterboarding has sued his former company, claiming that he felt like he was drowning.[25] The boss claimed he was trying to demonstrate that you should fight for sales the same way you fought for your life in this exercise. In this way you would be a good team player.

Proponents of these nonclassroom approaches to team building insist that such activities are excellent vehicles for building teamwork, along with leadership skills. Yet critics of offsite training are concerned that the skills learned in offsite training frequently do not transfer back to the workplace. When participants are coached about how what they have learned in the team-building activities applies to the workplace, the probability of acquiring valuable teamwork skills increases.[26] Yet another concern about demanding physical approaches to team building remains. Many people are physically injured in such activities as cliff climbing and walking over hot coals.[27]

When assigned to team training, the positive approach to team politics is to recognize that the process can work, and it is best to cooperate rather than join in with coworkers who might poke fun at the activity. Yet a person can be a good team player and still refrain from activities that are fearful to him or her, such as swinging from one high tree to another or whitewater rafting. Rather than stay behind, be a good sport and play the role of timekeeper or data recorder.

INDIVIDUAL RECOGNITION AND POSITIVE LATERAL RELATIONS

A major challenge to workers at all levels seeking to advance is how to attain the individual recognition needed for promotion while at the same time having positive lateral relations, including being a good team player. The ultimate paradox in corporate life is how to stand out while being a team player. The same issue has been expressed in more colorful terms by Blythe McGarvie, who has been a CFO at two large companies: "Someone once told me to be a team player, to hide in the tall grass. Later I learned that if you hide in the tall grass, you're going to get mowed under when it's time for a layoff or reduction. You have to stand out. Mowed around is better."[28]

Good lateral relations are typically a requirement for advancement, yet being perceived as a good team player is not sufficient for advancement in itself. Individual qualities such as imagination, strategic thinking, high motivation, and charisma are also key to promotion. A case in point is Mark Hurd, the celebrated CEO of Hewlett-Packard. He insists that being a team player is more important than individual contributions, yet he was chosen as the new CEO of HP in large part because of his reputation for bringing about organizational efficiency.

Exhibit 5.4 presents a model for being a good team player, including positive lateral relations, while attaining individual recognition.[29] Starting at the left, your many different contributions as a group or team member make it possible for your unit to achieve high performance. Yet, in order to achieve individual recognition, you also need to establish links with key people in your organization and the external environment.

Contributing to high performance sets the stage for achieving individual recognition. The back-and-forth arrows in Exhibit 5.4 between the high-performing team and influential people carry an important message. Assume

Exhibit 5.4 A Game Plan for Achieving Positive Lateral Relations and Individual Recognition

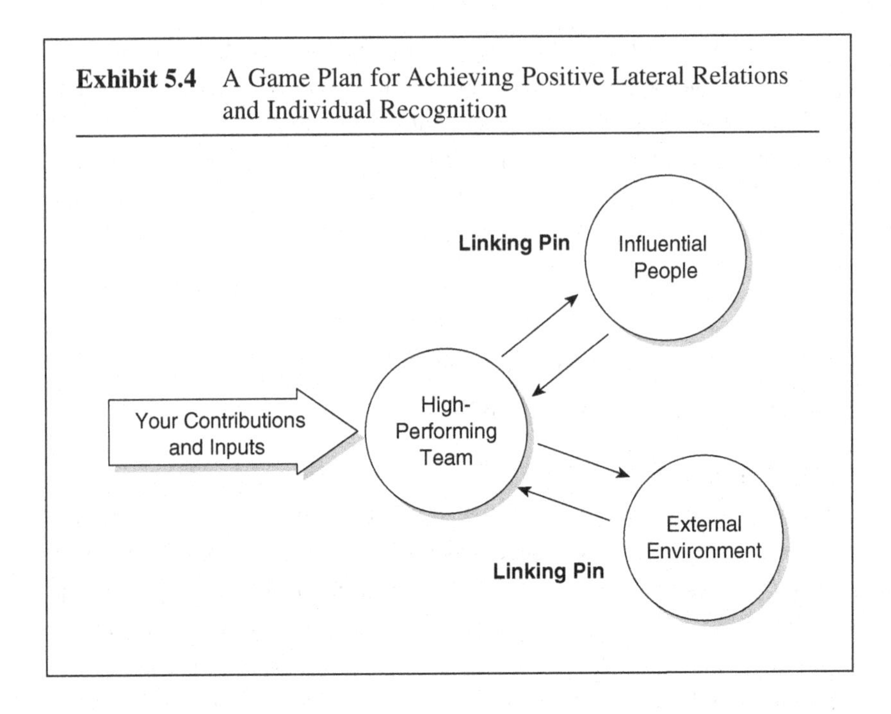

that your goal is to be identified as a major contributor to the success of the team. A sensible way to accomplish this is to inform influential people, such as senior managers and major stockholders, of how well your team is performing. Sunny Bates, a media executive recruiter, recommends that to make sure you stand out, establish a direct line of communication with someone above you. "Don't hit people over the head with a laundry list of what you've done," she cautions. "Just recap now and then. It's amazing how rare that is."

Talking about your accomplishments with a mentor is another valid link. At the same time, point appropriately to a breakthrough idea of yours that the team has accepted. For example, an IT worker at the supermarket chain Hannaford Bros. stood out from the team. He pointed out that steering shoppers to use debit cards rather than credit cards would save the chain millions of dollars in fees. The specialist followed up his recommendations with a technology plan for its accomplishment.[30]

If you hold the formal title of team leader, this liaison role is readily understandable. A senior manager would ordinarily think that the team leader is the natural spokesperson for the group. As a team member, you can also be a linking pin. Inform your teammates and team leader of what you are doing. For example, you might explain that you have a good working relationship with a particular executive and that you would like to keep that person informed of the group's activities. If you have already established trust with teammates, they will not suspect you of devious activity, such as being a corporate spy reporting on trouble spots.

Observe that in the model an arrow returns back to the team as well as pointing back toward influential people. An outstanding group member brings back nonprivileged information to the team. For example, an influential person might make a spontaneous favorable comment about the group's contribution. You can enhance your status as a strong team player or team leader by volunteering to share the successful methods your team uses with other teams. Also, be willing to draw up recommendations for making other teams effective. Spreading around useful information about your team's success will assist you in becoming the person associated with the success of your team.[31]

The other linking pin depicted in Exhibit 5.4 completes the model. A sophisticated team player stays focused on the external environment to understand how his or her team will be influenced by, or will influence, the outside world. This external focus is a key component of strategic thinking. Assume that a product development team member at the furniture manufacturer and retailer IKEA reads a few articles about the trend toward building of miniature houses, including those of approximately 400 square feet. The team member brings back this information to lead a discussion about developing a line of furniture for these small, energy-efficient homes.

SUMMARY

Good lateral relations have several positive consequences for the organization. Workers who have close friends are more likely to be engaged on the job, engage customers, have higher job satisfaction and fewer accidents, and focus on their strengths. Friendships satisfy key needs and motives. Getting along well with coworkers facilitates career advancement.

The political tactics for developing coworker relationships presented here are as follows:

1. *Engage in interpersonal citizenship behavior.* Coworker support, trust, perspective taking, and empathy are all related to interpersonal citizenship behavior. Interpersonal citizenship behavior works best when abusive supervision is low.

2. *Engage in positive coworker exchanges.* A high-quality exchange is characterized by mutual respect, trust, and obligation.
3. *Be positive.* Being discreet about your complaints is part of being positive.
4. *Make others feel important.* Coworkers play a key role in satisfying the recognition needs of each other.
5. *Be diplomatic.* Diplomacy is important when expressing disagreement.
6. *Participate in positive gossip and small talk.* Gossip helps establish bonds and small talk can convey warmth.
7. *Supplement e-mail with more personal contact.* Hearing a voice helps humanize a relationship.
8. *Repair damage quickly.* Problems between coworkers damage lateral relations.

The political tactics for enhancing team play described here are: (1) Contribute to the team culture (including following group norms); (2) demonstrate confidence and trust in teammates; (3) give credit to others; (4) follow the law of reciprocity; (5) participate in healthy competition; (6) assist teammates in trouble; and (7) cooperate during teamwork training.

A paradox in corporate life is how to stand out while being a team player. A model proposed here suggests that it is possible to achieve both individual recognition and still attain positive lateral relations. According to the model (shown in Exhibit 5.4), a person's many contributions to the group or team make his or her high performance possible. You then keep influential people outside the group, including a mentor, informed of your accomplishments. Nonprivileged information gathered from influential people is brought back to the team. The last component of the model involves the team player focusing on how developments in the outside world might affect the team's activities—a form of strategic thinking.

QUESTIONS AND ACTIVITIES

1. So what really is wrong with being a lone wolf on the job?
2. Provide an example of interpersonal organizational citizenship behavior in which you have engaged, or might engage in the future.

3. How specifically does being effective at small talk contribute to effective lateral relations?
4. What have you observed to be an effective technique for improving your relationship with an enemy or rival on the job or on a sports team?
5. Visualize the group of workers at a McDonald's, Taco Bell, or another fast-service restaurant. What are several of the group norms that appear to be in operation?
6. Give an example of the law of reciprocity from your own experiences.
7. Ask a few experienced workers what they think are a couple of frequent errors made in establishing good coworker relations.

CASE STUDY: PASSED-OVER PETE

Pete Gupta was enjoying his career as a real estate agent at Barclay Properties, a real estate development company. The business model adopted by the founders of Barclay is to purchase and then rehabilitate distressed office buildings. Many of the older buildings the company rehabilitated were then converted into mixed-use properties, such as office space, retail space, and loft condominium apartments. Part of the plan was to restore majestic older buildings, thereby fitting into the environmental trend of preserving what exists rather than consuming enormous amounts of energy and material in the construction of new office towers.

As Barclay Properties continued to expand, seven agents were working full time, all of them reporting to Katie Logan, the company cofounder. Gupta's major responsibility was to find tenants as well as condominium buyers for the rehabilitated buildings. His passion for the business, combined with his knowledge of the business and sales skills, enabled him to become the leading agent in terms of sales volume.

Logan specialized in supervising rehabilitation of the older buildings. Her role required her to spend considerable time with architects, construction firms, and local zoning boards. Ralph Parsons, the other cofounder, concentrated his efforts more on finding properties and working with financial institutions to fund the projects. Logan and Parsons agreed that Barclay had expanded enough to warrant hiring a manager to provide leadership to the sales group. Logan enjoyed working with the real estate agents, but she was too occupied with other activities to provide much assistance or direction to the agents.

Logan and Parson agreed jointly that it would be a plus for the firm to offer the promotion to sales director to one of the seven agents. The new director of sales would continue to contribute as a sales agent, but would also function as the manager of the group. After considerable discussion, the director of sales position was offered to Sara Morales, who readily accepted the offer. For the previous year, Morales was the third-highest producer in terms of dollar volume.

After learning of Morales's appointment, Pete Gupta demanded an explanation from Logan and Parsons. He said angrily, "I am the number one agent here, and you didn't even discuss the promotion with me. What's going on?"

Logan responded, "Ralph and I are well aware that you are a star performer, and we expect that you will make Barclay a long-term career. But we needed more of a team player for the sales director position. We see you as an individual star who doesn't get too involved with the rest of the sales group. The buzz we obtained from your colleagues is that you are great with clients, but that you are a lone wolf. You don't appear to have too much interest in working as a team member. You never share your expertise with the guys and gals in the group."

Gupta replied, "I thought the name of this game is bring in the big bucks. Spending time with colleagues seems less important."

Parsons said in response, "Sales volume is obviously very important. But we needed a little more of an internal person for this position."

Case Study Questions

1. In what way does this case study relate to lateral relations?
2. What do you think of the logic behind the decision of Logan and Parsons to pass over Pete Gupta?
3. What tactics should Gupta use if he wants to reverse his image as a lone wolf?
4. How ethical was it for the cofounders to listen to "buzz" about Gupta to help them reach their decision?
5. What should Logan and Parsons do to increase the chances that Gupta will not quit because he was passed over for promotion?

POLITICAL SKILL-BUILDING EXERCISE 5

High-Quality Exchanges With Coworkers

Groups of about six people each get together to simulate an ongoing work team. A suggestion would be to visualize the group as a product development team for Coca-Cola, attempting to think of a new product for the company that is not a beverage. Imagine that top-level management is applying heavy pressure on the product development team to arrive at an innovative idea today. (If you do not like the Coca-Cola scenario, invent another group problem.) At the same time, your group believes strongly that high-quality exchanges (as explained by TMX and CWX) will help you accomplish your task. As you discuss your potentially innovative ideas, engage in as many high-quality exchanges as feasible without going to the extreme of being a sickening office politician.

After you have completed the group role-play, have a brief debriefing session in which you analyze what were some of the best high-quality exchanges among group members. Also, make any observations you can about how the high-quality exchanges affected group creativity.

REFERENCES

1. Matlack, C. (2006, March 13). Vive les différences. *BusinessWeek,* 90.

2. Rath, T. (2006). *Vital friends: The people you cannot afford to live without.* New York: Gallup Press; Wilbert, C. (2006, July/August). You schmooze, you win. *Fast Company,* 109.

3. Keup, L., Bruning, N. S., & Seers, A. (2004). Members, leaders and the team: Extending LIX to co-worker relationships. *Administrative Sciences Association of Canada (ASAC),* Quebec, 1–15; Seers, A. (1989). Team member exchange quality: A new construct for role-making research. *Organizational Behavior and Human Decision Processes, 43,* 118–135.

4. Bruzzese, A. (2005, August 7). *Job advancement depends on building bridges to co-workers.* Gannett News Service.

5. Settoon, R. P., & Mossholder, K. W. (2002, April). Relationship quality and relationship context as antecedents of person- and task-focused interpersonal citizen behavior. *Journal of Applied Psychology,* 255–267.

6. Bennett, J., Tepper, M. K., Duffy, J. H., & Ensley, M. D. (2004, June). Moderators of the relationships between coworkers' organizational citizenship behavior and fellow employees' attitudes. *Journal of Applied Psychology,* 455–465.

7. Settoon, R. P., & Mossholder, K. W. (2002, April). Relationship quality and relationship context as antecedents of person- and task-focused interpersonal citizen behavior. *Journal of Applied Psychology,* 255–267.

8. Bennett, J., Tepper, M. K., Duffy, J. H., & Ensley, M. D. (2004, June). Moderators of the relationships between coworkers' organizational citizenship behavior and fellow employees' attitudes. *Journal of Applied Psychology,* 455–465.

9. Sherony, K. M., & Green, S. G. (2002, June). Coworker exchange: Relationships between coworkers, leader–member exchange, and work attitudes. *Journal of Applied Psychology,* 542.

10. Battaglia, E. (2006, November 9). Be a great coworker. *LifeScript,* 1. Retrieved 07/03/2007 from www.lifescript.com.

11. *Manager's Edge* (2003, January). Build allies for support. *Manager's Edge,* 8.

12. Research synthesized in Winerman, L. (2006, April). Have you heard the latest? *Monitor on Psychology,* 56–57.

13. Quoted in Pennington, A. Y. (2004, February). Breaking the silence. *Entrepreneur,* 25.

14. Cited in Brady, D. (2006, December 4). *!#?@the e-mail. Can we talk? *BusinessWeek,* 109.

15. Nadlerl, J. (2004). Rapport in legal negotiation: How small talk can facilitate email dealmaking. *Harvard Negotiation Law Review, 9,* 225–253.

16. Thackston, K. (2001). Overcoming poor coworker relationships. *Career Know-How.* Retrieved 07/17/2007 from www.careerknowhow.com.

17. Holmes, S. (2006, March 13). Cleaning up Boeing. *BusinessWeek,* 62–68.

18. Kiley, D. (2007, June 4). The new heat on Ford. *BusinessWeek,* 38.

19. Ehrhart, M. G., & Naumann, S. E. (2004, December). Organizational citizenship behavior in work groups: A group norms approach. *Journal of Applied Psychology,* 960–974.

20. Langfred, C. W. (2004, June). Too much of a good thing? Negative effects of high trust and individual autonomy in self-managing teams. *Academy of Management Journal,* 385–399.

21. *Fortune* magazine (2005, March 21). The best advice I ever got: Brian Roberts, 45, CEO of Comcast. *Fortune,* 112–113.

22. Quoted in Warsaw, M. (1998, April). The good guy's (and gal's) guide to office politics. *Fast Company,* 160.

23. *Chicago Tribune Career Builder* (2006, August 27). Game on: Healthy competition (even a good fight!) among co-workers can be helpful. *Chicago Tribune Career Builder,* 6–1.

24. Lepine, J. A., & Van Dyne, L. (2001, January). Peer responses to low performers: An attributional model of helping in the context of groups. *Academy of Management Review,* 67–84.

25. Vick, K. (2008, April 13). Team-building or torture? Court will decide. *Washington Post,* A04.

26. Woodward, N. H. (2006, September). Make the most of team building. *HR Magazine,* 73–75.

27. MacDonald, D. (2006, May). Why we all hate offsites. *Business, 2.0,* 79–80.

28. Conly, L. (2005, November). Credit where credit is due. *Fast Company,* 99–101.

29. DuBrin, A. J. (1995). *The breakthrough team player: Becoming the MVP on your workplace team* (pp. 165–168). New York: AMACOM.

30. Conly, L. (2005, November). Credit where credit is due. *Fast Company,* 99–101 [p. 100].

31. *Executive Strategies* (1994, October). Standing out on a team. *Executive Strategies,* 3–4.

SIX

DOWNWARD RELATIONS

LEARNING OBJECTIVES

After studying this chapter and doing the exercises, you should be able to do the following:

1. Explain how leader–member exchanges contribute to building downward relations.
2. Explain how the path–goal theory of leadership can be applied to building downward relationships.
3. Identify nine humanistic leadership practices that contribute to building downward relations.
4. Identify seven politically astute leadership practices that contribute to building downward relations.

Kim Simon moved from San Diego to Connecticut to become the first patient-advocacy director for Alexion Pharmaceuticals, a small biotechnology concern headquartered in the hamlet of Cheshire. He liked the idea of having a job that never existed before. "It was an opportunity for me to help shape this position rather than inherit somebody else's approach," said Simon, a 52-year-old with a trim gray beard and boyish grin. His fantasy of trailblazing soon clashed with harsh reality.

Ill-prepared for a wave of new hires, the company put Simon in its cafeteria with no phone or computer for days. He got another shock when he learned that his duties had shrunk. The first week "felt very much like a baptism by fire," he recalls. He survived his crises—assisted by an Alexion leadership coach—and is thriving. "He has done very well," reports his boss, Paul Finnegan.

Alexion picked the former Pfizer public relations manager to serve as its liaison with patient-advocacy groups worldwide. But when Simon arrived in October, the young enterprise was rushing to prepare for the imminent U.S. introduction of its first commercial product, a drug used to treat a rare blood disorder.

He needed to narrow his focus and work with the U.S. launch team for the new drug, Solaris. The team "wanted me to get up to speed as fast as possible," he remembers. Simon thought his new job would cover product public relations, too. "There was evolving clarification of the role," explains Dr. Finnegan, a vice president. He had spent a year amassing senior management support for a patient-advocacy spot.

The leadership coach, Lynda C. McDermott, told Simon to forge personal relationships with key players to gain credibility. "Find out what people want of you and establish your own internal network," she urged.

Simon met face-to-face with about a dozen coworkers in his first two weeks, gleaning clues about corporate politics. Without their insights, he believes, "I might have been at a disadvantage on some projects." He also walked down the hall at least twice a day to brainstorm and bond with the U.S. team. Simon deepened those ties and proved his value at a Florida scientific conference held six weeks after he began. He included team members in sessions he arranged with patient-advocacy groups. "We came back a much stronger team," he says.

To enhance his in-house visibility, Dr. Finnegan made sure his lieutenant was invited to important meetings—and suggested he attend others uninvited. Gatecrashing bothered Simon until he noticed that "nobody blinked an eye."[1]

The story about the manager of patient advocacy at a pharmaceutical firm illustrates several of the techniques of downward relations presented in this chapter. (Note that the person was building lateral as well as downward relationships because he appeared to be in the joint role of a manager and a staff professional.) Soon after arriving at the company, the manager went on a "listening tour" to gather ideas and build relationships. On the advice of a leadership coach, he forged relationships, thereby demonstrating the basic political technique of using face-to-face contacts to establish rapport.

LEADER–MEMBER EXCHANGE (LMX) AND DOWNWARD RELATIONS

According to **leader–member exchange (LMX) theory,** the quality of leader–subordinate exchange relationships determines the nature of many outcomes for the organization and subordinate. Among them would be favorable exchanges leading to higher satisfaction and productivity. Many of the exchanges are political in nature, such as certain members becoming part of the in-group.[2] We focus here on several aspects of LMX theory that are most directly related to the political aspects of downward relations.

To personalize the concept of leader–member exchange, you are invited to take the self-quiz presented in Exhibit 6.1.

Exhibit 6.1 The Leader–Member Exchanges Quiz

Directions: Respond “Mostly true” or “Mostly false” to each of the following statements about any specific manager you have worked for.

Attitude, Behavior, or Perception Involved in the Exchange	*Mostly True*	*Mostly False*
1. My manager and I think alike.		
2. My manager and I got along well from the start.		
3. My manager understands my problems and needs.		
4. My leader recognizes my potential.		
5. My manager and I have a good working relationship.		
6. My manager would use his or her power to help me in my work.		
7. My manager answers my e-mail messages and returns my phone calls quickly.		
8. My manager listens carefully to what I have to say and seeks my advice.		
9. My manager and I often talk on a personal level, rather than strictly at a work level.		
10. I can count on my manager to get me out of a tough situation.		
11. My manager and I are alike in a number of ways.		
12. I like my manager as a friend.		

(Continued)

Exhibit 6.1 (Continued)

Attitude, Behavior, or Perception Involved in the Exchange	*Mostly True*	*Mostly False*
13. My manager and I look out for each other's interests.		
14. My manager appreciates the work I do.		
15. My manager gives me good performance evaluations.		
16. My manager gives me higher than average salary increases.		
17. My manager would come to my defense if I were attacked by others.		
18. I do not mind working my hardest for my manager.		
19. I like my manager very much as a person.		
20. I am impressed by my manager's job knowledge.		

Total: "Mostly True" ____ "Mostly False" ____

Scoring and Interpretation: Count your number of "Mostly true" responses.

16–20 You probably have (or had) favorable leader–member exchanges with your manager, and you are or were part of the in-group.

1–15 You probably have (or had) below average leader–member exchanges with your manager and you are or were part of the out-group.

SOURCE: Statements 3–6 are adapted from Graen, G. B, & Uhl-Bien, M. (1995). Relationship-based approach to leadership: Development of leader–member exchange (LMX) theory of leadership over 25 years: Applying a multi-level domain approach. *Leadership Quarterly, 6,* 219–247. Statements 8, 9, and 13–16 are adapted from Lussier, R. N., & Achua, C. F. (2004). *Leadership: Theory, application, skill development* (2nd ed., p. 224). Mason, OH: Thomson/South-Western. Statements 17–20 are from Erdogan, B., & Enders, J. (2007, March). Support from the top: Supervisors' perceived organizational support as a moderator of leader–member exchange to satisfaction and performance relationships. *Journal of Applied Psychology,* 324.

Different-Quality Relationships

Leader–member exchange theory explains that leaders do not typically use the same leadership style in dealing with all members. Instead, they treat each member somewhat differently. The linkages (relationships) that exist between the leader and each individual team member differ in quality, on a continuum from low quality to high quality. With group members on the top half of the continuum, the leader has a good relationship. The leader has a poor relationship with those subordinates on the lower half of the continuum. Each of these pairs of relationships, or dyads, is judged in terms of whether a group member is "in" or "out" with the leader. The leader forms strong downward relations with member of the in-group, perhaps to the point of the in-group members being regarded as the favorites within the unit.

Based on their favored status, members of the in-group are invited to participate in important decision making, are given added responsibility, and are privy to interesting gossip. Members of the out-group are managed according to the requirements of their employment contract. They receive little warmth, inspiration, or encouragement, and might be regarded as political outcasts. In-group members tend to achieve a higher level of performance, commitment, and satisfaction than do out-group members. Furthermore, they are less likely to quit.

The in-group versus out-group status also includes an element of reciprocity or exchange. The leader grants more favors to in-group members, who in response work harder to please the leader. As part of pleasing the leader, in-group members are more likely to engage in citizenship behavior. The member going out of his or her way to help further cements the relationship between the member and the leader.

Evidence suggests that leader–member exchange depends on how frequently supervisors and subordinates interact. LMX is the most potent when interactions are frequent, such as many person-to-person and e-mail exchanges between the leader and group members. In contrast, LMX has substantially less effect when interactions are infrequent.[3] A warm, close supervisor would therefore be involved in different relationships with subordinates. As a consequence, he or she would develop strong downward relationships with some of them. In contrast, a cold, distant supervisor would not be involved in different relationships with group members.

The leader's propensity to engage in beneficial exchanges with group members is influenced by how much support each of them perceives they are receiving from the organization. Berrin Erdogan and Jeanne Enders conducted a study of this nature with 210 subordinates and 38 supervisors of a grocery store chain. Leader–member exchange was measured on a scale similar to the one presented in Exhibit 6.1. Perceived support from the organization was measured with a brief questionnaire that included statements such as, "My organization is willing to help me when I need a special favor."

A major finding was that the positive relationship between LMX and job satisfaction was stronger when supervisors had good support from the organization. Also, LMX was related to performance only when the supervisors had positive support from the organization.[4] The implication in terms of downward relations is that having good upward relations facilitates having good relationships with subordinates.

First Impressions

The leader's first impression of a subordinate's competency plays an important role in placing the group member in the in-group or out-group. Another key linking factor is whether the leader and team member have positive or negative chemistry. We can assume that group members who make effective use of political tactics, such as complimenting the boss, increase their chances of becoming members of the in-group.

A field study confirmed that first impressions make a difference. The researchers gathered ratings of six aspects of the manager–group member dyad. For example, one of the measures was feelings about the manager, such as, "I like my supervisor very much as a friend." Results showed that the initial leader expectations of members and member expectations of the leader were good predictors of leader–member exchanges at two weeks and at six weeks. An important interpretation of these results is that the quality of the leader–member relationship develops in the first days of the relationship, placing emphasis on the importance of making a good first impression.[5]

Exhibit 6.1 provides a quiz to measure the quality of leader–member exchanges with a present or past manager.

THE PATH–GOAL THEORY OF LEADERSHIP AND DOWNWARD RELATIONS

All theories of leadership should provide some suggestions for building downward relations because leaders in positions of authority have people reporting to them directly or indirectly. We described aspects of LMX theory because it so heavily focuses on interactions between the leader and group members. Robert House's path–goal theory is another leadership theory that focuses considerable attention on day-to-day interactions between the leader and group members. The *path–goal theory of leadership* states that, to be effective, leaders engage in behaviors that complement group members' environments and abilities in a manner that compensates for deficiencies and facilitates subordinate satisfaction and work unit performance.[6] Earlier versions of the theory are defined slightly differently, but all point to the idea of the leader helping subordinates to find the right path to attain goals.

Path–goal theory is quite complex in its latest reformulation. It includes eight classes of leadership behavior, individual differences of subordinates, and contingency moderator variables that are related to each other in 26 propositions. The moderators specify some of the situations in which the leader behaviors are likely to be effective or ineffective, such as giving more support when subordinates are facing ambiguity. Despite the complexity of the theory, many suggestions can be found for building downward relations, including the following:

1. Leader behavior is acceptable and satisfying to subordinates to the extent that the subordinates perceive such behavior to be helping them attain either immediate or future satisfaction. For example, the leader might talk about exciting work that the group will be doing.

2. Leader behavior will enhance subordinate motivation to the extent that such behavior (a) makes satisfaction of needs and preferences contingent on meeting performance standards, (b) makes the subordinates' task intrinsically satisfying, (c) makes rewards contingent on attaining goals, and (d) provides structure, support, and rewards necessary for effective performance. An example of the many behaviors included in this proposition would be for the leader to enable an achievement-oriented (ambitious) group member to work independently on a task important to the organization.

3. Leader behavior will enhance work unit performance to the extent that such behavior (a) facilitates collaborative relationships among group members, (b) maintains positive relationships between the unit and the larger organization, (c) ensures that adequate resources are available to the work unit, and (d) enhances the legitimacy of the work unit as perceived by other members of the larger organization. In this proposition, the leader builds relationships by helping members feel—and be—important to the rest of the organization. Publicizing the group's relevance would be one such leadership behavior.

HUMANISTIC LEADERSHIP PRACTICES FOR BUILDING DOWNWARD RELATIONS

The politically oriented manager or leader engages in many practices to build downward relationships that might be considered *humanistic* because they reflect a strong concern for human welfare, values, and dignity. Note that the term "humanistic" goes beyond "relationship oriented," a term that generally refers to the difference between focusing on people versus focusing on the task. We are dealing with a nuance between humanistic and relationship oriented rather than a concrete distinction. Exhibit 6.2 outlines the humanistic practices for enhancing downward relations.

Mix Humility With Self-Confidence

Self-confidence has been recognized as an important leadership trait for as long as leadership has been formally studied.[7] Unless the leader is self-confident, it will be difficult to provide direction to others. However, mixing humility with self-confidence provides a human touch that will often endear the leader to subordinates. As well, being somewhat humble results in sharing credit, which also builds bonds with group members. Stephen G. Harrison contends that there is

Exhibit 6.2 Humanistic Leadership Practices for Building Downward Relations

1. Mix humility with self-confidence.
2. Communicate trust and minimize micromanagement.
3. Engage in face-to-face communication.
4. Assist in the development of subordinates.
5. Be civil, yet maintain professional distance.
6. Give emotional support and encouragement.
7. Begin a new position with a listening tour.
8. Share credit with the team.
9. Avoid being the abominable no man or woman.

leadership value in humility. He writes, "Great leadership is manifested or articulated by people who know how to understate it. There is leadership value in humility, the leadership that comes from putting people in the limelight, not yourself. Great leadership comes from entirely unexpected places. It's understatement, it's dignity, it's service, it's selflessness."[8]

Communicate Trust in Others and Minimize Micromanagement

Being trustworthy is a key leadership behavior because subordinates are therefore more likely to take the leader seriously. At the same time, leaders who communicate by words and deeds that they trust subordinates will strengthen their downward relationships. Workers who feel trusted are likely to feel valued, such as the sales representative who has wide latitude in spending money to entertain customers and potential customers. Although the sales manager and the company are putting some money at risk, the payoff might be a sales representative who forms a stronger bond with the company because of being trusted to invest entertainment money wisely.

Terry Bacon, the CEO of a human resources consulting group, says that most employees relish knowing that their managers trust them. So a sensible approach is to delegate responsibility on important tasks and avoid micromanagement. Bacon notes, "If you don't trust them to do the work, you've got the wrong people."[9]

Micromanagement is the close monitoring of most aspects of a group member's activities by the manager or leader. The same approach to managing others might be referred to as compulsive meddling because the manager cannot resist contributing input to whatever task the subordinate is performing. For example, a micromanager will often tell a team member what size font looks best on a PowerPoint headline, or where to place an office plant. Micromanagement communicates distrust because the manager or leader communicates the feeling that he or she thinks the subordinate lacks enough skill or judgment to perform the task adequately. Also, the micromanager wants to make all the decisions, however small. The following steps are recommended for minimizing micromanagement, and at the same time communicating trust in group members' ability to perform the task:[10]

- *Put yourself in their shoes.* Reflect on a time that someone was micromanaging you. Try to remember the sense of always being watched and the lack of respect conveyed by the micromanagement.

- *Prove that you are not needed.* Identify a small project or task that you feel comfortable completely ignoring, then turn it over to an individual or the group. When they succeed, it will demonstrate that some work can get done without your input.
- *Hold yourself accountable.* Inform the staff that you are committed to turning over responsibility for the task or project to the group, and that you will punish yourself if you sway from your commitment. The "punishment" might take the form of paying for break-time refreshments one morning.
- *Stay informed, not involved.* It is not micromanaging to stay informed about your employees' progress. Employees welcome feedback, yet that does not mean you have to pore over every word of their report and then suggest minor changes.

Another way of looking at micromanagement is that it carries legitimate managerial behavior to excess.[11] An effective manager gives feedback to workers, whereas the micromanager gives constant feedback to the point of being disruptive. It is useful to recognize that being a *macromanager* (the opposite of a micromanager) can impair downward relations too. Consultant and trainer Bruce Tulgan observes that too many managers neglect getting involved in the work of subordinates. "At some point, the 'nice-guy or gal' manager came into fashion, and bosses started being afraid to act like bosses," he says. "But when we ask employees what they want from the people above them, the first thing they mention is never a raise. It's always more coaching, more guidance, clearer goals, more constructive criticism, and more recognition for achievements."[12]

Engage in Face-to-Face Communication

A potent vehicle for developing relationships in the workplace remains face-to-face communication, even if the face-to-face encounters are only a supplement to electronic communication. Political behavior in organizations depends on the human touch. Linda Dulye notes that a manager is the most significant communication channel in the workplace. Employees prefer to receive information from their direct manager in preference to e-mails, Web sites, intranet sites, town hall meetings, or the grapevine.

An effective channel for building downward relationships is the workplace walk-around, in which the manager drops by a group member's desk, sits down, and chats about work—yet not to the point of consuming too much of the worker's time. The power of the walk-around is illustrated by the experience of an aerospace manufacturer. A company spokesperson said that the walk-around was the most important improvement action recommended by employees as a solution to the lack of mutual trust between management and employees. The trust issue had been identified in an employee engagement survey.

Recommendations for enhancing the effectiveness of the walk-around include leaving behind electronic devices such as cell phones or personal digital assistants that might divert attention from the face-to-face visits. The visit should start slowly by exchanging small talk before jumping into an agenda. Eye contact and two-way communication are also important for relationship building. It is helpful to jot down issues uncovered that require follow-up, such as concerns expressed about a supplier. The worker should be thanked for his or her time. Finally, continue with the walk-around technique even if the first couple of tours feel awkward.[13]

Assist in the Development of Subordinates

A directly humanistic strategy for enhancing downward relations is to assist in the professional development of group members. Being a coach and mentor would be two such approaches, but so would occasional discussions with subordinates about their career growth. Larry Bossidy, the former business executive and then management author, said that while he was at GE one of his bosses was a mid-level manager who was a good performer but had reached a career plateau. The manager telephoned Bossidy one day and said he believed Bossidy had a chance to advance further than he. The mid-level manager also said he was going to do everything he could to help Bossidy reach his potential. From that moment forward, the manager was more interested in Bossidy's development than his own. He went out of his way to criticize or praise Bossidy when he needed it. The latter said, "I'll never forget him; he played a very meaningful role in my career."[14]

Bossidy also mentions the important personal growth principle of giving frequent, specific, and immediate feedback. The feedback is a signal to subordinates that the manager is interested in their growth, and that the manager sees a path for their future.[15] Specific feedback, assuming it is not cruel and hostile, provides useful guidelines for development. An example: "I like your presentation this morning, and you appeared friendly to the group. Yet you smiled so frequently, it made you appear to be nervous and unsure."

Assisting staffers to get promoted helps build downward relations in another important perspective: The people who receive the promotions are likely to be more loyal and motivated. Managers who help staff members advance their career often create lasting alliances over the long term. The people who were assisted in their advancement might engage in such activities as assisting the helpful manager in recruiting a new staff member or landing a new customer.[16]

Be Civil, yet Maintain Professional Distance

A straightforward tactic for establishing sound downward relations is to be civil toward group members, even under heavy work pressures. Although many readers might respond "Duh" in response to the importance of civility toward subordinates, many managers are uncivil. Terry Baker, the human resources consultant mentioned above, contends that most of the time people switch jobs because of a bad relationship with the boss. Yet learning to be more civil to group members does not mean the manager has to cross the line from manager to workplace buddy. According to Baker's findings, most workers would rather maintain an air of professionalism in the workplace. Baker says, "What they want is a professional, respectful manager who is honest, fair and has a strong work ethic."[17]

Being courteous is part of being civil. Being courteous to subordinates would include such acts as responding quickly to e-mail and text messages, returning phone calls, not multitasking when subordinates are talking to you, not keeping people waiting for you, and not belittling them.[18]

Give Emotional Support and Encouragement

Another humanistic and direct way of developing downward relations is to provide subordinates with emotional support and encouragement. A supportive manager or leader gives frequent encouragement and praise, such as, "Your graphics were exactly what we needed to demonstrate that we need to expand our budget. Thanks so much." One of the many work-related ways of encouraging people is to allow them to participate in decision making. Emotional support generally improves morale and sometimes improves productivity, and at the same time helps form ties between superior and subordinate. In the long term, emotional support and encouragement may bolster a person's self-esteem.[19] The consequence in terms of relationship building is that when a manager helps a person boost his or her self-esteem, that person is likely to feel more attached to the manager.

Begin a New Position With a Listening Tour

A standard technique for newly appointed CEOs is to start the job with a listening tour of workers, customers, suppliers, and sometimes union leaders. Hillary Clinton used this approach when she was first elected as a New York State senator, partly because she was relatively new to New York. The listening tour helps build downward relationships because the new manager expresses a genuine interest in the thoughts and feelings of organizational members. Also, listening carefully to people is a humanistic act.

Beginning a new position by listening to experienced workers is also useful in dealing with some of the resistance that might be encountered as a newly appointed manager. Jennifer, a 33-year-old systems analyst, took the listening approach when hired by an Atlanta retailer to take command of a team dominated by veterans older than she was at the time. "She had a lot of energy and a lot of fresh ideas, which the team didn't have," said her coach. Sensitive about being an outsider, she deliberately avoided telling teammates, "Things are bad and I'm going to make them better." Instead, she listened carefully and acknowledged their frustrations then invited suggestions about ways to serve internal clients better.[20]

Share Credit With the Team

Sharing credit with the team was described in Chapter 5 as an effective method of building lateral relations. The same technique is effective in building downward relations because team members often resent a manager receiving most of the credit for attaining objectives that actually required the efforts of many people. An example is that many CEOs receive credit for an increase in profits or share price, yet in reality the contributions of thousands of workers are necessary to achieve these financial objectives.

Mark Hurd, the chief executive of Hewlett-Packard, is a positive example of using credit sharing to solidify downward relations. At times he has refused to be photographed alone in stories about HP because he wanted to be flanked by members of his team. He also likes to be photographed surrounded by HP workers from different organizational levels. Hurd is regarded as a coaching-style executive partly because he involves himself in face-to-face encounters with his senior lieutenants and his factory-floor managers. In his informal discussions, he emphasizes how much different workers are contributing to the total corporate effort.[21]

Avoid Being the Abominable No Man or Woman

Too much negativity by the boss can dampen the enthusiasm of group members and ultimately interfere with establishing positive downward relations. Saying "no" is often necessary, such as rejecting expensive ideas that appear doomed to failure. Yet rejecting virtually every idea fosters a negative climate in which the group does not feel close to the manager. Here is an example of a manager who fits the "abominable no woman" mold, as reported by her former assistant. (The Abominable Snow Man is a creature of legend.) Whenever presented with work, the manager would disapprove of it, sending the administrative assistant to fix something a half-dozen times without ever explaining what she would give the green light to. If, during the course of planning an event, the assistant fixed an erroneous seating chart, then suddenly the napkins would have to be ecru, not white.

A possible explanation for a manager being so negative about the work of subordinates is that the manager believes that "yes" means standards have been lowered. Another possible explanation is that the negative manager is a perfectionist for whom no plan, proposal, or finished piece of work is ever quite right. Creativity specialist Teresa Amabile says that negative evaluation is a tactic people use when they are intellectually insecure.[22] Whatever the reason for the negativity, it creates distance from, rather than closeness with, group members.

POLITICALLY ASTUTE LEADERSHIP PRACTICES FOR BUILDING DOWNWARD RELATIONS

In this section, we describe additional practices by the leader or manager that help foster a good working relationship with members of the group, and all these tactics are meritorious. Exhibit 6.3 outlines the politically astute leadership practices for building downward relations.

Exhibit 6.3 Politically Astute Leadership Practices for Building Downward Relations

1. Use authority prudently.
2. Achieve buy-in for initiatives.
3. Encourage democracy, including power sharing.
4. Use a leadership style different from that of your predecessor.
5. Be prudent in dealing with former coworkers.
6. Encourage and welcome group members of superior intelligence.
7. Solicit and welcome feedback.
8. Be a servant leader.

Use Authority Prudently

Every leader/manager appointed to a formal position has some degree of position power and formal authority, or the right to make decisions. How the authority is used will help determine whether it helps build positive or negative downward relations. For purposes of building constructive downward relations, the leader/manager would make positive use of authority to help the group attain its goals. Statements reflecting positive use of authority would include, "Let me see if it is in the budget to buy that new equipment," "Keep up the good work, and I will see to it that you are recommended for a task-force assignment on a key project," and "What can I and other managers do to support your good work?"

Heavy-handed use of authority will often lead to poor relationships. Such misuse of authority often focuses on referring to formal authority and rules without an explanation of why the action has taken place. Visualize the hard-bitten bureaucrat who virtually defies people to get past his or her regulations. Statements reflecting harsh and imprudent use of authority include, "Do it because I said so," "I'm the boss, you're my subordinate," and "Please get my approval for taking any action that goes beyond your job description."

Jeffrey Pfeffer hints at finding the right balance in the use of authority in his analysis of understanding the role of power. He explains, "Subordinates obey not because the supervisor has the power to compel them; rather, they follow reasonable instructions related to the control of their work behavior because they expect that such directions will be given and followed."[23] The emphasis on *reasonable* instructions is well taken in terms of building downward relations.

Achieve Buy-In for Initiatives

A widely accepted tactic for gaining acceptance for change and breeding harmony is to attain buy-in for initiatives. A **buy-in** is a situation in which workers are willing to go along with an initiative because they feel they will benefit from the change or play an important role in it. A buy-in also implies that people accept a change because they perceive that the change will benefit them personally.

Carl Dickerson, the president and founder of Dickerson Employee Benefits, a general insurance agent located in Los Angeles, recognizes that it is natural for his 50-person staff to wonder, "What's in it for me?" when they work to attain company goals. At the same time, Dickerson intends to have amicable relationships with the staff. To generate buy-in for his vision of his small company becoming a major insurance resource, Dickerson offers his workers incentives such as insurance licensing classes, on-site workshops, and Las Vegas retreats. He believes that these incentives will make his staff feel personally vested in the company's success.[24]

Another standard approach to attaining buy-in is to have open communication about the initiative or plan. Workers should feel free to criticize the plan, such as global outsourcing, so they feel they have a voice in the changes. At the same time, the open communication helps build bridges between the manager and the employees.

Encourage Democracy, Including Power Sharing

According to David Butcher and Martin Clarke, the move to redistribute workplace power has a long history. It can be traced back to European feudalism, through the Industrial Revolution, attempts to encourage participation methods and cooperative enterprises over the past hundred years, and to the current emphasis on flat (de-layered) organizations and empowerment.[25] The manager who shares power with the group, or empowers the group, is likely to have improved downward relations for several reasons. First, sharing power gives people dignity and treats them as responsible adults. Second, having more power appeals to the needs for self-fulfillment and autonomy. The following suggestions are practical ways of sharing power with group members, thereby enhancing downward relations.

1. *Foster initiative and responsibility.* A manager or leader can empower team members by fostering greater initiative and responsibility in their assignments. Empowering phrases and instructions here include, "It's your baby," "You're in charge," and "What you will be doing might merit a bigger job title."

2. *Provide ample information.* To feel empowered, group members need loads of relevant information, including costs, prices, and quality standards. It is especially useful for workers to fully understand the impact of their actions on company costs and profits.[26] For example, an empowered sales representative, armed with cost information, is less likely to grant discounts that lose money for the company.

3. *Allow group members to determine how to achieve the objectives.* Consultant Norman Bodek says, "Allowing people to determine the most efficient work techniques is the essence of empowerment."[27] The downward relationship is enhanced because people who choose their own methods feel more professional.

4. *Communicate trust in employees.* This fourth requirement for effective empowerment underlies the three others. Unless the manager trusts employees, empowerment will not be effective or even take place. For example, when employees are trusted, they are more likely to be given the information they need and be granted the freedom to choose an appropriate method.

Use a Leadership Style Different From That of Your Predecessor

Leadership style is based somewhat on personality, so it cannot be readily changed—such as a brusque, hostile, and impersonal manager becoming warm and supportive to fit the occasion. Nevertheless, some aspects of style can be changed, such as giving more direction or listening more to suggestions from the group. Using a different leadership style from that of your predecessor is particularly important when he or she was ineffective or disliked.

An illustration of how choosing a leadership style different from that of the predecessor to help build downward relations took place at chip-maker AMD several years ago. AMD had long been dominated by the entrepreneurial, flamboyant, and autocratic Jerry Sanders. AMD executives said that Sanders had an answer for every question, whether or not he was informed on the subject. He also controlled business strategy single-handedly, making all major decisions. Hector Ruiz, the handpicked successor, took a different approach from the start of his tenure as CEO.

Ruiz had worked his way up from a poor border town in Mexico by relying on his intelligence, an almost photographic memory, and with the help of others. He was inclined to listen where Sanders might have talked. Sanders had conducted a quarterly management meeting labeled "Breakfast with Jerry." Ruiz kept the tradition but took his name off the meeting, and changed the title to "Management Committee Meeting." Sanders would talk for the entire 45 minutes, whereas Ruiz speaks for only 20. "Under Jerry, frankly, the company was very autocratic and power-centric," says Ruiz. "But I said we are going to die here if we don't do something different."

CFO Bob Rivet, who worked for both men, said, "Jerry's style was home-run or strikeout, with nothing in between. Either you had a great year or it was a flaming disaster. Hector is more process-driven. Now we worry more about getting people on base."

It appears that the change in leadership style has helped Ruiz build rapport with AMD managers. The company became an amalgam of the two business approaches: still being superb in technology but also managed for predictability and solid execution.[28] The managers also like the opportunity to have more voice at the executive meetings.

Be Prudent in Dealing With Former Coworkers

A substantial challenge for the newly appointed manager is to develop downward relationships with former coworkers for whom the manager is now responsible. Part of the problem is role confusion. When a coworker and perhaps friend now becomes your manager, his or her role can create confusion. Is this person still your buddy? Or is this person truly your boss? When a new manager has been romantically involved with a former worker, the political challenges are even greater. A *political challenge* here refers to the idea that the objective facts of the situation are only part of the problem.

A keen understanding of the human element and the power struggle between the former coworker and the new boss is required.

New managers often struggle to find the right approach to former peers, with some trying too hard to remain one of the gang and others asserting their authority too harshly. New managers are known to be inconsistent, confusing subordinates with intermittent or conflicting feedback.

A representative example of the problem of supervising former peers took place after mechanical engineer Donald Pierce was promoted to supervise a few employees at the National Institute of Standards and Technology. Pierce had to confront a group member about tardiness, the same person with whom he had been good friends, including taking an annual fishing trip together. Pierce decided to talk to the employee privately but firmly. "I didn't yell, but I was serious," he says. "I told him that part of my job is to make sure you're doing yours and that you're showing up on time." Although it was uncomfortable at first, Pierce says the employee was conciliatory and agreed to arrive to work on time.[29]

The anecdote illustrates the key principle that the newly appointed manager has to clarify his or her role to establish a good working relationship. Saying "it is part of my job" helps legitimatize the confrontation about the tardiness. The manager can also add, "Our personal friendship outside the job is not an issue. We are occupying two different roles."

Encourage and Welcome Group Members of Superior Intelligence

The manager who practices devious organizational politics works hard to avoid hiring a person so bright that he or she could become a rival for the manager's job. In contrast, a practitioner of positive organizational politics perceives hiring a group member of superior intelligence as an opportunity to multiply his or her effectiveness and power. As a result, the manager welcomes and supports the *brainiac* as a way of establishing a productive downward relationship.

Jack and Suzy Welch analyze the situation in this way: "Look, the best thing that can happen to you as a boss is hiring a person who is smarter, more creative, or in some way more talented than you are. It's like winning a lottery. Suddenly, you've got a team member whose talent will very likely improve everyone's performance and reputation, including yours."[30]

A justification for hiring a person who appears brighter than you is that leaders are generally not evaluated on their personal output. Rather, managers are judged on how well they have hired, coached, and motivated their staff, individually and collectively. The superior performance of a highly intelligent group member will show up in the manager's total accomplishments. In terms of building downward relations, Welch and Welch add that you have everything to gain from celebrating the growth of highly intelligent group members and nothing at all to fear.[31]

Solicit and Welcome Feedback

Many organizations today have systems in place whereby the manager receives feedback from subordinates on his or her performance and behavior. These systems are referred to as multirater surveys and 360-degree surveys. The information from these systems is used more often for leadership development than to evaluate the manager or leader's performance for administrative purposes.

The manager who solicits feedback from formal systems or has a more informal method of obtaining feedback gains several political points in terms of downward relations. A major advantage is that the manager demonstrates trust in the judgment of team members to assist in fine-tuning his or her leadership style. At the same time, the manager indicates that he or she is being open and flexible, rather than authoritarian and dismissive of criticism.

Some leaders and managers use ImproveNow.com, an anonymous service that enables employees to send their manager a performance review for about $10.00 per submitter. The dimensions measured are: generates trust, invents the future, articulates strategies, maintains awareness, realizes results, creates wisdom, and acknowledges freely. The recipient of the feedback is urged to share the results with subordinates and publicly explain action plans for improvement in weak areas, such as "I will work on presenting a clearer vision of where our division is headed."

A coach at ImproveNow.com contends, "Once people feel you're being authentic and genuine, you should apologize for letting them down on your weaker scores."[32] Such an approach would help gain the manager social capital for his or her honesty and humility.

Be a Servant Leader

A comprehensive and politically astute, as well as humanistic, method of building downward relations is to be a **servant leader**. A leader of this type serves constituents by working on their behalf to help them achieve their goals, not the leader's own goals. Servant leaders measure their effectiveness in terms of their ability to help others. Instead of seeking individual recognition, servant leaders see themselves as serving group members. Such a leader is self-sacrificing and humble—a quality already described here that contributes to building downward relations.

A servant leader might take over the responsibilities of a team member on a given day so the team member can be home with an ailing family member or partner. Servant leaders also focus on helping people develop, such as giving them the opportunity to acquire new skills. The humanistic approach of the servant leader also helps build community, or a sense of togetherness among the stakeholders. The servant leader uses his or her talents to help group members. For example, if the leader is a good planner, he or she engages in planning because it will help the group attain its goals.

Many academic administrators see themselves as servant leaders because they take care of administrative work so instructors can devote more time to teaching, advising, and research. Servant leadership is gaining in popularity as companies attempt to establish harmony between executives and workforce members who dislike all-knowing and powerful leaders.[33]

SUMMARY

Leader–member exchange (LMX) theory is useful in understanding many aspects of downward relations. LMX theory explains that leaders do not typically use the same leadership style in dealing with all members, and that these exchanges vary in quality. The leader forms strong downward relations with members of the in-group, whereas out-group members are treated more routinely. In-group members are more likely to be productive, satisfied, and engage in citizenship behavior. LMX is the most potent with frequent communication between the leaders and group members. Leaders who receive good organizational support are more likely to engage in beneficial exchanges. The leader's first impressions of a subordinate's competency play an important role in placing the group member in the in-group or out-group.

The path–goal theory of leadership states that, to be effective, leaders engage in behaviors that complement group members' environments and abilities in a manner that compensates for deficiencies and facilitates subordinate satisfaction and work unit performance. All versions of the theory point to the idea of the leader helping subordinates find the right path to attain goals. Certain aspects of path–goal theory foster positive downward relations.

Humanistic leadership practices for building downward relations described here are: (1) Mix humility with self-confidence; (2) communicate trust in others and minimize micromanagement; (3) engage in face-to-face communication; (4) assist in the development of subordinates; (5) be civil, yet maintain professional distance; (6) give emotional support and encouragement; (7) begin a new position with a listening tour; (8) share credit with the team; and (9) avoid being the abominable no man or woman.

Politically astute leadership practices for building downward relations described here are: (1) Use authority prudently; (2) achieve buy-in for initiatives; (3) encourage democracy, including power sharing; (4) use a leadership style different from that of your predecessor; (5) be prudent in dealing with former coworkers; (6) encourage and welcome group members of superior intelligence; (7) solicit and welcome feedback; and (8) be a servant leader. Being a servant leader includes several of the ideas for building downward relations described in this chapter.

QUESTIONS AND ACTIVITIES

1. Give two examples of exchanges the leader might initiate if the leader regarded a given support as a highly talented individual.
2. Give two examples of exchanges a leader might initiate if the leader wanted to increase the job satisfaction of a given group member.
3. How would a manager know whether he or she was finding the right balance between being a helpful coach versus a micromanager?
4. During a listening tour, a new manager is likely to hear some gripes and some suggestions for needed change. From a political standpoint, how do you think the manager should handle these gripes and suggestions?
5. Suppose you as a manager thought of a great idea that moved your organizational unit forward. How might you then authentically share credit with the team?
6. What should the manager who solicits feedback from the group and then finds that the feedback is almost all negative do?

7. What are several ways in which being a servant leader helps build downward relationships?

CASE STUDY: MICRO MIKE

Michael (Mike) Cochran is a principal and cofounder of Mesa Investments, a small company that manages financial portfolios for clients. Mesa clients are at the high end of personal investors, with a minimum portfolio of $500,000 required to become a client. Cochran supervises the work of six financial consultants who manage the portfolios of Mesa clients. In addition to his management responsibilities, Cochran carries a heavy client load and is also responsible for attracting new clients to the firm.

Cochran attributes much of his success as a financial consultant to his painstaking attention to detail when advising clients. For example, when a client suggests a possible investment, Cochran presents the client with fresh information about the investment, such as any change of direction anticipated in a mutual fund that the client might be considering. Cochran says his standards of excellence make him both a good financial consultant and a strong manager.

In describing his standards of excellence in working with clients, Cochran gave a recent example: "A couple I am working with said that it was time for them to get back into technology stocks and technology-heavy mutual funds. Yet I know that both of them like the security of seeing high dividends in their portfolio. So using our mammoth database, I located a few technology stocks and mutual funds that are poised for growth yet still pay reasonable dividends. Jake and Loretta (the names of the couple) were really appreciative."

Cochran also gave a couple of recent examples of his standards of excellence as a manager: "I review many of the client portfolios developed by group of financial consultants. If I see a buy or sell order that does not seem to fit the client's risk tolerance, I send an immediate e-mail to the consultant demanding an explanation. Also, if I see an application for becoming a client with the firm that is incomplete in any way, I demand that the consultant get the application correct. In one application I noticed that the new client had left off the social security number of one of the beneficiaries.

"Another way I hold high standards is that I insist on a professional look for all our consultants. I walked by one of our consultants' offices while she was working with a client. She actually had an old Pepsi can and a Styrofoam cup on her desk while talking to the client. After the client left, I told Carol [the financial consultant, Carol Reaves] that sloppiness like that would not be tolerated in our firm."

Reaves was then asked by the outside interviewer how she enjoyed working at Mesa, and for Mike. "Mesa has been great for me. I love my clients, and I'm making more money than I ever dreamed of six years out of college. I've learned a lot from Mike, but he's just too overwhelming as a manager."

Asked what she meant by *overwhelming,* Reaves replied: "My colleagues and I do not dislike Mike, yet we call him Micro Mike, as in micromanager. The man is too picky. He has given us instructions about which font to use in e-mails. Somehow he thinks that Rockwell looks more professional than Times Roman. He once told me that I should never wear heels to the office higher than two and a half inches. Mike insists on a quarterly review of our plans for each client. The review takes an enormous amount of time that could be spent speaking with clients or networking for new business.

"Larry [another financial consultant in the office] told me that Mike criticized one of his client portfolios because the ratio of investments for one of his clients was 63% equities and 37% debt. Mike's point was that the plan for the client was a ratio of 60/40.

"Larry and I, along with a couple of the other consultants, think that Mike is not giving us enough room to breathe professionally. When we hint at the problem with Mike, he just gets back to his theme of having high standards of excellence."

Case Study Questions

1. In what way is Mike Cochran being a micromanager?
2. What damage might Cochran be doing to his downward relations?
3. How might Cochran obtain the feedback he needs to more effectively manage his downward relations?
4. Why should Carol Reaves complain about Cochran's leadership style when she is making so much money?
5. What political advice might you give Reaves and her colleagues so they prosper in the firm yet be a little less micromanaged?

POLITICAL SKILL-BUILDING EXERCISE 6

The Effective Leader

The purpose of this exercise is to reflect on the practices of effective leaders. Organize into small groups to share experiences about the practices and attitudes of effective leaders for whom you have worked. After a few minutes of reflection, each person takes a turn describing what a particular former or present immediate manager did or does to be effective in terms of downward relations. Find a convenient way of recording these observations, at least to the extent of summarizing each one, such as "Would always listen to my problems."

After you have collected the brief descriptions of effective downward relations, classify them into two categories: humanistic and politically astute. As you study your lists, attempt to reach conclusions about what made for effective downward relations by a leader, at least for your small sample. If time permits, a spokesperson for each group will present the findings to the rest of the class. Again, attempt to reach a conclusion about effective downward relations as found in this informal analysis.

REFERENCES

1. Excerpted from Lublin, J. S. (2007, June 5). How you can ensure a newly created job has staying power. *Wall Street Journal,* B1.

2. James, K. (2006). Antecedents, processes, and outcomes of collective (group-level) politics in organizations. In E. Vigoda-Gadot & Drory, A. (Eds.), *Handbook of organizational politics* (pp. 53–74) [p. 59]. Northampton, MA: Edward Elgar; Ferris, G. R., & Judge, T. A. (1991). Personnel/human resources management: A political influence perspective. *Journal of Management, 17,* 447–488.

3. Kacmar, K. M., Zivnuska, S., Witt, L. A., & Gully, S. M. (2003, August). The interactive effect of leader–member exchange and communication frequency on performance ratings. *Journal of Applied Psychology,* 770.

4. Erdogan, B., & Enders, J. (2007, March). Support from the top: Supervisors' perceived organizational support as a moderator of leader–member exchange to satisfaction and performance relationships. *Journal of Applied Psychology,* 321–330.

5. Liden, R. C., Wayne, S. J., & Stilwell, D. (1993, August). A longitudinal study on the early development of leader–member exchanges. *Journal of Applied Psychology,* 662–674.

6. House, R. (1996). Path–goal theory of leadership: Lessons, legacy, and a reformulated theory. *Leadership Quarterly, 3,* 323–352. The definition and

presentation of the theory are from this source, which builds on earlier versions of path–goal theory.

7. Finney, M J. (1992). *In the face of uncertainty: 25 top leaders speak out on challenge, change, and the future of American business.* New York: AMACOM Books.

8. Hollenbeck, G. P., & Hall, D. T. (2004). Self-confidence and leader performance. *Organizational Dynamics, 3,* 254–269.

9. Quoted in *Manager's Edge* (2007, June). Strengthen workplace relationships. *Manager's Edge,* 1.

10. Adapted from Wuorio, J. (2004, March). 8 ways micromanagers can cure themselves. *MSN Business.* Retrieved 07/19/2007 from www.becentral.com.

11. Harry Chambers cited in Bruzzese, A. (2004, December 27). *Develop strategy on how to handle micromanagers.* Gannett News Service.

12. Quoted in Fisher, A. (2004, August 23). In praise of micromanaging. *Fortune,* 40.

13. Dulye, L. (2006, July). Get out of your office. *HR Magazine,* 99–101.

14. Bossidy, L. (2007, April). What your leader expects of you. *Harvard Business Review,* 61–62.

15. Bossidy, L. (2007, April). What your leader expects of you. *Harvard Business Review,* 64.

16. Hymowitz, C. (2003, December 9). Helping your staffers earn promotions builds broad alliances. *Wall Street Journal,* n.p.

17. Cited in McAleavy, T. (2007, February 18). Managers, mind your manners in the office. *The Record.*

18. DuBrin, A. J. (2008). *Human relations for career and personal success: Concepts, applications, and skills* (8th ed.) [p. 287]. Upper Saddle River, NJ: Pearson/ Prentice Hall.

19. Dinkmeyer, D., & Eckstein, D. (1995). *Leadership by encouragement.* Delray Beach, FL: St. Lucie Press.

20. Lublin, J. S. (2003, November 25). How to win support from colleagues at your new job. *Wall Street Journal,* B1.

21. Hardy, Q. (2007, March 12). The unCarly. *Forbes,* 82–90.

22. The anecdote and the citation of Amabile are from Sandberg, J. (2006, October 17). Some managers make it easy on themselves with a ready "No." *Wall Street Journal,* B1.

23. Pfeffer, J. (1981). *Power in organizations* [p. 6]. Marshfield, MA: Pitman.

24. Jenkins, M. (2005, September). All together now: The importance of generating "buy in" from your staff. *Black Enterprise,* 69.

25. Butcher, D., & Clarke, M. (2006) The symbiosis of organizational politics and organizational democracy. In E. Vigoda-Gadot & Drory, A. (Eds.), *Handbook of organizational politics* (pp. 286–300) [p. 287]. Northampton, MA: Edward Elgar.

26. Ettore, B. (1997, July). The empowerment gap: Hype vs. reality. *HRfocus,* 5.

27. Quoted in Perry, P. M. (1989). Seven errors to avoid when empowering your staff. *Success Workshop,* A supplement to *Manager's Edge,* p. 4.

28. The information and quotes are from Kirkpatrick, D. (2004, November 1). Chipping away at Intel: CEO Hector Ruiz came from humble roots to propel AMD into the big leagues. *Fortune,* 112.

29. White, E. (2005, November 21). Learning to be the boss. *Wall Street Journal,* B1, B5.

30. Welch, J., & Welch, S. (2006, July 24). The smarter they are. *BusinessWeek,* 102.

31. Welch, J., & Welch, S. (2006, July 24). The smarter they are.

32. Byrne, J. A. (2004, May). Do you make the grade? *Fast Company,* 101.

33. Greenleaf, R. K. (1998). *The power of servant leadership.* San Francisco: Berrett-Koehler; Hunter, J. C. (2004). *The world's most powerful leadership principle: How to become a servant leader.* New York: Crown Business.

SEVEN

INFLUENCE TACTICS

LEARNING OBJECTIVES

After studying this chapter and doing the exercises, you should be able to do the following:

1. Explain the meaning of influence and how it relates to organizational politics.
2. Identify and describe a variety of influence tactics aimed primarily at interpersonal relationships.
3. Identify and describe a variety of influence tactics aimed primarily at groups and the total organization.
4. Summarize information about the sequencing and relative effectiveness of influence tactics.

During a stretch of several months, nothing but bad news has emanated from the European Aeronautic Defence & Space Co. (EADS). The epic production delays plaguing the vaunted Airbus A380 super jumbo jet have saddled the company with a $3.3 billion cost overrun. They have also triggered the departure of several top officers, including two CEOs.

But there is one surprising bright spot for EADS—in the United States of all places, where the European aerospace giant has never been particularly well liked. Defying the skeptics, the company's U.S. defense arm, EADS North America Inc., is thriving. The unit's sales have steadily ballooned to more than $1 billion—up from just $400 million three years previously. And now, under the leadership of CEO Ralph D. Crosby Jr., a former senior Northrop Grumman Corp. executive, the European-American company is actually contending (with partner Northrop) for one of the richest Pentagon prizes in decades: the $100 billion contract to replace aerial refueling tankers. "Everybody thought the penetration of the North American market by anyone other than the British was near impossible—certainly not by a company with a heavy French accent," says an aerospace analyst.

Crosby's strategy has been simple: "Crawl, walk, run," as he puts it. He has been careful to bid only on U.S. defense contracts where EADS clearly brought something unique to the table. A good example is the light utility helicopters built by Eurocopter. It offered a noncombat chopper that cost less and could be delivered more quickly than the ones offered by U.S. competitors, the U.S. Army concluded. What's more, EADS boasted clearly superior copter technology. The U.S. Army purchased 322 helicopters in 2006, the single biggest Eurocopter order. "We were quite prudent about the expectations we had established and claims we made," Crosby said.

His experience in the domestic defense industry has given him discerning political antennae. One of Crosby's first moves was establishing stateside final production factories, which brought 645 high-paying assembly jobs in Texas, Mississippi, and Alabama. Plans were established to hire another 210 people in Mississippi as the helicopter factory there shifted into high gear. That has helped with the support of high-powered senators who sit on the influential Appropriations and Armed Services Committees.

Crosby has been savvy about partnering with big U.S. contractors. EADS North America, for example, is joining with Raytheon Co. and engine maker Pratt & Whitney in the bid to win the U.S. Army Joint Cargo Aircraft contract. The initial competition is for 33 small, off-the-shelf cargo aircraft worth $1.3 billion. But it could ultimately run as high as $6 billion for 145 planes. For Crosby and his staff of U.S. defense executives, the acid test is tankers. The initial contract is for 180 planes worth about $30 billion.

The real staying power of EADS North America will be tested during the decline in defense spending. "What happens when the budgets start going down is the small guys and the foreigners get squeezed out?" says another defense analyst. "The system only welcomes foreigners when the budgets are flush."

Crosby brushes off the criticism. "This is the largest defense acquisition for the next 20 years," he says. "We came here to win."[1]

The story about the European aerospace company and its American executive illustrates several ideas about influence and organizational politics. Crosby and his team gained advantage because of their expertise about helicopters and aerospace defense. His political skill in creating jobs for Americans also weighed heavily in EADS receiving giant U.S. contracts despite being mostly a European firm. In this chapter, we concentrate on influence tactics. Such tactics are as important for organizational politics as running is for football, especially because politics is often defined as the use of influence. **Influence** refers to the process of affecting the thoughts, behavior, and feelings of another person.[2] With influence, a person has the ability to affect the behavior of a person in a particular direction. Power gives you the potential or capacity to influence others. However, you can still influence others without having a lot of power, such as seeing a homeless child influencing a CEO to create more jobs in the community.

Influence has gained in importance because so many workers have to obtain the cooperation of other workers without much formal power or authority over them. For example, an enterprise sales representative at IBM said she might lead a team of up to 100 to 150 people for a large account. Those people do not report to her, so she has to rely on influence, as well as her standing in the company, to gain their cooperation to make and implement a sale.[3]

In this chapter, we first look at the theoretical link between influence tactics and political behavior. We group influence tactics into two major categories: those aimed primarily at one-on-one relationships, and those aimed at groups and the total organization. Exhibit 7.1 will help you differentiate the best-known and best-researched influence tactics from those that are less well-known and less researched, yet still useful for organizational politics. Most of the standard tactics will be mentioned in this chapter, either alone or incorporated into other tactics. For example, assertiveness is incorporated into "be in the alpha executive mode." We also present some information about the sequencing and relative effectiveness of the influence tactics mentioned.

Kelton Rhoads observes that we do not know how many influence tactics exist—much like we do not know how many branches there are on a tree. Do you count just the major branches, or do you count all the twigs? If you count the twigs, there are at least 160 influence tactics.[4] The left side of Exhibit 7.1 focuses on the well-researched major branches.

Exhibit 7.1 Influence Tactics Classified by Amount of Research Support and Level of Target

Well-Researched Influence Tactics	*Less-Well-Researched and Nonresearched Influence Tactics*
Individual Level	**Individual Level**
Ingratiation	Alpha executive mode
Persuasion	Negotiate sensibly
Exchange of benefits and favors	Be low key
	Be agreeable and apologize when necessary
	Apprise others of the usefulness of your demands
Group Level	**Group Level**
Coalition formation	Use charisma
Use of expertise	Display foreign language skill
Co-optation	Be a maverick or iconoclast
	Appeal to superordinate goals
	Remain cool under pressure
	Place negative spin on events

THEORETICAL AND CONCEPTUAL LINKS BETWEEN INFLUENCE TACTICS AND POLITICAL BEHAVIOR IN ORGANIZATIONS

Influence tactics are typically studied as part of organizational behavior or leadership, yet influence tactics are also an integral part of organizational politics. For those of you who like analogies, influence tactics are to political behavior what eggs are to an omelet. You cannot be political without using influence tactics, partly because political tactics are used to influence others. After an extensive review of definitions of organizational politics, Eran

Vigoda-Gadot concludes that influence tactics are a major component of political behavior.[5] Gerald R. Ferris similarly regards influence as one of the four underlying dimensions of political skill. (The other three dimensions are social astuteness, networking building/social capital, and genuineness.)[6]

Influence tactics are one process people use to get others to do their bidding or produce the response desired by the influence actor, such as accepting advice or agreeing with a decision. For instance, a manager might ingratiate himself with a vice president in order to be considered for promotion to division president.

Effective influence behavior includes a range of politically toned skill and knowledge. L. A. Witt and Gerald R. Ferris explain that socially skilled individuals are more likely than those with low levels of social skills to recognize the appropriate timing for an influence attempt. Socially skilled political actors will also know how to improvise when their planned impression management tactic looks like failing, and know when to be assertive or remain silent. Social skill therefore depends on the cognitive element of reading and understanding social situations. At the same time, social skill includes the behavioral or action component of capitalizing on that insight to influence others.[7]

INTERPERSONAL-LEVEL INFLUENCE TACTICS

In this section, we present influence tactics focused mostly on affecting the thoughts, behaviors, and feelings of another person in a face-to-face interaction. Most of these tactics were identified and researched before the widespread use of e-mail to influence others.[8]

Be Persuasive

Persuasiveness is also regarded as rationality, and includes such behaviors as using logic to convince subordinates, explaining reasons for a request, and presenting information to support a point of view. The modern manager and professional will often use benchmarks as a way of persuading others, such as mentioning the cost per sale or the revenue per employee of a competitor. The purpose of these benchmarks is to convince the group members to perform at least as well as the competitors. An illuminating example took place several years ago at Hewlett-Packard, when Mark Hurd was the new CEO. He pointed out that the company was "off benchmark" in numerous areas, including spending too much on information technology, the very product and service it sells to other companies. Specifically, HP was spending about $18,500 per employee on IT, whereas world-class companies such as GE were spending about $8,700 per employee.[9] Hurd then proceeded to get the ratio in line through cost cutting, including laying off thousands of people.

Exchange Favors and Benefits

Exchange of favors and benefits to influence subordinates includes specific behaviors such as offering to do something for the person if he or she does something for the manager. The manager might grant the worker a Friday afternoon off from work if the subordinate were willing stay until 10:00 p.m. one night to take care of an emergency. Exchange is the preferred tactic of lobbyists who contribute to political campaigns in the expectation of receiving favorable consideration when it comes time to vote for legislation needed by the lobbyist's client. Also, in the political realm, people who contribute to political campaigns often receive an appointed position if the politician wins. An extraordinary practitioner of this type of exchange was former New York State governor George Pataki. Throughout his administration, he regularly gave plum jobs to campaign contributors and their friends and families, often firing competent professionals in the process. In Pataki's early days in office, it was found that more than 100 persons appointed to jobs requiring state Senate confirmation had contributed nearly $1 million (in total) to his campaign and other state Republicans.[10]

Thomas H. Quinn, a high-level lobbyist, gives us insight into the skill involved in influencing others through lobbying: "Lobbying isn't all about wrapping your product in apple pie, God, and the flag. It's long hours, political maneuvering, and never forgetting the basic rules. First, never talk when a tape recorder is on. Never write anything down. Never talk on the telephone if you can talk face-to-face. And never talk if you can wink." We might add, never leave an electronic trail.

One might argue that lobbying as an influence tactic should be placed in Chapter 9 about negative tactics. Quinn argues to the contrary, in these words: "Lobbyist is the most noble profession. It used to be clergy and schoolteacher. But the highest calling is a lobbyist. The only business to protect the little man against the oppressive government is a lobbyist."[11] (A lobbyist is, by nature, a master of spin.)

Ingratiate Yourself With Others

Ingratiation deals with getting the other person to like you. It involves such behaviors as (a) acting in a friendly manner prior to asking what you want, (b) praising another person, and (c) making the other person feel important. We have twice previously mentioned research about the effectiveness of board members ingratiating themselves with a CEO in order to be invited to receive other board appointments. Ingratiation, as with all influence tactics, requires political skill (or sensitivity) to succeed. Without political skill or finesse, an influence tactic might backfire, such as giving an off-the-wall compliment for purposes of ingratiation.

A study with 337 employees in two retail firms demonstrated that subordinates with good political skill were more effective at ingratiating themselves with managers. The employees with high political skill were less likely than those with low political skill to have their ingratiation attempts perceived by targets as a manipulative influence attempt.[12] Political skill was measured by the questionnaire shown in Exhibit 7.2, which you are invited to take.

Exhibit 7.2 Political Skill Inventory

Directions: Using the following 7-point scale, write in each box the number that best describes how much you agree with the statement:

1 = strongly disagree; 2 = disagree; 3 = slightly agree; 4 = neutral; 5 = slightly agree; 6 = agree; 7 = strongly agree.

Statement	*Rating*
1. I spend a lot of time and effort networking with others.	
2. I am able to make most people feel comfortable and at ease around me.	
3. I am able to communicate easily and effectively with others.	
4. It is easy for me to develop good rapport with most people.	
5. I understand people very well.	
6. I am good at building relationships with influential people at work (or at school).	

(Continued)

Exhibit 7.2 (Continued)

Statement	*Rating*
7. I am particularly good at sensing the motivations and hidden agendas of others.	
8. When communicating with others, I try to be genuine in what I say and do.	
9. I have developed a large network of colleagues and associates at work (or school) on whom I can call for support when I really need to get things done.	
10. At work (or at school), I know a lot of important people and I am well connected.	
11. I spend a lot of time at work (or at school) developing connections with others.	
12. I am good at getting people to like me.	
13. It is important that people believe I am sincere in what I do and say.	
14. I try to show a genuine interest in other people.	
15. I am good at using my connections and network to make things happen at work (or at school).	
16. I have good intuition and am savvy about how to present myself to others.	
17. I always seem to instinctively know the right things to say or do to influence others.	
18. I pay close attention to people's facial expressions.	

Total: ____

Total ÷ 18: ____

Scoring and Interpretation: Compute your overall score by adding together your response scores on all the questions and dividing the total by 18. You will have an overall political score between 1 and 7. Larger scores identify people who have higher levels of political skill, and smaller scores identify people who have lower levels of political skill.

SOURCE: Adapted from Ferris, G. R., Treadway, D. C., Kolodinsky, R. W., Hochwarter, W. A., Kacmar, C. J., & Douglas, C., et al. (2005). Development and validation of the political skill inventory. *Journal of Management*, *31*, 126–153.

Be an Alpha Executive

A long-standing belief exists that an effective way of influencing others is to be bold, brash, assertive, and unrelenting. Many labels and concepts have been proposed to describe behavior of this nature, including the relatively recent **alpha executive.** Such an executive is ambitious, self-confident, competitive, and brash. When such behavior is within limits, it can be functional. Two executive coaches who work with alpha men and women contend that three out of four executives and half of all middle managers are alphas. Nonalphas who aspire to the executive suite apparently will not get there without adopting a few alpha traits.[13] Also, when the alpha characteristics are too exaggerated, the result can be an intimidating, disliked executive such as Bob Nardelli, the former GE and Home Depot executive, and now CEO of Chrysler LLC.

Alpha executives follow the law of power referred to as "Enter action with boldness." According to the law, if you are unsure of a course of action, do not attempt the action. Timidity is dangerous, so it is better to enter an engagement with boldness. Bold people are admired, whereas timid people are rarely admired.[14]

Chutzpah, or elevated audacity and nerve, is another term that gets at the boldness of alpha people. A manager with chutzpah might influence people by making demands that seem unreasonable—and often workers respond positively. When Jack Welch was the CEO at GE he would make such demands as telling suppliers that either they outsourced much of their manufacturing overseas (offshoring) or they would lose GE as a customer. In fear of losing a valued customer, most suppliers complied.

Negotiate Sensibly

Negotiation is an influence process, and all your negotiating skills would fit into your kit of influence tactics. Here we emphasize two related points about negotiation useful in influencing others. The first point is to consistently make high demands or low offers, yet still be realistic enough so the other side takes you seriously. For example, the politically insensitive negotiator might ask $2 million for a property for which he or she would be happy to receive $1 million. An unrealistic demand can readily make the other side lose interest. Bruce Wasserstein, the chief executive at the investment banker Lazard Ltd., built part of his reputation on his ability to win at the negotiating table.

Competitors gave him the nickname "Bid 'Em Up Bruce" for his mystical-like ability to induce clients to pay top dollar for acquisitions of other companies.[15] Wasserstein emphasized the potential value for clients, but did not ask for so much money that they lost interest.

A more subtle influence tactic during negotiation is to perceive negotiation as a way of building a long-term business relationship. The negotiator creates a feeling of goodwill by not attempting to capture as much as possible when beginning a business relationship with another party. Dick Parsons, the chairman and CEO of Time Warner, recalls the wonderful business advice he received from Steve Ross, his predecessor. "I was on the Time Warner board, and I was going to be coming over to the company from the banking industry, and we were talking about how to get things done. Steve said to me, 'Dick, always remember this is a small business and a long life. You are going to see all these guys come around and around again, so how you treat them on each individual transaction is going to make an impression in the long haul. When you do deals leave a little something to make everyone happy instead of trying to grab every nickel off the table.'"[16]

Be Low Key

In many situations, being the alpha leader is an effective technique for exerting influence. In contrast, in some situations acting low key will be more influential. Many employees, boards of directors, and shareholders became discouraged with the flamboyant, narcissistic CEOs of the late 1990s and early 2000s who appeared to be more focused on self-gain than helping the company. As a result, a leader being low key and centered on company welfare has become an effective influence tactic. According to one analysis, several of the best-publicized executive failures during that era could be attributed to management style.

Phillip Purcell of Morgan Stanley was an autocrat who treated his subordinates with contempt. Michael Eisner of the Walt Disney Co. was smart and creative but highly suspicious of others and unwilling to share power. Carly Fiorina of Hewlett-Packard was a wonderful roving ambassador and visionary but she was neglectful of the operations of the business. Boards have been disappointed too often by the self-proclaimed titans whose personalities are so domineering that they reject opposing points of view. So being overly charismatic has lost some currency.

Sydney Finkelstein, a professor of strategy and leadership and an expert on why executives fail, says that the new model leader is someone with "the highest ethical standards, who can lead by example, and who can build a strong effective team around him or her. Those are the hot buttons now, rather than the cowboy [or cowgirl] riding in to provide the magic answer for the company."[17] As a final illustration of this point, a successful leader referred to as Hal said, "The success of my organization isn't about me. It's about the great people who are working with me."[18]

Be Agreeable and Apologize When Necessary

Another tactic related to being low key is to emphasize your personality factor of *agreeableness* when attempting to influence others. Agreeableness, or likability, refers to such traits as selflessness, cooperativeness, helpfulness, tolerance, flexibility, generosity, sympathy, and courtesy. Because agreeableness is one of the five major personality factors, it is present in everyone, although people vary from low to high on agreeableness. You may not be able to change your personality to use agreeableness as an influence tactic, but at least you can look for ways to be agreeable.

Agreeableness is highly relevant to job performance in situations in which joint action and collaboration are required. In many situations, being agreeable will influence others to cooperate with you.[19] You may recall the example of the enterprise sales representative at IBM mentioned above. She needs to be tolerant and flexible in gaining the cooperation of others, such as giving them leeway in terms of providing technical information.

Knowing when to apologize is another way in which being agreeable can influence others. Apology can be a highly effective political tactic in working with insiders as well as customers and clients. Almost a decade ago, after a woman was paralyzed in a vehicular accident cased by faulty tires on a Ford Explorer, Ford attorneys apologized to the victim at her bedside. Apparently as a result of the apology, she settled her lawsuit for a third of the $100 million she originally had sought.[20]

With company insiders, an apology would often be directed at a mistake or missed deadline, such as, "I thought I could take care of that virus problem on your laptop by today, but I misjudged my workload. I am sorry, but I still want to help you." The apology in this case would influence the person with the problem to think kindly of the support technician and not verbalize complaints about the IT support group.

Apprise Others of the Usefulness of Your Demands

According to Gary Yukl, **apprising** refers to the influence agent explaining why a request or proposal is likely to benefit the target person individually. Apprising often takes the form of explaining the career benefits of going along with the agent's proposal, such as learning a new skill or acquiring valuable career experience, or meeting important people. A manager might influence a supervisor to manage night-shift operations because of the invaluable experience to be gained in managing a total operation.

Apprising is like persuasion except that part of the tactic is to provide benefits to the individual, such as the experience in managing a total operation. Apprising differs from exchange of benefits because the influence agent is not offering to give something to the target in return. Instead, the target acquires a beneficial experience.

For apprising to work well, the agent must understand what the target is seeking, and the target must trust the agent.[21] Too often, managers say "this will be great experience for you" without truly understanding how the subordinate will benefit from the experience.

GROUP- AND ORGANIZATIONAL-LEVEL INFLUENCE TACTICS

In this section, we feature tactics geared more toward influencing groups and total organizations than individuals. Recognize, however, that even if a person were attempting to influence 350,000 employees at the same time, it would still be individuals who would have to be influenced. A group or organization might have a distinctive culture, but both lack a brain that can respond to influence attempts.

Form Coalitions

At times it is difficult to influence an individual or group by acting alone. The actor will then have to form coalitions or alliances with others to obtain the necessary clout. A **coalition** is a specific arrangement of parties working together to combine their influence. Typically, the coalition target is several people. Coalition formation is effective as an influence tactic because, to quote an old adage, "there is power in numbers." The more people you have on your side the better, so the manager will often look to gain the support of several subordinates and perhaps those outside the department to support an initiative. An example of such an initiative would be attempting to get the company to only use suppliers who can guarantee that they or their subcontractors have not engaged in human rights violations.

Collaborative influence is one of the 10 leadership traits and behaviors that IBM emphasizes. The company urges leaders to form coalitions with other members of the company community. It is therefore recommended that the leader "create interdependence, building genuine commitment across organizational boundaries to a common purpose."[22]

Coalitions in the past were most often formed by managers chatting with their targets during lunch, at breaks, in the hallways, and while walking around.[23] E-mail, including instant messaging and perhaps even text messaging, plays a major role in coalition formation today. For example, the manager with an interest in combating human rights violations might send an e-mail to colleagues with an attachment about a supplier who hired a subcontractor who relied on slave labor to produce goods cheaply.

Forming coalitions often involves overcoming resistance to change, so the influence agent must think about how to sell others on the advantages of change. Part of overcoming resistance to change includes apprising. In the example at hand, the manager wanting to minimize human rights violations would have to sell the benefits of changing subcontractors, or getting these subcontractors to stop violating human rights. The reasons might include being a socially responsible company and avoiding negative publicity which could result in a consumer boycott against the company.

Engage in Co-Optation With the Other Side

Getting in bed with the enemy is an effective tactic for influencing a group of people, particularly when the other side is powerful. **Co-optation** is the merging or incorporating of another power group or individual for the purpose of controlling or silencing a counterpart.[24]

Assume that in one company, management and the union have an antagonistic relationship and that the company would like to influence union leadership to work more cooperatively with management. A co-optation technique would be for the board members to invite a key union leader to become a member of the board. In this way, leaders throughout the union might be prompted to work more cooperatively with management.

A few years ago, managers at four Hollywood studios, including Metro-Goldwyn-Mayer, used co-optation by going into business with one of their biggest adversaries, the peer-to-peer pioneer BitTorrent. The company whose technology enabled a wave of illegal file sharing on the Internet initiated the BitTorrent Entertainment Network on its Web site, BitTorrent.com. The digital media store began by offering about 3,000 new and classic movies and thousands more television shows, plus a thousand PC games and music videos. All of these offerings were legally available for purchase. At the same time, visitors to the site could use free downloads of their own video uploads. Doug Lee, the executive vice president of MGM's new media division, commented: "Somebody once said you have to embrace your enemy. We like the idea that they have millions of users worldwide. That is potentially fertile, legitimate ground for us."

Although co-optation by the four Hollywood studios is an effective technique, and politically savvy for gaining credibility with film fans, the solution was not 100% effective. BitTorrent executives say they cannot prevent illegal downloads in the larger file-sharing world. Yet, according to their studies, 34% of BitTorrent users would pay for content if a wide-ranging legal service were available.[25]

Display Expertise

Expertise was described in Chapter 3 as a key source of power. At the same time, the display of expertise is effective in influencing both individuals and groups. If a manager displays expertise in a business or technical area, he or she will be able to influence many people. Suppose an automotive executive has a strong track record in choosing vehicles that prove to be good sellers. As a result, when that executive has an unconventional idea about the introduction of a new model, he or she has a good chance of influencing others about the merit of the idea. Several years ago, a Mercedes Car Group executive was able to convince other key managers that the Smart Car (a tiny two-seat vehicle), which sold relatively well in Europe, was ready for introduction to the North American market—first Canada, then the United States.

An example of using expertise to influence thousands of people took place at Microsoft Corp. in 2006. Cofounder Bill Gates, with the agreement of CEO Steve Ballmer, brought Ray Ozzie on board in a key executive position. Ozzie was a renowned programmer who had created Lotus Notes. Ozzie's role at Microsoft was to influence people at all levels in the company to make every

Microsoft product and service compatible with the Internet. "Everything we do should have a presence on the Web," Ozzie said.[26]

Use Charisma

Being charismatic, which includes being charming, is a form of impression management and an influence tactic that can gain the cooperation of groups of people. Charismatic leaders are able to influence people from a distance as well as in face-to-face encounters. Many people will be influenced by your actions if they perceive you to be charismatic. An extreme example is Flavio Briatore, whose entrepreneurial ventures cater to the super-rich. His marquee project is the Billionaire Club, one of the world's most exclusive nightspots, located high on a hill on the Mediterranean island of Sardinia. In Italy, Briatore has climbed toward the top in the fashion, racing, restaurant, and nightclub industries. His friends and colleagues say much of his accomplishment can be attributed to a combination of organizational skills and uncanny charm, including exceptional taste.[27]

The use of charisma is a somewhat unreliable influence tactic because its effectiveness depends heavily on the perceptions of influence targets about the influence agent. In general, in order to be perceived as charismatic, research suggests that the person should be emotionally expressive, enthusiastic, eloquent, visionary, self-confident, and responsive to others.[28]

In recent years, many CEOs have purposely used charm to influence stakeholders to have a more positive attitude toward them and the companies they represent. At times, a more charming and charismatic CEO has been chosen to replace one who is less charming. A case in point is the American International Group (AIG). Hank Greenberg, the former CEO, was known as an impatient and prickly leader. He had successfully built a $99 billion financial services empire until he was forced out amid a financial scandal. Greenberg's replacement was Martin Sullivan, a jovial British person who is perceived by many to be cheerful and charming. He has quietly worked to boost morale and repair the AIG reputation.[29]

Display Skill in a Foreign Language

A low-key tactic to influence groups is to speak in their native language, when their language is your second language. One of the menu items on the customer service telephone lines of many companies is "Press 2 for Spanish."

Part of the rationale is to influence Hispanic people to think that the company has a genuine interest in the welfare of Hispanics. If the percentage of Spanish-speaking employees and customers is high, giving management a working knowledge of Spanish can improve employee training and customer service. Team building and a better cultural understanding can also result when managers speak Spanish in a U.S. workplace with many Hispanic employees and customers.[30]

English has become the official language for many international companies. Nevertheless, the influence agent who can speak a language other than English well may impress targets who are native speakers of his or her second language. An example would be a native English-speaking representative of an American company speaking German when working with customers in Germany. A note of caution is that unless your second language skills are highly advanced, you will lose political advantage because your target will usually respond to you in English. Yet a few introductory words and phrases—spoken well—in the target's native language are likely to be influential.

Be a Maverick or Iconoclast

Another potentially powerful influence tactic is to think differently than most people, which will capture their attention and influence them, providing your ideas appear to have merit. Being a maverick or an iconoclast is likely to influence many people at the same time. (An iconoclast is a person who attacks cherished beliefs, thus running counter to some icons.) A current example of an iconoclast in business is Patrick Le Quément, the design chief for Renault. His risk-taking designs are loved and detested by customers and critics in about equal numbers. One of the cars he designed is the Twingo, which has a front resembling a frog face. Another vehicle he designed, the Mégane, became Western Europe's best-selling car.

The point in terms of influence tactics is that, by being a maverick and iconoclast (attacking the existing line up of Renault cars), Le Quément captured the attention of company executives and eventually customers. Part of the designer's influence strategy was to widely expose his ideas through concept cars. Le Quément claims that the risk of the concept cars being copied is outweighed by them being fabulous accelerators of innovation.[31]

A historical example of how a contrarian insight can wind up influencing countless millions of people is Aaron Montgomery Ward (1844–1913). His contrarian insight was to eliminate the middleman. Ward founded the world's first mail-order business, Montgomery Ward Co., in 1872. An endless stream of catalog-based companies have followed the idea, including Amazon.com and other online retailers.[32]

Appeal to Superordinate Goals

A potentially effective way of influencing groups of people, as well as the entire organization, is to mobilize workers around an important, far-reaching goal such as guarding the environment, curing a fatal disease, or bringing happiness to thousands of people. For many years, the rallying cry at Coca-Cola Company was that the company was bringing moments of pleasure to millions of people all over the world every day. A **superordinate goal** is an overarching goal that captures the imagination of people.[33]

The superordinate goal is similar to a vision because it relates to an ideal, and is often inspirational. T. J. Rodgers, the founder of Cypress Semiconductor, at one point wanted to convince his board of the importance of purchasing SunPower, a then-struggling startup known for building efficient solar panels. In his third attempt, Rodgers held a silicon wafer in his hand. He told the board it would be worth a mere $600 if it were gold and $20,000 if it were used to make either computer memory chips or solar cells. "We turn silicon into something more valuable than gold," he said. "Now people want to get clean energy, and silicon can do that too."[34] The board finally agreed, and many Cypress Semiconductor employees were inspired by being part of a company that was helping produce clean energy. (Here, as in most situations of influence, the executive was using more than one influence technique. Appealing to the board's interest in potential profits was also influential.)

Be Cool Under Pressure

Performing well under pressure is influential for workers at every job level. The mechanic who can get a ski lift moving again while the skiers stuck on the chairs are panicking is a true hero. The mechanic might influence management to award him a bigger bonus. And the manager who can get a distribution center up and running after a hurricane will similarly influence other levels of management to regard him or her more favorably. The analogy is often drawn between an effective executive and a duck. On the surface, the executive appears cool, calm, and under control. Yet, underneath, he or she is paddling like all fury.

To retain coolness under pressure, many managers and professionals simply dig in and focus on attaining results rather than worrying too much about outside pressures. For a decade, Jeff Bezos, the founder of Amazon .com, faced continual criticism from outsiders that his company was burning money endlessly and had no sensible plan for profitability. Bezos continued to smile, while working at a feverish pace to implement his vision. After about 10 years of relentless effort by Bezos and workers at all levels, Amazon did become a profitable company. Bezos eventually influenced the critics to shut up, and to view his company more favorably as an investment.

Place Spin on Negative Events

An influence tactic aimed at hundreds, or even thousands, of people at the same time is **spin**, which means placing a favorable face on a negative situation or person. The spinner is not necessarily lying, but rather emphasizing a plausible positive aspect of a negative event. The spin usually has a kernel of truth, with a puffed message spun around the kernel. Spin is part of public relations except that public relations is also used to bring attention to favorable events, such as a company undergoing a major expansion or making a large contribution to charity. The term "spin" appears to have been derived from sports in which the player imparts a spin on the ball to gain advantage, such as a spin serve in tennis or spin on a bowling ball, helping it glide into the right position between two pins.

A representative example of spin took place at Yahoo! in 2007. At the time the company was under attack, including criticism of chief executive Terry S. Semel, who shortly thereafter gave up the CEO position and was appointed nonexecutive chairman of the company. Yahoo! had experienced a steady stream of executive departures, some planned but some stemming from disagreements over how the company should be operated. Two of the three newly formed Yahoo! operating units lacked a permanent leader. In addition, 17 executives at the vice president level or higher had left the company after the reorganization. Some of the executives left after their responsibilities changed, or their jobs were reduced in scope or eliminated. Top-level management responded with the spin that the company was not losing people at an unusual rate, saying that it had appointed about 80 vice presidents that year, with most of them being inside promotions.[35]

Here are a few representative examples of spin whose intent is to influence stakeholders—including employees, customers, and investors—toward a more favorable impression of the company.

- A company sells off a profitable unit to raise cash it desperately needs to reduce debt or pay other bills. The spin is that "By selling this non-core part of our business, the management team can get rid of a distraction that is diverting attention from the core business."
- A company enters into Chapter 11 bankruptcy, and offers this spin: "Declaring Chapter 11 is simply a balance sheet adjustment that will not adversely affect our operations. We will emerge as a stronger company soon with a great balance sheet."
- A giant retailer starts a new division of 75 stores to capture a larger market share in a specific segment of the market. The stores lose an enormous amount of money and are all closed within 18 months. The spin offered is that "We are glad we took this risk. A company that does not take risks with innovation will ultimately die."

A caution is that many scholars and consumers regard spin as a negative and unethical influence tactic. You might want to classify spin as rightfully being placed in Chapter 9 about negative politics, yet spin is widely practiced even by generally ethical organizations.

RELATIVE EFFECTIVENESS AND SEQUENCING OF INFLUENCE TACTICS

In deciding which influence tactic or tactics to choose, it is helpful to look at research about their relative effectiveness and the order in which they might be used (their sequencing). Here we look at some of the research evidence about both topics.

Relative Effectiveness of Influence Tactics

Research by Gary Yukl and J. Bruce Tracey provides insights about the relative effectiveness of influence tactics.[36] One hundred and twenty managers participated in the study, along with 526 subordinates, 543 peers, and 128 superiors, who also rated the managers' use of influence tactics. Half the managers worked for manufacturing companies, and half worked for service companies.

The people who worked with the managers completed a questionnaire to identify which of nine influence tactics the managers used. Defined for the participants, the tactics were many of those listed in the right side of Exhibit 7.1. Another question asked how many influence attempts by the agent resulted in complete commitment by the target respondent. The seven response choices were (1) none of them, (2) a few of them, (3) some (less than half), (4) about half of them, (5) more than half of them, (6) most of them, and (7) all of them. Respondents were also asked to rate the overall effectiveness of the manager in carrying out his or her job responsibilities. The item had nine response choices, ranging from the least effective manager I have ever known (1) to the most effective manager I have ever known (9).

The results suggested that the most effective tactics were rational persuasion, inspirational appeal, and consultation. (An effective tactic was one that led to task commitment, and that was used by managers who were perceived to be effective by the various raters.) In contrast, the least effective were pressure, coalition, and appealing to legitimate authority (legitimating). Ingratiation and exchange were moderately effective for influencing team members and peers. The same tactics, however, were not effective for influencing superiors.

The researchers concluded that some tactics were more likely to be successful. Yet they caution that the results do not imply that these tactics will always result in task commitment. The outcome of a specific influence attempt is determined by factors in addition to influence attempts, such as the target's motivation and the organizational culture. Also, any tactic can trigger target resistance if it is not appropriate for the situation or if it is applied unskillfully. Tact, diplomacy, and insight are required for effective application of influence tactics.

Which influence tactic a manager might consider effective—and therefore choose—depends to some extent on how much group members are trusted. When we distrust people, we are likely to attempt to control their actions. Carole V. Wells and David Kipnis conducted a survey about trust involving 275 managers and 267 employees. The managers answered questions about subordinates, and subordinates answered questions about their managers. The two groups, however, were not describing each other. A key finding was that both managers and employees used strong tactics of influence when they distrusted the other party—either a manager or a subordinate. The strong influence tactics studied were appeals to higher authority, assertiveness, coalition building, and sanctions.[37]

Sequencing Influence Tactics

Another important consideration in using influence tactics is the sequence or order in which they should be applied. In general, begin with the most positive, or least abrasive, tactic. If you do not gain the advantage you seek, proceed to a stronger tactic. For example, if you want a larger salary increase than that initially assigned you, try rational persuasion. If persuasion does not work, move on to exchange. Use a more abrasive tactic such as upward appeal only as a last resort. The reason is that abrasive tactics trigger revenge and retaliation. Many people who have brought their complaints to an outside agency such as a governmental office have found themselves with a limited future in their organization. Although the appeal is legally justified, it is politically unwise.

In addition to the sequencing of tactics, the influence agent must also consider the direction of the influence attempt as a contingency factor. In general, the more position power one individual exerts over another, the less the need for being cautious in the use of influence tactics. When you have more power, there are likely to be fewer negative consequences from using more powerful tactics, such as blaming or attacking others.

SUMMARY

With influence, a person has the ability to affect the behavior of another person in a particular direction. Power gives you the potential or capacity to influence others. Influence helps gain cooperation among people over whom you do not have formal authority.

Influence tactics are a major component of political behavior. Influence tactics are one of the processes people use to get others to do their bidding or produce the response desired by the influence actor, such as accepting advice or agreeing with a decision. Effective influence behavior includes a range of politically toned skills and knowledge. Social skill therefore depends on the cognitive element of reading and understanding social situations. At the same time, social skill includes the behavioral or action component of capitalizing on that insight to influence others.

The interpersonal-level influence tactics studied here are: (1) Be persuasive; (2) exchange benefits and favors; (3) ingratiate yourself with others; (4) be an alpha executive; (5) negotiate sensibly; (6) be low key; (7) be agreeable and apologize when necessary; and (8) apprise others of the usefulness of your demands.

The group and organizational-level influence tactics studied here are: (1) Form coalitions; (2) engage in co-optation with the other side; (3) display expertise; (4) use charisma; (5) display skill in a foreign language; (6) be a maverick or iconoclast; (7) appeal to superordinate goals; (8) be cool under pressure; and (9) place spin on negative events.

Research suggests that influence tactics vary in their effectiveness. One study indicated that the most effective influence tactics of managers were rational persuasion, inspirational appeal, and consultation. Effectiveness was defined in terms of task accomplishment and being perceived as effective. However, any tactic can trigger resistance if not appropriate to the situation and not applied skillfully. Another study showed that when we distrust people, we are likely to use strong influence tactics, such as sanctions.

In sequencing influence tactics, it is best to begin with the most positive or least abrasive tactic. If you do not gain the advantage you seek, proceed to a stronger tactic. The more position power an individual exerts over another, the less the need for caution in the use of influence tactics.

QUESTIONS AND ACTIVITIES

1. Identify several influence tactics described in this chapter which you think would be effective in influencing your behavior. Explain your reasoning.
2. Identify one or two influence tactics described in this chapter which you regard as unethical. Explain your reasoning.
3. Identify one or two influence tactics described in this chapter which you think that, when used by managers, would be helpful to a business organization.
4. Reach into your network to find an industrial sales representative or a retail sales associate. Ask that person which techniques he or she finds the most useful in influencing customers to make a purchase. Be prepared to bring your findings back to class.
5. Why are lobbyists often referred to as *influence peddlers?*
6. Why bother developing proficiency in a second language when you can purchase a handheld computer that will translate thousands of different phrases for you?

7. Visualize yourself as a CEO of a large company. Place a positive spin on the fact that you are going to lay off 15% of the workforce.

CASE STUDY: THE COAL MAN SPEAKS

Robert E. Murray is a 67-year-old, straight-talking coal mine owner. You won't hear many of Murray's energy biz colleagues mention him; they tend to avoid his name, much as nephews avoid talk of their crazy uncle. GE's Jeffrey Immelt, Duke Energy's Jim Rogers, Exelon's John Rowe—these political titans have been basking in an intense media glow ever since they claimed to have seen the light on global warming and backed a mandatory government program to cut CO_2 emissions.

And yet there's Robert Murray, killjoy-in-chief at the global warming love-fest. "Some elitists in our country can't or won't, tell fact from fiction, can't understand what a Draconian climate program will do to the dreams of millions of working Americans and those on fixed incomes," says on the chairman and CEO of Murray Energy, one of the largest private coal concerns in the United States.

He's incensed by his fellow energy CEOs' "shameless" goal of fattening their bottom lines at the "expense of the broader economy." So a couple of years ago, he emerged from his quiet Cleveland office and jumped on the national stage, calling out the rest on his industry's CO_2 collaborationists. He's testified in front of Congress, become a regular on television and radio programs, sat for profiles by journalists, and written letters to other energy companies exhorting them to think of the broader consequences.

It seems unlikely that his campaign will slow the runaway global-warming train now hurtling through Washington. But Murray is certainly making the ride less comfortable for some corporate players. "For me, global warming is a human issue, not just an environmental one," he says in his slow gravelly way, nursing a cup of coffee at a local shop in Washington, D.C. Murray was in town to give congressional testimony.

"The science of global warming is speculative. But there's nothing speculative about the damage a CO_2 capture program will do to this country. I know the names of many of the thousands of people—American workers and their families—whose lives will be destroyed by what has become a deceitful and hysterical campaign perpetuated by fear-mongers in our society and by corporate executives intent on their own profits or competitive advantage. I can't stand by and watch."

Unlike other energy executives—at industrial firms such as GE which make millions on wind turbines, or utilities such as Duke or Exelon who are making big financial bets on "clean energy"—coal CEOs such as Murray are the bad boys on the global-warming scene, and will see zero upside in a global-warming program. While the industry has made advances on one pollution front (sulfur dioxide/ nitrogen oxide), coal still accounts for the vast majority of all electricity-related CO_2 emissions.

The only way to really cut carbon emissions would be to severely limit the use of coal-fired power plants and manufacturing facilities, which is exactly what environmentalists have wanted for years. "We're one of the targets of this campaign," says Murray. "Putting in place a global warming program is about putting limits on the coal business and low-cost energy." The Ohio coal miner therefore has nothing to lose by speaking hard truths.

Murray hails from a long line of coal miners proud of their roots and industry. A no-nonsense guy, Murray became the family provider after his father was paralyzed in a coal-mining accident. By 16, he was mowing lawns every day after school, using a coal miner's cap with a light on the front so he could continue his work past dark. He'd set his sights on a medical career when he was unexpectedly offered a chance at a scholarship to become a mining engineer.

He then spent 31 years at North American Coal Corporation, where he rose to CEO then left in 1987 after a disagreement. Striking out on his own, he mortgaged his home to buy his first mine. Today, Murray Energy operates 11 coal mines in four states, producing 32 million tons of coal annually ($800 million in sales). He employs about 3,000 people, although he estimates that if you look at all the secondary jobs created to provide goods and services for miners, his company has created some 36,000 jobs.

Those jobs are top of Murray's list of concerns, and he's been determined to make people hear about them. After the 1990 Clean Air Act, "In Ohio alone, from 1990 to 2005, nearly 120 mines were shut down, costing more than 36,000 primary and secondary jobs. These impacted areas have spent years recovering, and some never will. Families broke up, many lost homes, and some were impoverished." He finishes the thought by noting that a global warming program would make those prior coal cuts look like small potatoes. Murray notes that 52% of this country's electricity is generated from coal, and there is nothing to replace it at the same cost.

He further notes, "Even if the politicians believe 100% that humans are causing global warming, they still have an obligation to discuss honestly just what damage they want to inflict on American jobs and workers and people on fixed incomes, in the here and now, with their programs."

Case Study Questions

1. How influential does Robert Murray appear to be to you?
2. Which influential tactics is Murray using?
3. How credible is Murray in terms of his vantage point for delivering his message?
4. If Murray is right about the job losses that would be associated with an anti–global warming program, what do you recommend the coal workers do?
5. How would you rate Murray's political skills?

SOURCE: Adapted from Strassel, K. (2007). The weekend interview with Robert E. Murray: Coal man. *Wall Street Journal,* May 19–20, A9.

POLITICAL SKILL-BUILDING EXERCISE 7

Applying Influence Tactics

Divide the class into small teams. Each group assigns one leadership influence tactic to each team member. During the next week or so, each team member takes the opportunity to practice the assigned influence tactic in a work or personal setting. Hold a group discussion with the same class teams after the influence attempts have been practiced. Report back the following information: (1) under what circumstances the influence tactic was attempted; (2) how the influence target reacted; and (3) what results, both positive and negative, were achieved.

Practicing influence tactics directly contributes to your political effectiveness because being influential is a subset of political skills. If you want to exert leadership as a nonmanager, you will have to be particularly adept at using influence tactics because your formal authority will be quite limited.

REFERENCES

1. Holmes, S. (2007, April 9). EADS' unlikely American ascent. *BusinessWeek,* 68.

2. Nelson, D. L., & Quick, J. C. (2000). *Organizational behavior: Foundations, realities, & challenges* (3rd ed.) [p. 352]. Mason, OH: Thomson/South-Western.

3. Levin, M. L. (2007, February 13). Enterprise sales executives require an array of skills. [Special advertising section]. *Wall Street Journal,* B8.

4. Rhoads, K. (n.d.). *How many tactics are there?* Retrieved 10/10/2007 from www.workingpsychology.com.

5. Kurchner-Hawkins, R. & Miller, R. (2006). Organizational politics: Building positive political strategies in turbulent times. In E. Vigoda-Gadot & A. Drory (Eds.), *Handbook of organizational politics* (pp. 328–352) [pp. 338–339]. Northampton, MA: Edward Elgar.

6. Ferris, G. R., Treadway, D. C., Kolodinsky, R. W., Hochwarter, W. A., Kacmar, C. J., & Douglas, C., et al. (2005). Development and validation of the political skill inventory. *Journal of Management, 31,* 126–153.

7. Witt, L. A., & Ferris, G. R. (2003, October). Social skill as a moderator of the conscientiousness–performance relationship: Convergent results across four studies. *Journal of Applied Psychology,* 811.

8. The pioneering studies here are Kipnis, D., Schmidt, S., & Wilkinson, I. (1980, December). Intraorganizational influence tactics: Explorations in getting one's way. *Journal of Applied Psychology,* 440–452; Schriesheim, C. A., & Hinkin, T. R. (1990, October). Influence tactics used by subordinates: A theoretical and empirical analysis and refinement of the Kipnis, Schmidt, and Wilkinson subscales. *Journal of Applied Psychology,* 246–257.

9. Lashinsky, A. (2005, June 13). Take a look at HPO. *Fortune,* 118.

10. Associated Press. (1995, December 14). *Paper finds many Pataki appointees are major donors.*

11. Both quotes are from Javers, E., & Woellert, L. (2006, March 20). It's hard out here for a lobbyist. *BusinessWeek,* 88.

12. Treadway, D. C., Ferris, G. R., Duke, A. B., Adams, G., & Thatcher, J. B. (2007, May). The moderating role of subordinate political skill on supervisors' impressions of subordinate ingratiation and ratings of interpersonal facilitation. *Journal of Applied Psychology,* 848–855.

13. Park, A. (2006, May). Taming the alpha executive. *Fast Company,* 88.

14. Greene, R. (1998). *The 48 laws of power.* New York: Viking.

15. Bianco, A. (2006, November 6). The taking of Lazard. *BusinessWeek,* 56.

16. *Fortune* magazine (2005, March 21). Dick Parsons, 56: Chairman and CEO of Time Warner. *Fortune,* 103.

17. Tischler, L. (2005, September). The CEO's new clothes. *Fast Company,* 27–28.

18. Goldsmith, M. (2004, October). It's not about the coach. *Fast Company,* 120.

19. Witt, L. A., Burke, L. A., Barrick, M. B., & Mount, M. K. (2002, February). The interactive effects of conscientiousness and agreeableness on job performance. *Journal of Applied Psychology,* 164–169.

20. Kiger, P. K. (2004, October). The art of the apology. *Workforce Management,* 57–62.

21. Yukl, G. (2002). *Leadership in organizations* (5th ed.) [p. 161]. Upper Saddle River, NJ: Prentice Hall; Yukl, G., Chavez, C., & Seifert, C. F. (2005). Assessing the construct validity of two new influence tactics. *Journal of Organizational Behavior, 6,* 705–725.

22. Tischler, L. (2004, November). IBM's management makeover. *Fast Company,* 13.

23. DeLuca, J. M. (1992). *Political savvy: Systematic approaches to leadership behind-the-scenes* [p. 90]. Horsham, PA: LRP Publications.

24. Gunn, J., & Chen, S. (2006). A micro-political perspective of strategic management. In E. Vigoda-Gadot & A. Drory (Eds.), *Handbook of organizational politics* (pp. 209–229) [p. 218]. Northampton, MA: Edward Elgar.

25. Stone, B. (2005, February 25). Software exploited by pirate goes to work for Hollywood. *New York Times.* Retrieved 02/25/2007 from www.nytimes.com.

26. Kirkpatrick, D. (2006, May 1). Microsoft's new brain. *Fortune,* 58.

27. Freedman, M. (2007, March 26). La dolce vita. *Forbes,* 122–123.

28. Research synthesized in Greer, M. (2005, January). The science of savoir faire. *Monitor on Psychology,* 28.

29. Brady, D. (2006, June 26). Charm offensive: Why American CEOs are suddenly so eager to be loved. *BusinessWeek,* 76–79.

30. Hoff, C. (2006, February 27). English-only not always best course in language programs. *Workforce Management,* 38, 40.

31. Wylie, I. (2004, December). Please dis-please me. *Fast Company,* 90–91.

32. Lev-Ram, M. (2007, May). Two centuries of contrarian thinkers. *Business 2.0,* 20.

33. Latham, G. (2003, November 3). Goal setting: A five-step approach to behavior change. *Organizational Dynamics,* 309.

34. Lev-Ram, M. (2007, May). The sun king. *Business 2.0,* 68.

35. Helft, M. (2007, June 12). *For Yahoo, an ordeal of dissent. New York Times.* Retrieved 06/12/2007 from www.nytimes.com.

36. Yukl, G., & Tracey, J. B. (1992, August). Consequences of influence tactics used with subordinates, peers, and the boss. *Journal of Applied Psychology,* 525–535.

37. Wells, C. V., & Kipnis, D. (2001, Summer). Trust, dependency, and control in the contemporary organization. *Journal of Business and Psychology,* 593–603.

EIGHT

SOCIAL NETWORKS WITHIN ORGANIZATIONS

LEARNING OBJECTIVES

After studying this chapter and doing the exercises, you should be able to do the following:

1. Present an overview of social network theory.
2. Explain the basics of social network analysis, including drawing a diagram.
3. Give several examples of internal and external networks in organizations.
4. Present information about the relationship between social networks, and group and organizational performance.
5. Explain how social networks assist career advancement.
6. Summarize suggestions for building and maintaining social networks.

In his 19-year career at BMW, Norbert T. Reithofer has worked his way up from maintenance planner to head of production, and finally to chief executive. A quintessential BMW man, Reithofer led the company's drive for greater factory flexibility and customization, helping to give the automaker its competitive edge.

Like every successful BMW manager, Reithofer has learned how to build informal networks of associates across the company to make sure his ideas are embraced. And he definitely has a gold-plated network. When Reithofer ran BMW's factory in Spartanburg, South Carolina, the U.S. chief was Helmut Panke, who was later promoted to CEO. And Reithofer's thesis advisor in graduate school was Joachim Milberg, Panke's predecessor as CEO and now chief of BMW's supervisory board.

But that's not the kind of network that really matters at BMW. While it never hurts to have friends in high places, 50-year-old Reithofer has excelled at forging alliances at all levels. About eight years ago, for instance, he and development chief Burkhard Goerschel wanted to halve the time it took to reach full production of the next-generation 3 Series, from six months to three. That would slash startup costs and boost margins by allowing the company to pump more cars onto the market while interest in the new model was still superhot.

Skeptics said it couldn't be done without compromising quality. But Reithofer and Goerschel reached deep into the organization to assemble a team of R&D production aces who worked three years to reach their target. The cars were introduced in March, and by June the factory was cranking out its full-scale production of 800 cars a day. "Managers have to be role models and work together," says Reithofer.[1]

Many people reading this book are probably BMW fans. However, you don't have to be one to admire how skillfully the BMW chief executive uses networking to gain support for his ideas and to assemble a team that can accomplish an outstanding production feat. Social networking in organizations preceded social networking on the Internet, such as with MySpace, FaceBook, and Friendster. Networking merits a chapter of its own because developing contacts with influential people is the most fundamental principle of organizational politics. Several years ago, Jack Welch gave a guest lecture at the Sloan School of Management at MIT. A student asked, "What should we be learning in business school?" Welch replied, "Just concentrate on networking. Everything else you need to know, you can learn on the job."[2] As with many other popular management gurus, Welch is prone to exaggeration and simplification, but he does remind us that networking is an essential skill.

A **social network** (as opposed to a computer network) is a specific set of linkages among a defined set of individuals.[3] Social networking in organizations is used for several interrelated purposes. The major purpose is to develop social capital in the form of smooth-working relationships with a variety of people. These smooth relationships can then be used to enlist the cooperation of others in accomplishing tasks (as in the BMW example). Also, people in your network become part of your coalition to support initiatives you think are important, such as a manager seeking support for starting a Six Sigma quality program.

In this chapter, we look at social networking from several perspectives. First we review the theory behind social networking, before examining social network analysis (who contacts whom to accomplish work). We then explain many types of social networks that exist within and across firms, followed by information about how networks improve performance and advance careers. Then comes advice about a cornerstone topic of political behavior in organizations: how to establish and maintain an effective social network.

SOCIAL NETWORK THEORY

Networking has come to mean almost any approach to developing contacts with people, yet theory helps explain many aspects of the process. **Social network theory** regards social relationships in terms of nodes and ties. **Nodes** are the individuals (or actors) in the network, while **ties** are the relationships between and among the actors.[4] Many types of ties exist between the nodes, such as one pair of nodes being a mentor and the person mentored, or two people in different parts of the organization exchanging technical information. The most basic social network is a map of all the relevant ties among the nodes under surveillance. As will be shown later in the chapter, a social network diagram is often used to illustrate the nodes and ties, with the nodes being circles and the ties being lines. Here, we describe several aspects of social network theory most useful to an understanding or political behavior in organizations.

Social Capital and the Importance of Ties

Social network theory helps evaluate the social capital of individuals by understanding the links one person has with others. An actor with strong social capital has an advantageous network position and can draw on the resources of many people. He or she is *well connected.* The more mappings or links a person has in the social network, and the more mappings these people have, the more knowledge, influence, and power the actor has. If you are connected to many influential people, you will have more social capital and political clout. In summary, the better connected you are, the greater your social capital.

Social network theory emphasizes the ties among people rather than the individual attributes of the actors within the network. For example, instead of attempting to understand the intelligence and motivation of Brenda in the network, it focuses on the type of relationship she has with Gus and Sylvie in other parts of the organization. Much of Brenda's success and failure in her company will then be attributed to her connections rather than her intelligence and motivation. Social networks can also go outside the organization, such as the many ties professionals and managers might have with members of other organizations. In an era of strategic alliances, interorganizational ties are quite important, such as a product developer at the Jaguar division of Tata getting advice about door knobs from the Land Rover division of the same company.

Strength of Ties Among Network Members

Another key part of social network theory is the *strength-of-ties perspective.*[5] For any particular actor, the most relevant part of the network has to do with the strength of the ties. A key proposition of the theory is that there are different densities in different parts of the network. A high-density network consists of close friends linked together. In contrast, a low-density network consists of acquaintances linked together. The relationships among the different actors in a network can broadly be classified into two major types: strong versus weak ties and direct versus indirect ties. An acquaintance would be a weak tie, whereas a close friend would be a strong tie. Strength of ties would ordinarily be measured by frequency of contact, yet some contacts could be relatively superficial and others might be more emotional and intimate. Brenda might ask Gus for status reports on his predictions about currency fluctuations, whereas she talks to Sylvie about her career and her relationship with her boss.

Some disagreement exists about the importance of strong ties in a network. One line of argument is that weak ties among actors are quite important. According to this reasoning, weak ties improve an organization's performance because more diverse information emerges from a larger environment, such as obtaining input on a project you are working on from a wide variety of people with whom you have a limited association. The people with whom a person has weak ties are less likely to be connected to each other. In sociological jargon, the person is embedded in a *structural hole.* The strength or value of these weak ties is that they are less likely to be redundant, and more likely to be unique. As a result, they are information rich. If you lack weak ties, you might suffer from only receiving information from a close group of friends. Strategic thinkers tend to widen their network so they can capitalize on ideas from many sources.

The opposite argument is that small networks characterized by strong ties are more functional to the organization because they provide the loyalty and coordination that enhance organizational performance. In the case at hand, it would be better to obtain more thoughtful input from a few people you knew well than collecting less well-thought-through input from casual contacts.

SOCIAL NETWORK ANALYSIS

The most widespread application of social network theory is to conduct a **social network analysis**, the mapping and measuring of relationships and links between and among people, groups, and organizations.[6] The nodes in the network are the people, and the links show relationships or flow between and among the nodes as shown in Exhibit 8.1. Notice that Ram is an important node in the network because he is linked with Ginny, Anna, and Kent. Social network analysis helps explain how work gets accomplished in a given unit, such as shown in the interactions among Laura, Todd, and Misty on the right side of Exhibit 8.1. Perhaps the three of them mutually discuss credit risks. The interrelations can become quite complicated because of the large number of people and the many interactions between and among them.

An example of how a business firm might use social network analysis took place at MWH Global, an engineering and environmental consulting firm in Cheshire, England. To help with a reorganization in the IT division, the company analyzed the interactions among workers. Employees were asked which colleagues they consulted most frequently, who they relied on for expertise, and who either boosted or drained their energy. The answers were then analyzed in a social network analysis software program, and then laid out as a web of interconnecting nodes and lines. Ken Loughridge, the executive in charge of the new IT division, used the map to identify how work really got accomplished among the workers. The map also helped him to visualize the informal connections that do not appear on a traditional organization chart.

The new IT head used the map to identify well-connected technical experts with whom he should meet first. Six months later, when a key manager left the company, the executive referred back to the social network map in

Exhibit 8.1 A Basic Unit of a Social Network Analysis

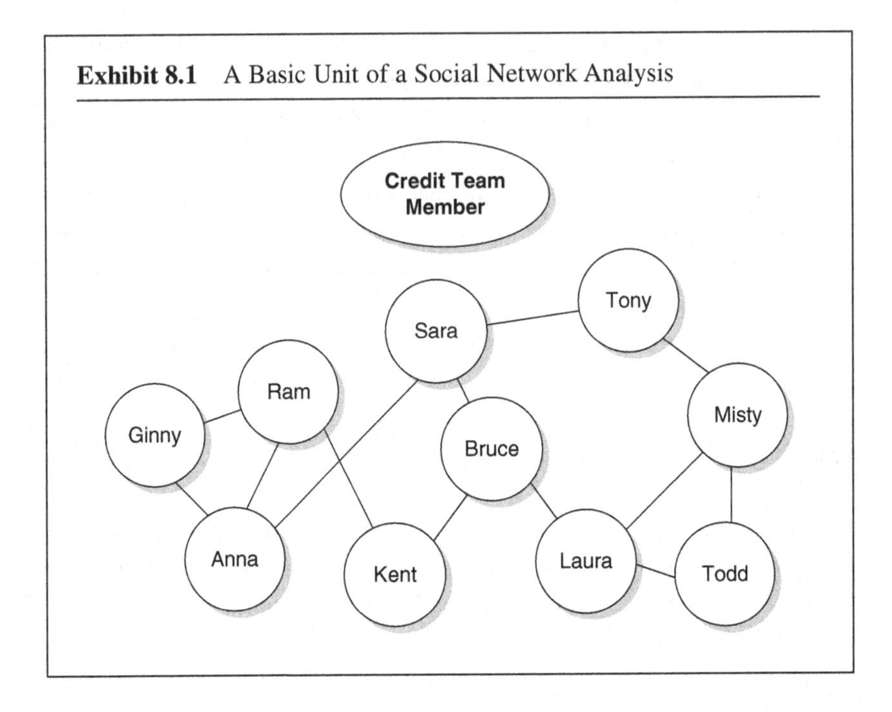

order to reach out to the departed manager's closest contacts, and thus minimize disruption. Loughridge said of the analysis, "It's as if you took the top off of an anthill and could see where there is a hive of activity. It really helped me understand who the players were."[7]

Social network analysis helps management survey the informal interactions among employees that can lead to innovative ideas. At the same time, the maps can point to areas where workers should be collaborating but are not. In this way, the maps help facilitate knowledge sharing. The maps can also be used to pinpoint the interactions one manager has so he or she can give the information to a successor.

Another insight gleaned from social network analysis is that the lines indicate who trusts whom because they exchange ideas and go to each other for advice. Knowing who the *hubs, gatekeepers,* and *pulse keepers* are helps identify valuable employees and unearth innovative ideas. According to corporate anthropologist Karen Stephenson, knowing who trusts whom is as important as knowing who reports to whom. Finding out who trusts whom is part of the social network analysis, and is revealed by asking employees questions such as the following:[8]

- Who do you go to for a quick decision?
- Who do you hang out with socially?
- Who do you turn to for advice?
- Who do you go to with a good idea?
- Who do you go to for career advice?

A subtle political point about social network analysis maps is that more connections aren't necessarily the best for the organization. If one person is too connected, he or she could be a bottleneck. Also, it is okay for some workers who spend a lot of time with customers or have expertise in highly specialized areas to show up on the outside of the web of interactions.

INTERNAL AND EXTERNAL NETWORKS IN ORGANIZATIONS

As you probably have already inferred from social network theory, organizational members develop networks both within and outside their own organization. For example, a purchasing agent might have an important contact at a comparable company with whom he or she exchanges useful ideas about efficient purchasing. A powerful political player is usually connected both internally and externally. In this section, we describe internal and external networks, as well as information that bridges the two types of networks.

Internal Networks

A highly political purpose of an internal network is to gather intelligence information that might affect your welfare or that of your unit. By exchanging gossip with your intelligence agents, you might learn of an important development such as a pending merger that could result in consolidation of your unit with a comparable unit in the joint organization. With this knowledge in hand, you might begin preparing an analysis of what your unit has accomplished to present to high-level management. A positive use of an internal network would be to learn what type of technology the company might be adopting in the future so you might have time to prepare early for adapting to the new technology. If your company were going to drastically reduce in-person meetings with videoconferencing, it would be helpful for you to learn in advance how to present yourself comfortably in front of a camcorder.

In recognition of the importance of internal networks for accomplishing goals, some large firms establish formal networking groups. An example is the corporate women's networks, the aim of which is to recruit and retain top achievers. One of these groups is the GE Women's Network, which has 40,000 active members worldwide. The focus of the GE Network on leadership, advancement, and career-broadening opportunities has helped the company get to the point where women run businesses generating 20% of total company revenues. Women outside GE are invited to some of the key networking events, which helps the GE women strengthen their external as well as internal networks. Also, the company outsiders are key customers who might develop ties with the GE women that lead to a better working relationship and more sales.[9]

External Networks

One of the major reasons that an external network is important is that high-level business is facilitated by contacts, providing the business firm associated with the contact is capable of performing the work. An example of how personal contacts facilitate business took place after Hurricane Katrina in 2005. Several of the contracts for debris removal and reconstruction were hastily given to politically connected firms and were extended without warning months later. Criticisms of awarding these contracts on the basis of network membership were that they promoted waste and unfairly hurt small businesses.[10]

Powerful people develop powerful external networks, often because their power and influence enable them to attract influential people as nodes. A penultimate example of power contacts is the Carlyle Group, a private equity firm. Members of the group all have high-level contacts in business and government. Among the past power players have been former President George H. W. Bush, former Secretary of State James A. Baker III, President George W. Bush, and former British Prime Minister John Major. Recent power players have included former IBM chairman and CEO Louis V. Gerstner Jr., former SEC chairman Arthur Levitt, former General Electric vice-chairman David L. Calhoun, and former Time Inc. editor-in-chief Norman Pearlstine.

Carlyle has used its partners' collective relationships to build a highly profitable business buying, transforming, and selling companies, with a specialty in defense companies. Carlyle owns 200 companies that employ a total of 200,000 people. It has been predicted that Carlyle will have $300 billion under management by 2012. Observe that having powerful nodes in your network makes you influential.

In addition to the well-connected nodes, Carlyle also hires associates who are help operate the company, and are expected to help build the future. The new hires must have good political skills. In the words of the manager in charge of recruiting, "We don't want isolationists. We also don't want cry-babies. And we don't want mercenaries—people who are here to put a notch on their own gun. We want people to help us build a cannon."[11]

Internet-Mediated Social Networking for Business

Networking via the Internet supplements, and sometimes replaces, the more traditional approaches to business networking such as the Rolodex and the power lunch. The major network of this type is Linkedin, a Web site that takes a personal business network online. Linkedin is a community of more than 8 million people who rely on one another to accomplish work. The membership includes leading venture capitalists and entrepreneurs plus tens of thousands of employees from Google, Microsoft, and other technology firms that use Linkedin for employee recruiting. The service is also used extensively for deal making—such as one company purchasing another—and for raising capital. Linkedin members are free to invite other members, who then have to accept the invitation, to become part of the network. The service shows a maximum of 500 connections on a profile page.[12]

Another approach to networking via the Internet is Jigsaw.com, an online market that enables people to trade their contacts for more contacts (nodes) or cash. Every time you enter a nonmember's information on its sight, you receive 10 points, enough to purchase two contacts from Jigsaw's database. People who enter at least 25 contacts become members without charge. Without contributing new members, a person pays $25 per month to access 25 contacts. Note that people can be entered without their approval. Jigsaw makes it easy to search for contacts based on name, company, geographic location, job category, and business size. Jigsaw, in essence, is a way of buying contacts or "friends" for $1.00.[13]

Another method of social networking within organizations is to encourage workers to communicate with each other on popular social networking sites such as Facebook and MySpace. The Web sites enable the workers to form contacts in a relaxed, natural manner. The social networking site becomes a virtual water cooler, leading to relationship building. Serena Software Inc. was a pioneer in using Facebook to enhance in-company social networking. CEO Jeremy Burton said in a press release, "Social networking tools like Facebook can bring us back together, help us to get to know each other as people, help us understand our business and our products, and help us better serve our customers."[14]

To make contacts from a social networking site more focused, some companies develop an in-company social networking site. One application is to collect individual contact data including past employment histories. You can type in a name such as Dell Computer, and then find that a colleague in another division worked there in the printing department. With the contact's permission, you can then get in touch with a worker at your target company (in this case, Dell).[15] From a political standpoint, your expectation is that the Dell worker would become a useful member of your social network.

Online business networking has an extraordinary reach, with some members claiming around 28,000 contacts. The reach is also a limitation, with most of these links being quite thin rather than dense. Many of the relationships are superficial and therefore not particularly useful when you need help from a friend. Another concern about social networking sites is that they generate hundreds of unwanted e-mail messages from people wanting you to be part of their network.

How Leaders Use Internal and External Networks

A way of integrating knowledge about internal and external social networks is to understand how leaders create and use these networks. Based on their interviews with 30 leaders, Professors Herminia Ibarra and Mark Hunter discovered three distinct forms of networking: operational, personal, and strategic.[16]

- *Operational networking* is geared toward accomplishing one's assigned tasks more effectively. To execute operational networking, one must cultivate strong relationships with colleagues whose membership in the network is unambiguous because they are stakeholders. The people (or nodes) in the operational network are the people the manager depends on to accomplish immediate tasks, and most of the contracts are internal.
- *Personal networking* is an external type of networking which engages people of similar interests outside the organization in a leader's efforts to grow professionally and find opportunities for personal advancement. Professional associations and alumni groups are often included

in personal networking, as might be a mentor. Other people in the network might help the manager reach the person he or she needs, such as finding an executive coach who might be a good fit. Maintaining contact with an executive recruiter might help the leader/manager to gain insight into what types of skills are in demand in the industry. The leader might also learn of a position for which he or she is qualified that would represent a promotion, more compensation, or both.

- *Strategic networking* is aimed directly at attaining business goals. At this high level of networking, the manager creates the type of network that will uncover and capitalize on new opportunities for the company, such as a tractor and lawnmower company contemplating diversifying into the production of windmills. Both internal and external network members might help the leader deal with strategic issues. The ability to network at the level of attaining business goals is characteristic of a strong and strategically minded leader.

The effective manager or leader uses all three forms of networking, and the three types are often interdependent. An example would be someone in the personal network—such as a mentor—asking questions that triggered strategic thinking. For example, the mentor might challenge the manager to think through what type of services his or her unit should be providing to the organization. One mentor asked a manager why her unit, a human resources group, was not providing retirement counseling, considering all the baby boomers on the payroll who would soon be eligible for retirement.

SOCIAL NETWORKS AND GROUP AND ORGANIZATIONAL PERFORMANCE

It is widely assumed that when an organization has many members with good connections, both organizational units and the total organization will perform better. Why else would the Carlyle Group pay huge compensation to former high-level politicians, government officials, and business executives? Here we look at three research studies supporting the proposition that social networks enhance group and organizational performance. We assume that if social networking is improving group and organizational performance, individual worker performance is also enhanced because individual workers are the building blocks of work groups and organizations.

Group Performance and Social Networking

Prasad Balkundi and David A. Harrison conducted a meta-analysis of 37 studies of teams in natural contexts such as factories and laboratories. A total of 3,098 teams were represented in the study. All of the studies included in the meta-analysis had used social network analysis or similar methodology to map the networks, and had objective measures of team performance.[17]

A major finding is that teams with dense interpersonal ties attain their goals better and are more committed to staying together; both team task performance and viability are higher. It was also found that teams with leaders who are central within the team's intragroup (internal) network tend to perform better. It is also of note that when the team is a central part of its intergroup network, the team performs better. The point here is that the entire team can be a node in a group social network. The ties among people in the study were classified as either advice/instrumental or friendship/affective. An advice/instrumental tie is more task-oriented, such as asking a node how to convert British pounds into U.S. dollars, and vice versa. A friendship/affective tie is more relationship oriented, such as asking a node to listen to your complaints about a coworker or the team leader.

Looking at the study in question in more detail, seven hypotheses were supported as listed next. We choose to include the hypotheses most directly related to the relationship between social networks and team performance.

1. Density of ties in a team's instrumental social network is positively associated with team task performance. (The team gets the job done better with close friends in the group who help each other with tasks.)

2. Density of ties in a team's expressive social network is positively associated with team task performance. (The team gets the job done better when the members have friendly interactions.)

3. Density of ties in a team's instrumental social network is positively associated with team viability. (When teammates have close ties with others and assist each other with tasks, low turnover results.)

4. Density of ties in a team's expressive social network is positively associated with team viability. (When teammates have close ties with people with whom they have friendly interactions, better team performance results.)

5. Relationships between network density and team outcomes reflect a match of tie content in that expressive network density is more strongly related

than instrumental network density to team viability. (Having emotional attachments among teammates is more important for low turnover than ties related to task performance.)

6. Centrality of a team's formal leader in a team's informal network is positively associated with team task performance. (A well-connected leader helps the team perform well.)

7. Team centrality in an intergroup network is positively associated with team task performance. (A well-connected team is in a better position to accomplish work.)

A study conducted with small businesses in Korea included an examination of how group social capital is related to group effectiveness. A group with high social capital has the right types of social connections that make it possible to effectively employ other types of capital they possess, such as financial resources and skills. Group effectiveness was measured by upper management's evaluation of a team in relation to such factors as quantity and quality of work, and ability to complete work on time. A general finding was that greater group social capital contributes to group effectiveness because these groups (a) have better access to important resources necessary to improve their performance and (b) quickly respond to challenges that arise.

The type of informal socializing ties within a group also has an impact on group effectiveness. The optimal configuration of ties is a moderate degree of internal closure, with *closure* being defined as all members being connected to one another. The study also found that the optimal configuration of these informal socializing ties across groups is a large number of bridging relationships to other groups' leaders. A *bridging relationship* is defined as ties among heterogeneous people.[18]

Organizational Performance and Social Networking

Social networks grow in importance if they can elevate the performance of an entire business firm. Christopher J. Collins and Kevin D. Clark conducted a study in 73 high-technology firms to investigate the possibility that specific network building practices by top management teams enhanced firm performance. The network building human resource practices measured in the study included training, performance assessment, and rewards designed to encourage executives to build relationships with external and internal actors.

An example of a network-building HR practice was giving top-management team members expense accounts for developing job-related personal contacts.

External and internal social contacts were measured by respondents evaluating the size, range, and strength of ties for their contacts in nine external and internal categories of actors. Among the contacts were suppliers, customers, and financial institutions; internal contacts included sales and marketing, research and development, and operations. Firm performance was measured in terms of sales growth and stock performance.

A major finding of the study was that top-level managers' networks mediated or influenced the relationship between human resources practices and firm performance. Human resources practices lead to higher performance by developing and reinforcing employee-based resources that are valuable in a competitive environment. In short, the HR practices help build the internal and external networks of the executives, and the networks help improve firm performance. An example of a specific finding was that a one standard deviation increase in specific network-building practices yielded an 18.7% growth in sales and a 2.55% stock return.[19]

SOCIAL NETWORKS AND CAREER ADVANCEMENT

Virtually all career guides emphasize the importance of social networking in both finding a job and advancing one's career. Contacts help you get into a firm, and then enable you to advance. Although the association between contacts and career advancement is as certain as the link between exercise and weight loss, a few examples of this relationship may prove helpful.

- George O'Leary was the Notre Dame head football coach for five days in December 2001, before being fired because it was discovered that he fibbed on his job résumé about lettering in football at the University of New Hampshire and earning a master's degree from New York University. However, in 2002 Mike Tice, the head coach of the Minnesota Vikings, hired O'Leary as the defensive line and assistant head coach of the Vikings. Tice was a former student of O'Leary's, and also a close personal friend. A few years later, O'Leary continued his career rehabilitation and became the head coach of the University of Central Florida football team.

- An effective route to becoming a board member is to have personal contact with executive recruiters. The executive recruiting firm Korn/Ferry estimates that about one half of all new board appointments come through headhunters. The recruiter acts as a matchmaker.[20] Building relationships with recruiters will also give a person access to other managerial positions because most companies do not advertise the positions recruiters are hired to help fill.[21]
- An interview study of 15 high-level executives revealed that, for managers in the modern workplace, career advancement is closely associated with having a network of multiple mentors. These mentors have the potential to help protégés continually acquire knowledge which they can leverage for career and personal success within and across organizational boundaries.[22] Mentors represent powerful nodes in a person's network.

SUGGESTIONS FOR BUILDING AND MAINTAINING SOCIAL NETWORKS

A key part of systematic knowledge about social networks is to follow suggestions for building and maintaining them. Effective networking involves far more than making "friends" on Web site networks or handing out business cards to any person who comes within 3 feet of you. The suggestions that follow are divided into those based on scholarly research about social networking, and those based mostly on experience and intuition. Exhibit 8.2 gives you the opportunity to think through your level of networking activity and skill.

Networking Suggestions Based on Scholarly Research

A modest amount of research has been conducted about how to network more effectively for career advancement. A starting point is recent research by N. Anand and Jay A. Conger, based on observations of effective networkers. Four capabilities were found to be characteristic of effective networking behavior: (1) seeking out the most influential individual in any given situation, (2) matchmaking people who are compatible or have complementary needs to get things done, (3) taking the initiative to enlarge the number of people one is connected to, and (4) interacting in a friendly manner with others to build positive relationships.

Exhibit 8.2 My Networking Activity and Skill

Directions: Indicate whether each of the following statements is "Mostly true" or "Mostly false."

Statement	*Mostly True*	*Mostly False*
1. I have loads of up-to-date business cards ready to hand out to contacts.		
2. I have an electronic business card capability built into a hand-held electronic device.		
3. I maintain a database of all influential people I meet.		
4. I regularly update my database of all influential people I meet.		
5. I initiate conversations with people in public places such as airports, just to see if they might fit into my network.		
6. I regularly attend business networking events in my community.		
7. I have given my business card out to hundreds of people.		
8. For me, it would be okay to hand out my business card to potential network members at a wedding, engagement shower, or similar gathering of family and friends.		
9. I belong to an Internet social networking site like MySpace or Friendster, and use it to make contacts for business or my career.		
10. At school I attempt (or did attempt) to make personal contact with professors who might be able to help me in my career.		
11. I already have my own Web site, and I let other people know about it.		
12. When somebody I know receives a significant promotion, I will contact that person by e-mail or phone to offer my congratulations.		
13. When I attend a formal networking event, I am quite active in introducing myself to many people.		
14. I attend a professional meeting, trade meeting, or student professional group in my field at least twice a year.		

Statement	Mostly True	Mostly False
15. When I ask anybody in my network or potential network for a favor, I explain how I will reciprocate.		
16. I regularly send e-mails or postcards to most of the people in my network.		
17. The people in my network are diverse in terms of age, sex, race, ethnic background, and field of specialty.		
18. Loads of people know who I am.		
19. I have asked people in my network to suggest the names of other people who might fit into my network.		
20. I am prepared to give a one-minute presentation about myself and my accomplishments.		
21. For most challenges and problems I face, I know people I can count on to help me.		
22. At least once, I have contacted a well-known person such as a famous business executive to make him or her aware of my presence.		
23. I almost always thank people for any favor related to work or school.		
24. My name can be found for a neutral or positive reason on at least one of the major Internet search engines.		
25. I have made a systematic effort to contact my relatives throughout the country to let them know who I am and the type of work I do.		

Total: "Mostly True" ____ "Mostly False" ____

Scoring and Interpretation: Count your number of "Mostly true" responses.

20–25 You are quite active in networking, and this activity should boost your career and help you solve problems.

8–19 It appears that you do enough networking to help you solve problems and advance your career, but some more positive networking would benefit you.

1–7 Unless you have some rare talents that are in high demand, you need to network more to help you in your career.

The matchmaking capability generally assumes that the person is a manager with enough power to bring people together, such as building relationships between departments. A typical comment of a matchmaker is, "I think you should meet . . ." The connections between people are designed to help the organization, such as matching up one worker with a new product idea with an executive who has some seed money to invest.

The study found that just about 2% of executives excel at all four capabilities. A challenge in developing these capabilities is that they are dependent in part on personality, such as a person who scores high on the trait of agreeableness finding it easier to interact with others in a friendly manner. Yet people who are less agreeable can put extra effort into being amiable. Overall, Anand and Conger recommend that you focus on one of the capabilities and learn from someone who might be "best-in-class" in that capability.[23] For example, you might observe how a particularly gregarious manager or professional meets and greets contacts.

A study by Tiziana Casciaro and Miguel Sousa Lobo of 10,000 work relationships in five organizations found that nodes in a social network tend to be chosen not by ability but on the basis of likability. The authors classified people in the network into four types: The *competent jerk* has a lot of knowledge but is unpleasant; the *lovable fool* doesn't have much knowledge but is delightful to work with; the *lovable star* is both knowledgeable and likable; and the *incompetent jerk* has limited knowledge and is unlikable. The lovable fool is usually chosen over the competent jerk as a node. The implication for effective networking is not to be so readily taken in by the lovable fool. Because a person is fun to work with, it doesn't mean that he or she will be a valuable node in your network. At the same time, find a way to build a bridge to the *competent jerk* because that person might have some wonderful knowledge and skills to share. Use a technique like ingratiation to establish rapport with him or her.[24]

Based on case studies and some published research, Brian Uzzi and Shannon Dunlap conclude that strong personal networks do not just happen around a water cooler or at reunions with old classmates. Much of their advice relates to having your ideas disseminated personally to people you do not know by using the people you gather into your network. An idea to plant in the network might include a new product or service that could benefit from outside funding. Many personal networks are highly clustered in the sense that network members share the same friends. A stronger network occurs when you develop ties with people who have a different set of contacts from yours.

Networks have to be constructed through relatively high-stakes activities that bring you into contact with diverse people. Diversity in terms of culture, industry, and functional specialty is particularly helpful. The shared activities Uzzi and Dunlap recommend include sports teams, community service activities, voluntary associations, board membership, cross-functional teams, and charitable groups. The diverse people in your network might then inform others in their networks about your ideas.[25]

Networking Suggestions Based on Experience and Intuition

The focus on social networking for purposes of career advancement is to develop and maintain contacts with influential people who might be in a position to help you with respect to your career. Also, regard networking as a long-term strategy in which you gradually build contacts that will serve you now and in the long run. The popular literature about career networking is vast, yet much of it overlaps around a few similar themes. Following are 10 representative suggestions for effective career networking.

1. *Create a visible identity.* The ideal base for effective career networking is to find some way to stand out from the crowd, based on reputation, talent, appearance, or personality. Yet even without one or more of these attributes, being able to start a conversation at a networking event will give you a small edge. Making a comment about the weather or a recent major sporting event is overdone, so you might be more creative with a question of this nature: "What is your link to this event?" or "What is your specialty within corporate finance?" In general, asking the other person about him or herself is a good starting point in getting the conversation rolling.

2. *Listen actively to your target.* Another way of distinguishing yourself at a networking event or other opportunity is to listen actively to the other person. In review, active listening involves an intense focus on the other person, including observing body language and what is *not* said. The target will appreciate being listened to, and will probably give you your turn to say something about yourself. An effective question to keep your target talking is, "What is the most exciting part of your work?"[26]

3. *Be prepared to hand out your business card.* The humble business card remains a standard networking tool. The card should have an impressive,

uncluttered appearance, and preferably be engraved rather than using flat printing. A person who is not employed at the time can still have an impressive card that mentions his or her specialty and city, such as "Jennifer Green, production scheduler, Jacksonville, Florida." Electronic business cards in which you download a copy of your card to the personal digital assistant of your target should also appear professional and uncluttered. Microsoft Office Online offers a selection of impressive electronic business cards.

4. *Develop a polished 30-second presentation about yourself.* Another standard networking tool is to rehearse a brief (less than one minute) presentation describing who you are. This presentation is sometimes referred to as an *elevator speech* because it is used for brief meetings with people, such as in an elevator in an office tower. The brief presentation is a useful way to get started presenting yourself at networking events, at job fairs, and when meeting potential network members at social events. Here is a 30-second presentation for the woman mentioned above: "Hi, I'm Jennifer Green, a production scheduler. I majored in business administration at the University of Florida, and also studied manufacturing engineering. I am looking to make an impact in a domestic manufacturing setting to help the plant compete more successfully on an international scale. I am pleased to meet you." The presentation is particularly valuable when attempting to network with people of high status, who tend to guard their time carefully.

5. *Be sensitive to the fact that some networking targets are overloaded with requests.* Too many networking agents are chasing the same networking targets. People of the stature of Donald Trump, Bill Gates, or Martha Stewart receive thousands of unsolicited requests each month from people who would like to team up with them on a breakthrough money-making idea. When attempting to invite a busy person to become part of your network, it is best to ask for a specific, small favor such as that person mentioning you to a particular hiring manager. Kenneth Norton, the director of product management at Yahoo!, has developed the term *snam,* for unwanted e-mail generated by Web sites like Friendster and Linkedin. (*Snam* = social networking spam.)[27] One way of overcoming resentment to yet another network request is to state, "I recognize that you are probably overloaded with personal requests, but what I need will only take about two minutes of your time. And I am willing to reciprocate in any way feasible." Inviting a busy, influential person to have breakfast, lunch, or dinner with you is usually asking for too much time.

6. *Explain how you will reciprocate any favors.* Most networking involves asking the target for some favor, such as a job lead, source of funding for a business, mentoring, or technical assistance. A fundamental principle of effective networking is to explain how you will reciprocate in such ways as referring business in the other person's direction, preparing some computer graphics for your target, or getting his or her vehicle serviced. A major mistake in networking is to regard it as a method of obtaining favors from people rather than an exchange of benefits. The buzzword is that you have to add value. A subtle way of networking is to assist people in advance of when you might need help from them. You might be able to receive a favor in return should you need one.

7. *Capitalize on networking opportunities.* The successful networker searches for natural opportunities to interact with people inside and outside the organization. Among these diverse activities would be company social events, happy hour, local networking groups, national trade groups and professional organizations, and management or professional development programs. It is also helpful to attend company meetings where executives might be present. Examples of networking groups include Breakfast Club of America, the Northern Virginia Technology Council, and Women of Power Summit.

8. *Justify your networking request.* When approaching someone to be part of your network, explain how you received his or her name or refresh the person's mind as to how you met previously. Potential nodes are forced to say too often: "Who is this person? He (or she) is nobody I ever heard of."

9. *Notify network members of a change in status.* When you have a change of status, such as accepting a new position, let this be an opportunity to notify network members. Let all network members know should you change your e-mail address or telephone number. Notifying others of a change of status may help them remember you.

10. *Play golf reasonably well.* This same networking suggestion could have been made 100 years ago, and will probably be valid for the indefinite future. Many valuable career contacts and business deals are made on the golf course and in the clubhouse. Real estate professional Kristen Schwark neatly sums up the networking advantages of golf: "One thing I've found is that if a man finds out you play golf, they [he] think that's really neat. So if in conversation, a prospective client says they [he] play golf a little bit, I might just

suggest we go play a round. Golf can be an excellent common ground."[28] Whether playing on public links or a private golf course, your skill in golf must be high enough not to appear to be playing golf exclusively for making contacts.

At a handful of elite golf courses whose membership consists mostly of powerful business executives, the club culture frowns upon talking directly about business. Short pants on the course are also forbidden, even in the most sweltering heat. One of these clubs is the Pebble Beach Golf Links in California.[29] Nevertheless, playing golf together is a relationship builder that facilitates business talk back at the office. Chris Sullivan, the Outback Steakhouse founder and golf course developer, long ago recognized the networking value in golf, and has frequently capitalized on it during his career. He has played with several people who later became Outback franchisees and suppliers.[30]

SUMMARY

Developing contacts with influential people is one of the most fundamental principles of organizational politics. A social network is a specific set of linkages among a defined set of individuals. Social network theory regards social relationships in terms of nodes (people) and ties (relationships between and among people).

An actor with strong social capital can draw on the resources of many people because he or she is well connected. If you are connected to many influential people, you will have more social capital and political clout. Social network theory emphasizes ties among people rather than the attributes of the actors within the network.

The strength of ties perspective explains that there are different densities (closeness of friendships) in different parts of the network. The relationships among actors in the network can be strong or weak. One argument is that weak ties improve an organization's performance because more diverse information emerges from a larger environment. Also, the people with whom a person has weak ties are more likely to be connected to each other. The ties are less likely to be redundant. The counterargument is that strong ties are functional to the organization because they provide the loyalty and coordination that enhance organizational performance.

Social network analysis allows for the mapping and measuring of relationships between and among people and organizations. Social network analysis helps management survey the informal interaction among employees that can lead to innovative ideas. The same type of analysis indicates who trusts whom because they exchange ideas and go to each other for advice. Social network analysis is based on answers to such questions as, "Whom do you go to for a quick decision?" and "To whom do you turn for advice?"

Internal networks are useful for gathering intelligence. In recognition of the importance of internal networks for goal accomplishment, some firms establish formal networking groups, such as the GE Women's Network. One of the major reasons why an external network is important is that high-level business is facilitated by contacts. Powerful people develop powerful external networks, partly because they are influential.

Networking via the Internet supplements, and sometimes replaces, the more traditional approaches to business networking. Linkedin takes a personal business network online. To make contacts from a social networking site more focused, some companies develop an in-company social networking site.

One study showed that leaders use three distinct forms of networking: operational, personal, and strategic. The effective leader uses all three forms, and the three types are often interdependent—such as a personal contact triggering strategic thinking.

Research evidence suggests that social networks enhance group and organizational performance. One study showed that teams with dense interpersonal ties attain their goals better, and are more committed to staying together. Also, team leaders who are central within the team's internal network tend to perform better. A study in Korea showed that greater group social capital contributes to group effectiveness because of better access to resources, and quicker responses to challenges. A study in high-tech firms found that top-level managers' networks influenced the relationship between human resources practices and firm performance. The HR practices helped build the networks, and the networks helped improve performance.

Social networking is useful for job finding and career advancement. Several networking suggestions have been based on research. Two suggestions stemming from one study are: (1) Take the initiative to enlarge the number of your contacts; and (2) interact in a friendly manner to build positive relationships. A second study showed that too much networking takes place on the basis of likability rather than knowledge. A third study recommended developing a strong network by building contacts with people with different contacts than your own. Your ideas will then receive wider dissemination. High-level shared activities are useful in building the contacts.

Networking suggestions based most on experience and intuition presented here are: (1) Create a visible identity; (2) listen actively to your target; (3) hand out business cards; (4) develop a 30-second presentation to describe yourself; (5) recognize that some network targets are overloaded with requests; (6) explain how you will reciprocate; (7) capitalize on networking opportunities; (8) justify your networking request; (9) notify nodes of your change in status; and (10) play golf reasonably well.

QUESTIONS AND ACTIVITIES

1. What can you do today to help strengthen your social network?
2. In what way does social network analysis reveal more information than one might find in an annual report?
3. Suppose a node in a social network does not have enough lines pointing to him or her. What can political tactics can that person implement to attract more lines (relationships)?
4. If you were a business owner, would you invest in a social network analysis of your company? Why or why not?
5. How credible to you was the research reported in this chapter that top-level management membership in internal and external networks was associated with the financial performance of the firm?
6. How do you think joining a social networking Web site such as Linkedin would help you advance your career?
7. Ask a couple of the most successful people you know what they do to network. Be prepared to share your answers with classmates.

CASE STUDY: NETWORKING ASHLEY

Ashley Gomez worked for several years as an accounts payable supervisor at a hospital. She enjoyed the work, the group she supervised, and the hospital setting. Yet Ashley craved a more adventurous career, work with more flexible hours, and the opportunity to earn a higher income.

In her words, "Brad, my husband, and I both work, but we are struggling to break even. We need to build up an investment portfolio so we can send our children to college. Shauna, our oldest, starts college in three years."

While searching several job boards on the Internet, Ashley saw an opening for a mortgage broker in White Plains, New York—the same town in which she and her family lived. Shortly after sending a résumé and cover letter to Regency Brokers, Ashley received a phone call from Keith Rowe, the Regency owner. She agreed to an interview and was offered the job during her second interview. The job offer meant that Ashley would represent Regency in obtaining contracts for the company to place residential and commercial mortgages. Ashley would work on commission only, receiving 50% of the value of the contract. The borrowers would pay a $250 fee for having Regency find them a suitable mortgage. In addition, Ashley would receive about 25% of the fee the mortgage holder paid Regency.

Before agreeing to quit her job at the hospital and sign up with Regency, Ashley asked what it would take for her to be successful as a mortgage broker. Keith replied, "I have a single answer for you. Network like crazy. There are hundreds of people out there who need a mortgage now or in the future, or who would like to refinance. You just have to find them before another mortgage broker does or they go directly to their bank or credit union.

"A few years back, some mortgage brokers in our office were making over $300,000 per year. The business has cooled down somewhat, but there is still lots of opportunity. Residential and small business sales are not going away. You create your own destiny in this business."

With some trepidation, Ashley accepted the position. She and Brad agreed that she already had a lot of contacts, and that she could add all of Brad's contacts to her network. Ashley became a certified representative for Regency on March 1, just before the peak home-buying season. She maintained a Word diary of her networking activities, with nine of her entries as follows:

> *March 8:* While getting my hair done at Chez Pauline, I gave out my card to all nine women at the salon, along with the owner and two other stylists. I explained to them that if any of them needed a new mortgage, or wanted to refinance, they should just contact me. I also told them to please refer to me anybody they heard of who wanted an original mortgage or to refinance.

March 19: I sent e-mail messages to the 50 people I knew best in my graduating class at college, informing them of my new position and how I could help in finding the best mortgage for them.

April 1: I went to a large home furnishing store, and started up conversations with several of the shoppers. I gave each one a card, with the same pitch about their own needs or referring to me anybody who was mortgage shopping.

April 17: While taking a break at Starbucks, I overheard a couple talking about their plans for home ownership. I quickly introduced myself and gave the couple my business card. Unfortunately, I happened to splatter my coffee on the man's shirt.

May 3: We had a plumbing problem with the air-conditioning unit dumping water all over the floor. The plumber was a friendly guy, so I popped him my business card just in case he was looking for a mortgage. I asked him to tell others in his plumbing company about me also.

June 25: I attended a 10-year high-school reunion, and gave about 50 people my card after striking up a conversation with them.

July 1: I hit five garage sales in one day. I struck up conversations with as many people as I could and gave them my card. One lady seemed interested.

July 15: I asked dear old mom and dad to give me the names, e-mail addresses, and phone numbers of their 10 closest friends. I contacted every one, explaining how I might be able to obtain the best possible mortgage for them.

August 16: I attended the White Plains chapter of Finance Women in Business, and gave my card out to 26 members. However, most of the women said they were not looking for a mortgage.

After 7 months of searching for sales leads through networking and some random telephone calls, Ashley had earned a total of $1,850 in commissions. Feeling discouraged and beaten down, she asked Keith for advice. Keith replied, "You are doing a good job of networking. But remember, you are just planting seeds. It will take time for you to develop a successful mortgage broker business. Just dig into your savings to tide you over until you are making as much money as you want. Also, have you and Brad or your parents thought about refinancing your mortgage? You would get credit for those fees."

Case Study Questions

1. What is your evaluation of Ashley's networking technique and skills?
2. What suggestions can you offer Ashley so she can develop a more useful set of leads?
3. What is your evaluation of Ashley's political skill?
4. What is your evaluation of Keith's political skill?
5. What career advice might you offer Ashley about staying with Regency?

POLITICAL SKILL-BUILDING EXERCISE 8

Building Your Network

Networking can be regarded as the process of building a team that works with you to achieve success. You can start the following exercise now, but it will probably take your entire career to implement completely. To start networking or make your present networking more systematic, take the following steps:

Step 1: Jot down your top three goals or objectives for the following three months, such as obtaining a new job or promotion, starting a small business, or doing a field research study.

1. ______________________________
2. ______________________________
3. ______________________________

Step 2: List family members, friends, or acquaintances who could assist you in meeting your goals or objectives. Prepare a contact card, database, or Internet social network entry for each person on your list, including as many details as you can about the person and the person's family, friends, employers, and contacts.

(Continued)

(Continued)

Step 3: Identify what assistance you will request of your contact or contacts. Be realistic in light of your prior investment in the relationship. Remember, you have to be a friend to have a friend.

Step 4: Identify how you will meet your contact or contacts during the next month. Could it be for lunch or at an athletic field, nightclub, sports club, recreational facility on campus, cafeteria, and so forth? Could it be on a professional social networking site? Learn more about your contacts during your face-to-face meetings. In some cases, you may have to use the telephone or e-mail to substitute for an in-person meeting. Look for ways to mutually benefit from the relationship. At the beginning of each week, verify that you have made a small investment in building these relationships.

Step 5: Ask for the help you need. A network must benefit you. Thank the contact for any help given. Jot down on your planner a reminder to make a follow-up call, write a letter, or send an e-mail message to your contacts. In this way, you will have less work to do before you make another request for help.

Step 6: For each person in your network, think of a favor, however small, that you can return to him or her. Without reciprocity, a network fades rapidly.

SOURCE: The idea for this exercise derives from Kitter, C. (1998, March). Taking the work out of networking, Success Workshop, supplement to *The Pryor Report,* pp. 1–2. The exercise presented here is modernized.

REFERENCES

1. Edmondson, G. (2006, October 16). A role model for the team player. *BusinessWeek,* 78.

2. Quoted in Fisher, A. (2007, April 30). The trouble with MBAs. *Fortune,* 49.

3. Robbins, S. P. (1998). *Organizational behavior* (8th ed.) [p. 245]. Upper Saddle River, NJ: Prentice Hall.

4. *Social network theory.* Retrieved 08/17/2007 from www.istheory.yorku.ca./socialnetworktheory.htm; Suarez, F. F. (2005, August). Network effects revisited: The role of strong ties in technology selection. *Academy of Management Journal,* 710–720 [p. 712]; Ethier, J. (2005). *Current research in social network theory. Retrieved* 06/20/2007 from www.ccs.new.edu/home/perrollle/archive/Ethyier-SocialNetworks.html.

5. Granovetter, M. (1983). The strength of weak ties: A network theory revisited. *Sociological Theory, 1,* 201–233; Kurchner-Hawkins, R., & Miller, R. (2006). Organizational politics: Building positive political strategies in turbulent times. In

E. Vigoda-Gadot & A. Drory (Eds.), *Handbook of organizational politics* (pp. 328–352) [p. 342]. Northampton, MA: Edward Elgar.

6. Krebs, V. (2007). *Social network analysis: A brief introduction.* Retrieved 08/10/2007 from www.orgnet.com.

7. McGregor, J. (2006, February 27). The office chart that really counts: Mapping informal relationships at a company is revealing—and useful. *BusinessWeek,* 48–49.

8. Watters, E. (2006, April). The organization woman. *BusinessWeek,* 106–110.

9. Bradym, D., & McGregor, J. (2007, June 18). What works in women's networks. *BusinessWeek,* 58–60.

10. Yen, H. (2006, March 25). Katrina fraud likely to balloon past $1B. *The Los Angeles Times.*

11. The story and the quote is from Thornton, E. (2007, February 12). Carlyle changes its stripes. *BusinessWeek,* 46–59.

12. Copeland, M. V. (2006, December). The missing link. *Business 2.0,* 118–124.

13. Taylor, J. (2006, June). Card shop. *Fast Company,* 101.

14. Quoted in Roberts, B. (2008, March), Social networking at the office. *HR Magazine,* 81.

15. Kirsner, S. (2004, April). Networking overload, *Fast Company,* 38.

16. Ibarra, H., & Hunter, M. (2007, January). How leaders create and use networks. *Harvard Business Review,* 40–47.

17. Balkundi, P., & Harrison, D. A. (2006, February). Ties, leaders, and time in teams: Strong inference about network structure's effects on team viability and performance. *Academy of Management Journal,* 49–68.

18. Oh, H., Chung, M.-H., & Labianca, G. (2004, December). Group social capital and group effectiveness: The role of informal socializing ties. *Academy of Management Journal,* 860–875.

19. Collins, C. J., & Clark, K. D. (2003, December). Strategic human resource practices, top management team social networks, and firm performance: The role of human resources practices in creating organizational competitive advantage. *Academy of Management Journal,* 740–751.

20. Fisher, A. (2005, June 27). Winning a corporate board seat. *Fortune,* 204.

21. Needleman, S. E. (2006, November 7). Links to recruiters might reveal opportunities. *Wall Street Journal,* B9.

22. De Janasz, S. C., Sullivan, S. E., & Whiting, V. (2003, November). Mentor networks and career success: Lessons for turbulent times. *Academy of Management Executive,* 78–91.

23. Anand, N., & Conger, J. A. (2007). Capabilities of the consummate networker. *Organizational Dynamics, 1,* 13–27.

24. Casciaro, T., & Lobo, M. S. (2005, June). Competent jerks, lovable fools, and the formation of social networks. *Harvard Business Review,* 92–99.

25. Uzzi, S., & Dunlap, S. (2005, December). How to build your network. *Harvard Business Review,* 53–60.

26. The first two suggestions are based on Hillard, B., & Palmer, J. (2003). *Networking like a pro.* Atlanta, GA: Agito Consulting; Capell, P. (2006, June 6). Tongue-tied when networking? Develop foundation for dialogue. *Wall Street Journal,* B9.

27. Kirsner, S. (2004, April). Networking overload, *Fast Company,* 38.

28. Quoted in Hutchens, T. (2005, June 26). *Tee time an icebreaker for women executives.* Retrieved 08/15/2007 from www.detnews.com.

29. Cook, D., & Jenshel, L. (2003, April 14). Golf and power. *Fortune,* 163–174.

30. Foust, D. (2005, May 30). Working to play. *BusinessWeek,* 104.

PART III

NEGATIVE TACTICS, BLUNDERS, AND OVERCOMING DYSFUNCTIONAL POLITICS

NINE

NEGATIVE POLITICAL TACTICS AND BLUNDERS

LEARNING OBJECTIVES

After having studied this chapter and done the exercises, you should be able to do the following:

1. Identify and describe negative and devious political tactics focused primarily on hostile behavior toward others.
2. Identify and describe negative and devious political tactics that are classified as shrewd tricks.
3. Identify and describe political blunders classified as career-retarding blunders.
4. Identify and describe political blunders classified as leading to embarrassments and minor setbacks.
5. Describe how to recover from relatively minor political blunders, as well as major errors.

A few years ago, on a Friday morning in November, Justen Deal, a 22-year-old Kaiser Permanente project supervisor, blasted an e-mail throughout the giant health maintenance organization. His message charged that

HealthConnect—the company's ambitious $4 billion project to convert paper files into electronic medical records—was a mess.

In a blistering 2,000-word treatise, Deal wrote: "We're spending recklessly, to the tune of over $1.5 billion in waste every year primarily on HealthConnect, but also on other inefficient and ineffective technology projects." He did not stop there, however. Deal cited what he called the "mis-leadership" of Kaiser Chief Executive George Halvorson and other top managers, who he said were jeopardizing the company's ability to provide quality care. "For me, this isn't just an issue of saving money," he wrote. "It could very well become an issue of making sure our physicians and nurses have the tools they need to save lives."

Deal signed the e-mail. Before sending it, he says, he printed out a copy and handed it to his boss. "She gave me a look like, 'I think you are going to be fired,'" he recalls. Soon afterwards, his office phone was ringing off the hook. IT staffers later arrived to seize his computers, and Deal was placed on paid leave from his $56,000-a-year job.

Kaiser refuted Deal's assessment of its custom software system, developed by Epic Systems Corp. The company said HealthConnect was doing fine despite some missteps. Ultimately the company fired Deal, who worked on patient-education booklets and provided technical support to the department. On Monday, Halvorson sent his own Kaiser-wide e-mail dismissing Deal's attacks as "an unfortunate combination of partial facts, old data, incomplete data, 'conspiracy' thinking, and naiveté."[1]

Some people might regard Justen Deal as a whistleblower who was trying to protect his employer from financial ruin. Yet at the same time we cannot overlook how Deal committed an enormous political blunder—one that cost him his job, and most likely will prevent him from working as an IT professional in a large organization for the rest of his career. In this chapter, we look at the underbelly of political behavior in organizations: negative (or devious and unethical) tactics, along with political blunders, and how one might recover from a blunder. Studying a sampling of these tactics and faux pas can help raise your awareness level so as to avoid committing them.

NEGATIVE POLITICAL TACTICS

People engage in negative political tactics for many of the same reasons that people engage in other forms of organizational politics. Yet why people engage in negative rather than positive tactics is also partially attributable to their personal makeup. A negative disposition contributes to the choice of negative tactics. **Negative affectivity** is a tendency to experience aversive emotional states. In more detail, the tendency is a pervasive predisposition to experience emotional stress that includes feelings of nervousness, tension, and worry. The same disposition includes such emotional states as anger, scorn, revulsion, guilt, self-dissatisfaction, and sadness. Negative affectivity is likely to be triggered by the circumstances a person faces.[2] The type of highly competitive work environment that contributes to organizational politics might also trigger the symptoms of negative affectivity. Two personality traits that foster negative political behavior are aggressiveness and a strong need for power. For example, a major reason executives fire their enemies is to retain power by removing a potential threat to them remaining in office.

For purposes of simplification, we place negative and devious political tactics into two categories: hostile behavior toward others, and shrewd tricks, as outlined in Exhibit 9.1. All the tactics described in this chapter might be regarded as outright unethical, or at best ethically questionable. The model mentioned in Chapter 2 for examining the ethics of political behavior might readily be applied to negative political tactics.

Exhibit 9.1 Negative and Devious Political Tactics

Hostile Behavior Toward Others	*Shrewd Tricks*
1. Machiavellianism and bullying	1. Favoritism and nepotism
2. Bitter rivalries	2. Stealing ideas from job candidates
3. Holding a grudge and seeking revenge	3. Creating a false impression
4. Backstabbing	4. Strategic incompetence
5. Eliminating enemies	5. Abuse of contacts
	6. Territorial games
	7. Corporate espionage

Hostile Behavior Toward Others

Although all negative and devious political tactics are fueled in part by hostility, the tactics in this category are particularly hostile. For example, backstabbing placed in this category is meaner than strategic incompetence, placed under *shrewd tricks.*

Machiavellianism and Bullying

When Machiavellian tendencies are expressed, they often result in the manipulation and intimidation of others to gain personal advantage. A Machiavellian, for example, might keep offering drinks to a subordinate at an office party. Finally the subordinate becomes inebriated, and later receives a reprimand for being drunk at a business function.

Manipulation is also a negative influence tactic. The manipulator makes untrue statements or fakes certain behaviors, even to the point of engaging in blackmail. A manipulator might say to his or her boss, "After I receive a generous performance evaluation, I will probably forget about the fact that you accepted a rather generous gift from one of our suppliers." Another form of manipulation is to name drop to get one's way, such as saying, "Sally (the chief marketing officer) will be very happy if you get this report done for me."

Several case histories collected in Canada indicated that intimidating employees lowers their productivity and feelings of security, and can trigger violence. In one case, a worker named Pierre LeBrun killed four other employees, and then took his own life. An investigation revealed that LeBrun had been intimidated and mocked by coworkers for several years, but the company did not intervene to control the problem.[3]

Another form of Machiavellianism is intimidating people through bullying, which might also be classified as a devious influence tactic. Bullying usually involves persistent, offensive, abusive, intimidating, malicious, or insulting behavior. Bullies often attempt to control their victims through fear and intimidation. A specific example of bullying would be name-calling, insults, and teasing. Much bullying is conducted by managers attempting to control their subordinates, as found in a study of bullying conducted in the National Health Services in Britain. Two thirds of the respondents in the study had tried to take action when the bullying occurred, but most did not defend themselves well. Staff who had been bullied had lower levels of job satisfaction, and higher levels of job stress, depression, and intention to leave the job.

Emotional support at work had a positive effect in protecting people from some of the damaging effects of bullying.[4]

Bitter Rivalries

Another hostile political tactic is to maintain a bitter rivalry with a superior, subordinate, or coworker. A person who regards another person as a rival might be prone to badmouth the other person. A rivalry between divisions—such as between the commercial and retail divisions—might lead to poor cooperation and duplication of effort. One situation that frequently breeds an intense rivalry is when an outsider is brought into a company as a head of a group. The rivalry surfaces because one or more of the manager's subordinates believe that he or she should have received the promotion. Sometimes the person passed over will attempt to hijack the manager's authority, or give him or her wrong information.

An energy company hired a man named Richard Guha to lead a key division. He soon learned that he had been chosen over an official who was a longtime buddy of the founder and board chairman. The passed-over official soon complained to the chairman that Guha would wreck the business. "He thought he was the right answer and I was the wrong answer," Guha recalls. He believes that the badmouthing hurt his effectiveness. Guha went to the chairman, but the latter refused to stop the official from complaining. So Guha initiated a series of dinners with the official, and solicited his advice on business problems. Eventually the rival became an ally.[5]

Holding a Grudge and Seeking Revenge

Disputes with others in the workplace are almost inevitable because of the mix of personalities and goals. Many people are either able to resolve the dispute or let it rest in order to work well with the adversary in the future. A minority of workers hold a grudge against the other person as a way of keeping the conflict alive and exerting control over the other person. The grudge holder has a feeling of ill will toward the person who created the alleged wrong, and often thinks of ways to even the score. As a result, the person with the grudge is predisposed to blame or criticize the other person, and is reluctant to give the other person a second chance.

An example of a grudge took this form: Coworker A laughed at a marketing suggestion of coworker B during a meeting. After the meeting, B told A that he was quite upset at the laughter. A apologized, but that was not good enough for B. When it came time for completing the peer evaluation form, B made several negative statements about A, including the fact that he routinely stole ideas from others.

Going beyond disputes between two individuals, the research of Robert J. Bies suggests a series of events that can trigger employees to take revenge: layoffs without warning, public beratings, and budget cuts without explanation. One example of such revenge would be giving extremely poor customer service. Bies also observes that few people admit to taking revenge. As he began his research, he would ask people, "Do you guys engage in revenge?" The response would be, "Oh no, we never engage in revenge." Yet when asked whether they try to get even with people, the answer would be "All the time."[6] A research study with government employees showed that revenge often takes place when the other side is blamed for a negative event. An employee might seek revenge against a manager who reduced his or her pay, yet would be unlikely to seek revenge against the manager if every employee in the company had received a pay cut. The study also found that employees were more willing to exact revenge against less powerful offenders.[7] Revenge seekers probably take into account the potential for counterrevenge.

Based on their position power, spurned CEOs can engage in high-level revenge, sometimes by turning around a struggling competitor. Millard "Mickey" Drexler, the merchandising expert who was ousted from Gap Inc. in 2002 after 19 years at the helm, left behind a hefty severance package and its noncompeting restrictions. That decision enabled him to accept a position at the preppy retailer J. Crew Inc. Since joining J. Crew, Drexler has hired at least two dozen executives away from his former employer.[8] To make the revenge even sweeter, J. Crew has been more profitable than Gap since Drexler left Gap and joined J. Crew.

Backstabbing

A widely known devious political tactic is **backstabbing**, in which another person pretends to be nice to you but is really plotting to damage or ruin your reputation. During times of less job security, including downsizings due to mergers and acquisitions, workers are more likely to say negative things about coworkers to gain advantage. Also, when a promotion is at stake, coworkers are more likely to say negative things about each other to a common boss.

A frequent form of backstabbing is to initiate a conversation with a coworker about the weaknesses of a common boss. When these comments are passed along to the boss, the rival appears disloyal and foolish. E-mail has become a convenient medium for backstabbing, such as documenting a mistake made by a rival and distributing it widely. A devious political actor might write an e-mail of this nature, sending it to her rival and a few key managers: "Wanda, I am so sorry that your sales forecast overestimated sales by 45%. But I am attaching a reference that offers a few refined sales forecasting techniques. And please let me know if I can help you with your next forecast."

Backstabbing is an attempt to sabotage another person and is sometimes a symptom of a character disorder on the part of the political actor, says Fred Nader. At other times, an organizational culture prone to dishonesty will foster backstabbing.[9]

Eliminating Enemies

The ancient strategy of *embrace or demolish* suggests that you remove from the premises rivals who suffered past hurts through your efforts or those who oppose you for other reasons. Wounded rivals might retaliate at a vulnerable moment. The origin of this strategy is found in Machiavelli's advice regarding the conquest of smaller nations, as follows:[10]

> Upon this, one has to remark that men ought to be either well-treated, or crushed, because they can avenge themselves of lighter injuries, of more serious ones they cannot; therefore the injury that is done to a man ought to be of such a kind that one does not stand in fear of revenge.

A common form of eliminating enemies by executives is to fire subordinates who are rivals for their jobs, or who simply disagree with them over strategy issues. Stanley O'Neal, the former CEO and chairman of Merrill Lynch, believes strongly in eliminating enemies. Within a couple of years of being appointed CEO, O'Neal demoted or fired dozens of veteran executives, many of whom disagreed with his cost-cutting initiatives. His primary rival, asset-management chief Jeff Peake, was dismissed in 2001 through means of a press release. Next on the hit list was Win Smith, another division chief whose father once was head of Merrill Lynch. Also terminated was every member of the executive management committee built by his predecessor. (All of these members might have been perceived as not being loyal to O'Neal.) In O'Neal's words, "Ruthless isn't always that bad."[11] The financial losses

Merrill Lynch experience in 2007 in relation to high-risk, mortgage-related investments led to the dismissal of O'Neal.

Shrewd Tricks

The tactics described in this section are perhaps less hostile than those described in the previous section, and therefore are categorized as being shrewd tricks. However, people with high ethical standards would still describe the tactics described here as negative and devious.

Favoritism and Nepotism

When workers complain about office politics, the reference is frequently to **favoritism**, or giving preferential treatment to people the manager likes personally. *Cronyism* refers to the same concept as favoritism, because cronies (companions or chums) are given plum assignments even if they are not the best-qualified persons for them. Cronyism is widely practiced in business and public life, including old friends getting plush political appointments after a close friend is elected to office.

The leader–member exchange (LMX) theory mentioned several times in this book substantiates the idea that leaders give unequal treatment to group members, often based on personal preferences. Examples of favoritism include (1) giving the largest salary increases to personal friends within the department, (2) giving an outstanding performance evaluation rating to an average employee whom the manager is dating, (3) giving the most desirable assignments to favorites within the department, (4) giving the least desirable assignments to those personally disliked within the department, and (5) keeping personal favorites off the list of people to be downsized.

Nepotism is a form of favoritism based on family membership. The definition sometimes extends to close friends. When the family member given a key job is more or equally competent than other contenders for the position, nepotism is hardly devious. The owners of a family business, for example, may have more trust in a family member. However, nepotism is regarded as a devious tactic in situations such as when a family member collects full salary and benefits yet contributes little value to the company.

Stealing Ideas From Job Candidates

A sensible approach to screening job candidates for higher-level positions is to ask how they might tackle a real problem facing the company. However, job tryouts of this nature can lead to two different devious political tactics. The most devious trick is to have no intention of hiring any candidate, but simply to use the fictitious job opening as a way of gathering potentially useful ideas from job applicants. The more frequent shrewd trick is to steal ideas from the rejected candidate or candidates who present useful proposals. An example of this unethical political tactic took place as follows.

While jobless a few years ago, Vincent A. Gaglione Jr. pursued a middle-management position at an Ohio insurer. The company asked him to create a marketing strategy focused on its independent field agents. He spent about 50 hours drafting a 25-page plan, then presented his detailed proposal to 20 officials over the next two days. "We shook hands," Gaglione recalls. "There was a lot of backslapping and they said, 'We'll be in touch.'"

He didn't get the job. Gaglione soon found out that the insurer was test marketing a key piece of his plan, even used the name he had given it. He left angry messages for two executives there. "I didn't appreciate you guys taking up my time and taking my work," his voicemail said. They never called back.[12]

An intellectual-property attorney suggests that the candidate add a copyright symbol © to the report, plus a confidentially warning stating: "This information is being provided solely for the purpose of the job interview and may not be used for other purposes without the author's permission."[13]

Creating a False Impression

Impression management is often a positive strategy, yet creating a false impression is devious and shrewd. A false impression can take many forms. One example is pretending to buy into a company strategy of being environmentally friendly yet at the same time wasting considerable energy in your private life. Another example is pretending to have strong connections with powerful people you have never met. A type of false impression in the executive suite can involve a disparity between how the executive actually manages a company and the principles he or she publicly espouses.

In 2007, Lord John Browne was forced out of office as CEO of BP (British Petroleum), partly because of lying about his personal lifestyle. BP has long held a public image of self-righteousness, including a heavy concern for protecting the environment. Browne had launched a $200 million image campaign with the tagline that "BP stands for 'Beyond Petroleum.'" The principles embedded in the campaign included "delivering performance without tradeoffs" in areas ranging from worker safety to environmental protection. Yet in reality BP was not such a caring company.

Greenpeace presented Browne with an award for the "Best Impression of an Environmentalist." Browne's cost-cutting after a merger was cited as a cause of a refinery explosion in Texas City, Texas, killing 15 and injuring dozens of others. Other instances were found of deadly accidents resulting from not meeting safety standards. Also, two large oil spills at BP's Prudhoe Bay, Alaska, oil fields had a serious negative environmental impact.[14]

Strategic Incompetence

Avoiding work one prefers to shun because it does not fit one's role is referred to as **strategic incompetence**. In years past, some women used strategic incompetence to avoid performing work stereotypical of their gender. During the 1970s, when more women entered the managerial and professional ranks in business, many of these women felt forced to defend themselves against performing clerical support work and errand running. When asked to type a letter, the professional woman might say, "I don't know how to type."

Steven Crawley, a human resources executive, says, "The inability to grasp selective things can be very helpful in keeping your desk clear of unwanted clutter. I have developed a very agile selective memory across a wide range of nonvalue-added activities." His proudest moment of strategic incompetence took place when the president of an automotive parts manufacturer asked Crawley to organize the company picnic. Not liking to do party planning, he responded to inquiries with comments such as "How do you do that?" or "Help me remember why we are talking about this." The responsibility for the picnic was soon assigned to another worker.[15]

A strong disadvantage of using strategic incompetence is that the political actor might be perceived as a poor organizational citizen, and therefore not promotable. It is politically wiser to take on a few undesired tasks to create the impression of being a strong team player.

Abuse of Contacts

Making effective use of contacts is the essence of networking, and therefore highly recommended. Yet some political actors use contacts to the point of being devious, such as knowing a public official who gets the person's law violation reduced from a felony to a misdemeanor. At one time, Jack Grubman was Wall Street's most influential telecommunication analyst. Eventually he was barred from the securities industry for recommending to investors telecom stocks he knew were in decline because of his business relationship with the telecom companies in question. Grubman was forced to pay a $17 million fine.

An example of how Grubman abused his contacts (and simultaneously engaged in exchange of favors) took place at Citigroup. Sanford Weill, at the time the co-CEO of Citigroup, asked Grubman to "take a fresh look" at his rating for AT&T. Grubman informed Weill of "his progress with AT&T" and asked Weill for help in getting his twin daughters accepted at an elite nursery school in Manhattan. Grubman upgraded AT&T to "buy" from neutral, and Grubman's unit of Citigroup later received $45 million in fees from AT&T for underwriting new stock. Citigroup began donating $1 million a year to the nursery school (the 92nd Street Y). Later, when an e-mail was uncovered documenting the arrangement with Weill, Grubman protested that his e-mail was simply a lie to inflate his own importance.[16]

A personal contact with an executive recruiting specialist is sometimes used to remove a rival or enemy. Suppose you have a boss who dislikes you, or thinks poorly of your contribution. It appears that you cannot change your boss's perception of you, and you therefore want him or her out of the way. To achieve your goal, you highly tout your boss to an executive recruiter who in turns finds a company that is looking for a person of his or her expertise.[17] Although this tactic has been used for a long time, it will often backfire. Most headhunters are aware of the tactic, and they use multiple references before pursuing a candidate.

Territorial Games

Many aspects of life in organizations are territorial. Workers make claims on and defend their control of a variety of organizational objects, spaces, roles (positions and jobs), and relationships. Manifestations of territoriality include nameplates outside offices or cubicles, family photos on desks, and reluctance to let others join a key project. Territoriality has its benefits, such as protecting physical space and increasing the feeling of belonging to a social group, leading to less turnover and higher productivity. Territoriality can also have negative consequences, such as employees protecting proprietary claims about being responsible for a certain project, and diverting their attention away from attaining company goals. Moreover, when territoriality is part of the organizational culture, workers may be reluctant to cooperate and share information with others for fear of infringing on their territory.[18]

Much of why territoriality can result in political maneuvering is summed up in a definition of the concept developed by Graham Brown, Thomas B. Lawrence, and Sandra L. Robinson: "**Territoriality** is an individual's behavioral expression of his or her feelings of ownership toward a physical or social object. This definition includes behaviors for constructing, communicating, maintaining, and restoring territories around those objects in the organization toward which one feels proprietary attachment."[19] An implication of this definition is that people will sometimes engage in political behavior to protect what they consider to be their territory, resulting in *territorial games.* One example would be a tech support group attempting to forbid people in other departments from working on virus protection for their desktop computers—because virus protection is part of the tech-support group's territory.

An example of territorial games, or turf battles, took place at Ford Motor Company in the 1990s. Top-level management attempted a sweeping reorganization to function as one company, globally, rather than as a collection of regional fiefdoms. However, these major efforts failed, partially because top-level and middle managers resisted the pressure to surrender their turf. In the current era, CEO Alan Mulally is attempting to eliminate fiefdoms at Ford and better integrate the company's divisions.[20]

Corporate Espionage

An old trick that has received renewed visibility is to hire a detective to spy on workers. The purpose of spying is to discover whether workers are violating company policy, such as leaking news to the press or doing anything embarrassing that could be used to their discredit. Spying to determine whether employees are selling trade secrets should not be considered a political trick because divulging proprietary information is a crime.

A celebrated case of corporation espionage took place at Hewlett-Packard in 2006. The case began when the online technology site CNET published an article containing information about long-range strategy at HP that could only have been obtained from a director. Upset with the leak, chairwoman Patricia Dunn authorized a team of independent electronic-security experts to spy on the January 2006 personal telephone accounts of the 10 other HP directors. Dunn acted without informing the rest of the board of her spying. One of the directors, Tom Perkins, told Dunn that her behavior was illegal, unethical, and a misplaced corporate priority. Perkins resigned in protest, but the reasons for his resignation were hidden from the public. Dunn soon resigned and later pleaded not guilty to California misdemeanor charges that were eventually dropped. The most embarrassing part of espionage authorized by Dunn is that it involved *pretexting,* or using false pretenses to get another individual's personal private information. In one type of pretexting, a person pretends to be the person spied upon in order to obtain telephone records. The Federal Trade Commission contends that pretexting is illegal, but opinions vary on the legality of representing yourself as a customer to obtain information.[21]

Wal-Mart is another highly visible company that has practiced corporate espionage directed at employees and outside critics of the company. The Threat Research and Assessment Group within Wal-Mart was first formed to detect theft and pro-union sympathies among workers. Soon the group's activities grew into surveillance of certain outside critics, consultants, stockholders, and even Wal-Mart's board members. One security technician was accused of unauthorized wiretapping of a *New York Times* reporter.[22]

POLITICAL BLUNDERS

Many people get into trouble with their manager and organization, and damage their career, because they commit **political blunders**, or insensitive acts. Blunders are also referred to as "putting your foot in your mouth," or committing a faux pas. We approach blunders from four perspectives: why they occur, those most likely to damage a career, those most likely to lead to embarrassments and minor setbacks, and recovering from blunders. The blunders described here are outlined in Exhibit 9.2.

Political Blunders and Emotional Intelligence

As implied from their definition, political blunders usually arise from being insensitive, or not stopping to carefully size up the situation. The Apple employee who brings a BlackBerry to work instead of an iPhone does not stop to think of the consequences of his or her actions. Insensitivity can also be framed as being deficient in two aspects of emotional intelligence—self-management and social awareness:[23]

- **Self-management** is the ability to control one's emotions and act with honesty and integrity. The right degree of self-management helps prevent a person from throwing temper tantrums when activities do not go as planned. With a reasonable degree of self-management, a political actor would not commit such blunders as insulting the boss in a meeting,

Exhibit 9.2 Political Blunders

Career-Retarding Blunders	*Blunders Leading to Embarrassments and Minor Setbacks*
1. Public humiliation of others	1. Being politically incorrect
2. Violation of company code or ethics	2. Displaying impatience for promotion
3. Out-of-control avarice	3. Gossiping about taboo subjects
4. Disseminating negative messages and misdeeds electronically	4. Attacking sacred cows
5. Bypassing the boss	5. Refusing to take vacations
6. Being revengeful and hostile during an exit interview	6. Insensitivity to cross-cultural differences
7. Indiscreet behavior in private life	7. Rejecting business social invitations
8. Improperly conducted office romance	8. Wearing overly sexy clothing
	9. Inappropriate consumption of alcohol
	10. Insensitivity to public opinion

NOTE: What constitutes a blunder depends upon the context, such as the organizational culture or type of industry. One example is No. 4, about sacred cows. In a very open organization, challenges to the status quo are welcome. Another example is No. 8, about overly sexy clothing. In some retail establishments, "overly sexy clothing" is almost required for customer contact positions.

crying over a poor performance review, or getting even with the company during an exit interview.

- **Social awareness** includes having empathy for others, and having intuition about organizational problems. A person with good social awareness would not commit such blunders as out-of-control avarice, attacking sacred cows, and being insensitive to public opinion.

You are invited to take the quiz in Exhibit 9.3 to help you think through your tendencies toward committing political blunders.

Exhibit 9.3 The Blunder Quiz

Directions: Indicate whether you agree or disagree with the following statements.

Statement	*Agree*	*Disagree*
1. It's fine to criticize your manager in a meeting as long as the criticism is valid.		
2. I generally refer to females on the job and at college as "girls."		
3. I would not hesitate to ask a coworker how much he or she was paid.		
4. If I worked for Microsoft I would still use whatever search engine I pleased (instead of Live.com) while at the office.		
5. If I objected to a decision made by top management, I would send a company-wide e-mail explaining my objection.		
6. I am willing to insult any coworker if the insult is deserved.		
7. During a national election, I would place campaign banners for my favorite candidate outside my cubicle or office.		
8. I see no problem in using competitors' products or services and letting my superiors know about it.		
9. If I thought the CEO of my company were way overpaid, I would send him or her an e-mail making my opinion known.		
10. Never bother with company-sponsored social events, such as holiday parties, unless you are really interested.		
11. I like the idea of firing an employee by sending him or her an e-mail about being fired.		
12. If I disagreed strongly with top-level management, I would ridicule them during conversation in the office.		

(Continued)

Exhibit 9.3 (Continued)

Statement	*Agree*	*Disagree*
13. I openly criticize most new ventures my company or department is contemplating.		
14. I avoid any deliberate attempt to please or impress coworkers or superiors.		
15. I would only attend a company picnic or other company social gathering if the activity were something I really wanted to do.		

Total: "Agree" _____ "Disagree" _____

Scoring and Interpretation: The greater the number of statements you agree with, the more prone you are to political blunders that can damage your career. You need to raise your awareness level of blunders in the workplace.

Career-Retarding Blunders

The blunders mentioned here are usually serious, often leading to a severe career setback such as being fired and being unable to find new employment at one's accustomed job level.

1. *Public humiliation of others.* The oldest rule in human relations is to praise in public but criticize in private. Yet many people lose career momentum through criticizing an immediate manager or company executive in public. Also, destructive criticism of a subordinate in public can damage the manager's reputation as an effective boss. A few years ago, Judith Regan, the head of ReganBooks imprint, intended to publish a book and a television series about a hypothetical confession by O.J. Simpson of the assassination of his former wife and her friend. However, the parent company nixed the project. Regan's response was to criticize on radio the executives at the parent HarperCollins. She also made offensive remarks about Jane Friedman, head of HarperCollins, to a company lawyer. Friedman then quickly fired Reagan.[24]

2. *Violation of company code of ethics.* Acceptance of generous gifts from suppliers and the misuse of company resources are two violations of ethical

codes that often lead to being fired. The case study in this chapter deals with a former Wal-Mart executive who was fired because she violated the company ethical code in several ways. Using company jets for family travel is an example of an ethical violation that has led to the dismissal of many executives.

3. *Out-of-control avarice.* Being too greedy is a political blunder because it leads to shame and humiliation for the greedy person. Even if the executive is able to extract extraordinary sums of money from the company, being publicly humiliated and never being invited to hold an executive position again are severe negative consequences. Richard A. Grasso, the former chairman and CEO of the New York Stock Exchange is a legendary example of out-of-control avarice. Based partly on his ability to develop close contacts with powerful people, Grasso negotiated a $187 million compensation package for himself. Public news of this giant payout led the exchange's board to turn against Grasso, even though they had approved the giant payment. Soon after submitting his resignation, the dispute over Grasso's pay became one of the ugliest fights in modern corporate history. For years, Grasso was embroiled in court battles, with an appeals court finally ruling that he would have to return $100 million of his compensation. A later New York Appeals Court ruling made it uncertain how much of this sum Grasso would have to pay.[25] Although still an extremely rich person, Grasso became a symbol of corporate greed and the butt of jokes about executive pay.

4. *Disseminating negative messages and misdeeds electronically.* The chapter opener illustrated how sending an extremely negative e-mail message about your company can wreck a career. Another example is a Wal-Mart cashier who posted a joke on his MySpace Web page suggesting that average IQs would increase if a bomb were dropped on every Wal-Mart store. He was fired after the company perceived it as a threat. Company officials had him sign an acknowledgment that he had been fired for "gross misconduct and integrity issue." Because his joke was interpreted as a threat, the man did not qualify for unemployment insurance.[26]

5. *Sending e-mail messages about misdeeds.* An example of another electronic blunder would be sending back and forth love notes about an office romance that violates company policy. Sending e-mail messages poking fun at company management is also a blunder. As is well-known, even deleted e-mail messages can be traced. Another e-mail caution is to not hit Reply to All when your insults about an executive's broadcast message to company employees were intended for just one coworker.

6. *Bypassing the boss.* If you have a problem or conflict with your immediate manager, it is best to resolve the problem directly with him or her. Going around your boss by attempting to resolve the issue with your boss's boss almost always backfires because the boss bypass is a taboo, even in a democratic organization. You are likely to be perceived as a troublemaker by higher management, and your relationship with your immediate manager will be permanently damaged. Bypassing the boss is only legitimate when the boss engages in outrageous behavior such as illegal and criminal activity, including frequent sexual harassment of subordinates.

7. *Being revengeful and hostile during an exit interview.* After resigning a position, many companies conduct an exit interview in which departing employees are asked to discuss the true reasons for them quitting. Under the best of circumstances, the employee who quits would offer constructive suggestions that would improving the working conditions and work climate for present and future employees. This would enhance a person's reputation, and perhaps lead to a stronger reference in the future. The exiting employee is invited to be frank, but being frank to the point of getting revenge by saying hostile things about the company and the manager is a career-retarding error. Often the employee will receive a negative employment reference.[27] An employee who fell into this category said to the exit interviewer, "Our company adds no value to society. And my manager was a pathetic excuse for a boss."

8. *Indiscreet behavior in private life.* Employees are representatives of the company, so their behavior off the job is considered to contribute to their performance—particularly in the case of managers. Embarrassing the company will often lead to dismissal, combined with a negative reputation that will be difficult to shake for purposes of future employment. Indiscreet behavior in private life that can lead to dismissal includes being caught shoplifting, a citation for drunk driving, being arrested for a drug offense, charges of rape, and assault and battery against another person. Several years ago, top-level managers at Time Warner asked Chris Albrecht, CEO of its Home Box Office unit and a high performer, to resign after he was accused of assaulting his girlfriend in a hotel parking lot in Las Vegas.[28] (Note that the company did not wait for a judge or jury to declare Albrecht guilty.)

9. *Improperly conducted office romance.* The workplace is a major place for meeting romantic partners, so office romances are inevitable. (Bill Gates married a woman who he began dating when she was a Microsoft employee.) A discreetly conducted office romance is therefore not a political blunder.

In contrast, office romances that are embarrassing to the company can lead to punishment, including dismissal. A romance with a subordinate is particularly sensitive because if the romance cools down, it can lead to charges of sexual harassment. Other taboos include public displays of affection on company time, a married manager getting involved with a worker other than his or her spouse, and extending business travel to conduct a romance.

Another reason an office romance can be a political blunder is that approximately 25% of companies have rules forbidding or restricting office romance. Even without such rules, the company might be concerned about (a) the abuse of power when a manager becomes involved with a subordinate and (b) the productivity-lowering distraction of the romance.[29]

Blunders Leading to Embarrassment and Minor Setbacks

The political blunders in this section tilt toward leading to embarrassment and minor setbacks. Nevertheless, if carried out in the extreme or in the wrong organizational culture, the blunder could have serious consequences. For example, having three drinks at a business lunch just once could block you from promotion in an ultra-conservative firm.

1. *Being politically incorrect.* Political correctness involves being careful not to offend or slight anyone, and being extra civil and respectful.[30] An effective use of political correctness would be to say, "We need a ladder in our department because we have workers of different heights who need access to the top shelves." It would be politically incorrect—and therefore a political blunder—to say, "We need ladders because we have some short workers who cannot reach the top shelves." To avoid being politically incorrect, many people will almost never mention a person's race, sex, ethnicity, or health status when referring to another worker. To avoid political incorrectness, it is better to err on the side of caution. Although many men and women in the workplace are returning to the language of yesteryear by referring to adult females as "girls," it is still preferable to refer to females over 17 as "women."

2. *Displaying impatience for promotion.* Appearing too eager for promotion, such as frequently mentioning your desire to be promoted, is often a political blunder. Part of the problem is that people in power want to think that promoting you is their idea, not yours. Also, it may violate protocol to campaign too heavily for a promotion. At one point, Mike Roberts was heir

apparent to the CEO position at McDonald's Corp., partially because he was the chief architect of a remarkable turnaround at the company. Roberts pushed so hard for the big promotion, including being outspoken about his ambitions, that he antagonized the board. The board then decided that Roberts should stay in the number-two role longer, so he soon resigned.[31]

3. *Gossiping about taboo subjects.* Gossiping about taboo subjects is a political blunder that can erode the political player's relationship with coworkers. A survey conducted by a consulting firm revealed the following topics to be off limits, whether they were in reference to oneself or other workers: sexually transmitted disease, domestic violence, mental illness, alcohol/drug abuse, and fertility problems. Topics to avoid were political beliefs and religious beliefs.[32] In general, it is best to not talk about topics that include considerable intimate detail or are so emotional that someone who feels differently would be offended. Also, malicious gossip can be career threatening because it can be regarded as libel. For example, four town employees in New Hampshire lost their jobs because they referred to the town administrator in derogatory terms, and discussed a rumor than he was having an affair with a female employee.[33]

4. *Attacking sacred cows.* The lore of many organizations includes fond beliefs about what is positive and effective, such as certain products, services, and values. If you attack these sacred cows, you run the risk of being perceived as disloyal. A sacred cow at Burger King is that frontline experience in a company store (restaurant) is essential for success. A sacred cow in most business organizations is that management and leadership skill is worth more money than technical skill. As a result, the CEO might earn $20 million per year and the inventor whose product helped the company become successful might earn $100,000 per year.

5. *Refusing to take vacations.* In companies in which work–life balance is heavily emphasized, taking vacations without bringing along work or being wired to the office is expected behavior. To refuse to take a vacation is therefore a political blunder. A manager who refuses to take a vacation risks projecting the image of a micromanager who has failed to develop anyone enough to take over while he or she is away. PricewaterhouseCoopers is one company where refusing to take vacations is a blunder. The company tracks employees who have not taken enough vacations, and sends reminders to them and their managers that they should schedule a vacation.[34]

6. *Insensitivity to cross-cultural differences.* In a global workplace, insensitivity to cross-cultural differences can be a blunder that will make you appear unsophisticated. An amusing example took place when the president of Toyota, Katsuaki Watanabe, visited San Antonio, Texas, to celebrate the opening of a new assembly plant. Watanabe jumped behind the wheel of a Tundra full-size pickup that had just rolled off the assembly line. To the cheers of workers and guests, Watanabe pressed on the horn and leaned out the window, waving and smiling. The Texas governor, Rick Perry, could not control his enthusiasm about the new plant. He hugged Watanabe, violating the "no touching" rule of Japanese business etiquette. Watanabe endured the hug with a smile, but the press later brought attention to Perry's faux pas.[35]

7. *Rejecting business social invitations.* Business social activities including company activities, meals, and after-work drinks with coworkers can rightfully be perceived as another work activity taking time away from personal life. However, it is a political blunder to reject too many of these activities. When invitations are rejected, they should be rejected only with a valid and important excuse. Employment lawyer Richard C. Busse explains that these social events are one of the 12 steps you can follow to build up currency in the workplace. These social invitations are good networking opportunities, and avoiding them sends the signal that you are "too good" to socialize with the group.[36]

8. *Wearing overly sexy clothing.* Most people are aware that obeying dress codes in business is important, and that a worker might be negatively judged if his or her attire is inappropriate. An experiment published in the *Psychology of Women Quarterly* supports this contention with respect to women. Male and female undergraduates viewed a woman on videotape who was dressed in either sexy or businesslike attire, and allegedly either a manager or a receptionist. Participants in the study showed more negative emotion toward the sexily attired manager and rated her less competent than the neutrally attired manager. In contrast, the difference in attire had no effect on emotions or competence ratings of the receptionist. The conclusion drawn to the study was that a sexy self-presentation harms women in a high-status job.[37] It is probably also true that men in high-status positions should avoid overly sexy clothing to avoid committing a political blunder.

9. *Inappropriate consumption of alcohol.* Consuming alcohol at work-related functions is much less prevalent today than in years past, partly because of stricter DWI regulations and concerns about employer liability. Nevertheless,

drinking alcohol remains part of business for the simple reason that big deals are still conducted over meals. Anything more than light drinking (usually two beverages) is most likely a political blunder. A study of 501 human resource professionals provides some data to ponder. Respondents were asked, "At which of the following work-related events is drinking alcohol accepted at your organization?" The answers were: holiday party, 70%; meal with a client/customer, 40%; retirement party, 32%; celebration of company milestone, 28%; meal with a coworker, 22%; none, 14%; and meal during a job interview, 4%.[38]

10. *Insensitivity to public opinion.* An executive blunder is insensitivity toward public opinion because the consequence might be negative publicity and a temporary dip in sales. Insensitive acts include an airline canceling too many flights or bumping too many passengers, and awkward firings of workers. In 2006, executives at Radio Shack received considerable negative publicity for firing 400 employees via this e-mail message: "Unfortunately, your position is one that has been eliminated." The e-mails told employees they were to meet with their managers at 9:15 a.m. to discuss their severance packages.[39]

Recovering From Blunders

We have mentioned recovering from mistakes and misdeeds at two other places in this book: in relation to impression management in Chapter 4, and in terms of influence tactics in Chapter 7. Here we look at recovering from blunders. A recommended way of recovering from a blunder is to admit you made a mistake, apologize, and then refrain from committing the same blunder again. Mel Fugate describes an approach for overcoming a blunder with a boss that would also apply to most of the blunders described here. You have to earn back your trust. Do not wait or try to smooth over the blunder with a quip. Apologize immediately face-to-face, while speaking slowly to sound remorseful. Next, accept responsibility for what you did or said. Empathize with the discomfort you caused. ("You must have felt horrible when I challenged your figures in this morning's meeting.") Offer a credible explanation for the blunder, and perhaps ask for assistance to prevent repeating the mistake. ("How do I overcome being such a data freak?")[40]

Damage Control After a Major Error on the Job

A large blunder sometimes shifts into the more severe category of having made a major error on the job, such as a trader at an investment bank having lost several million dollars of the company's money on a risky investment. Marion Thomas offers this eight-step procedure for damage control:

1. *Take responsibility.* Taking responsibility for a major error makes you appear strong and in control. Making excuses makes you look weak and inept.

2. *Analyze the failure.* Invest time in analyzing what really went wrong—and devise a plan for preventing the problem from happening again. The trader mentioned above might consult with a colleague or the manager before making such a risky investment in the future.

3. *Avoid berating yourself.* One mistake does not convert a person into an incompetent, or destroy a person's career. Negative self-talk only worsens the situation.

4. *Keep it in perspective.* Ask yourself, "How much will this mistake matter within my company in five days? In five weeks? In five months? In five years? Making a major mistake on the job is only a *temporary* setback.

5. *Talk it over with someone you trust.* Talking to a trusted person outside the organization can be a useful method of dealing with the emotional upset associated with having made a major mistake on the job. Talking over your problem with an insider might lead to you being backstabbed by your confidant.

6. *Consider training.* If the error can be attributed to lack of a specific skill or technical expertise, seek out training or coaching. The trader mentioned above might need more coaching in excessive risk assessment.

7. *Give it time.* Give yourself time to recover and regroup from the major error you have committed, but do not wallow in misery for too long. Put on your game face, even if you still feel beaten down.

8. *Get over it.* Perceive your mistake as a learning experience, and profit from it. Now move on, and do not be paralyzed by the big mistake you made. Keep in mind that most successful people make at least one big mistake in their career, and later recover from the experience.[41]

SUMMARY

One reason why many people engage in negative rather than positive organizational politics is because of a group of personality traits referred to as negative affectivity. Negative political tactics referred to as hostile behavior toward others include (1) Machiavellianism, including bullying; (2) bitter rivalries; (3) holding a grudge and seeking revenge; (4) backstabbing; and (5) eliminating enemies.

Negative political tactics referred to as shrewd tricks include (1) favoritism and nepotism, (2) stealing ideas from job candidates, (3) creating a false impression, (4) strategic incompetence, (5) abuse of contacts, (6) territorial games, and (7) corporate espionage.

Many political blunders can be attributed to low emotional intelligence, particularly poor self-management and social awareness. Career-retarding blunders include (1) public humiliation of others, (2) violation of company code of ethics, (3) out-of-control avarice, (4) disseminating negative messages and misdeeds electronically, (5) bypassing the boss, (6) being revengeful and hostile during an exit interview, (7) indiscreet behavior in private life, and (8) an improperly conducted office romance.

Political blunders leading to embarrassment and minor setbacks include (1) being politically incorrect, (2) displaying impatience for promotion, (3) gossiping about taboo subjects, (4) attacking sacred cows, (5) refusing to take vacations, (6) insensitivity to cross-cultural differences, (7) rejecting business social invitations, (8) wearing overly sexy clothing, (9) inappropriate consumption of alcohol, and (10) insensitivity to public opinion.

To recover from a blunder, admit you made a mistake, apologize, and refrain from committing the same blunder again. If a blunder is committed with a boss, trust must be regained. To bring about damage control after a major error, consider this eight-step process: Take responsibility; analyze the failure; avoid berating yourself; keep it in perspective; talk it over with a trusted person; give it time; consider training; and get over it.

QUESTIONS AND ACTIVITIES

1. Give two examples of negative organizational politics you have observed in any workplace. To what extent were coworkers aware that the person in question was engaged in negative politics?

2. Provide a workplace example of backstabbing that you have personally witnessed. What do you think was the motivation of the backstabber?

3. Identify a couple of disadvantages to a person's career from practicing *strategic incompetence.*
4. How might an employer convert the tactic "stealing ideas from job candidates" into an ethical and responsible tactic?
5. How does a political player know when he or she is abusing personal contacts?
6. Assume that you have recently joined a new employer. How would you be able to identify what types of behavior are likely to constitute political blunders?
7. What right does a company have to make judgments about an employee based on indiscreet behavior in private life?
8. Give an example from your own observations of insensitivity to cross-cultural differences being a political blunder.

CASE STUDY: THE WAL-MART ADVENTURES OF JULIE ROEHM

Julie Roehm was a high-profile ad executive from the auto industry. Wal-Mart hired the 36-year-old executive away from carmaker DaimlerChrysler AG in January 2006 to shake up the marketing department. As an automotive industry marketing executive, Roehm was known for her aggressive and contemporary car ideas. Her ads were edgy and memorable. She worked with rock bands, and created the idea of a football game with lingerie-clad models. The idea was nixed, but the "lingerie bowl" eventually ran on another channel during the Super Bowl.

Although she wanted to bring about a more daring and creative marketing approach for Wal-Mart, she knew that she was not a good cultural fit with the conservative Bentonville, Arkansas, retailing giant. One of her early moves was to paint the walls in her office chartreuse, covering up the former battleship gray.

In her new job as Wal-Mart's senior vice president for marking communications, Roehm moved swiftly. She produced new ads that took pokes at rivals, sponsored football on ESPN, and hired a new agency for Wal-Mart's $580 million account, the Interpublic Group of Draft FCB.

Roehm said she was ready for cultural friction, but she had learned that this was what change agents should expect: "Any time there's someone new or who represents change, you always get a feeling that's not always welcoming." She conceded: "My visibility created a general amount of animosity."

Wal-Mart Dumps Roehm

Wal-Mart fired senior vice president Julie Roehm and former company vice president Sean Womack in December 2006, backed up by a court filing in March 2007. The company accused the two of violating its policies against fraternization, and later claimed they carried on an affair and inappropriately extended business travel in order to spend additional time with each other at Wal-Mart's expense. The company also accused Roehm of accepting gifts from suppliers, misusing her company expense account, and pursuing a job with the Interpublic Group.

Wal-Mart has explicit rules in relation to supplier relationships. The policy states that its employees "must avoid conflicts of interests in supplier selection, such as directing business to a supplier owned or managed by a relative or friend." It also warns that executives aren't allowed to "have social or other relationships with suppliers, if such relationships would create the appearance of impropriety or give the perception that business influence is being exerted."

The Wal-Mart policy labeled "Gifts and Gratuities" states: "It is our policy that associates of the Company, regardless of their capacity, do not accept for their personal benefits, gratuities, tips, cash, samples, etc., from anyone buying from us or selling to us, or in any way serving our company." Even a cup of coffee as a gift is forbidden.

Revenge and Counterattack

In May 2007, Roehm began her counterattack on chief executive Lee Scott and other Wal-Mart executives. She claimed they accepted sweetheart deals and free airplane rides, and engaged in improper personal relationships. In a court filing, she contended that Wal-Mart applied its rules of conduct arbitrarily. Among her specific claims were that Scott accepted "preferential prices" on boats and jewelry from financier Irwin Jacobs, whose companies do everything from selling boats to Wal-Mart to buying unsold goods from the retailer. She also contended that Scott's relationship with Jacobs went "beyond a business relationship" and violated the corporation's conflict-of-interest guidelines.

Wal-Mart management dismissed the assertions, made in a filing in the U.S. District Court in Michigan, as did Jacobs. He called the accusations of preferential treatment "totally outrageous" and said they were without any substance. However, Jacobs acknowledged a long friendship with Scott. The two were close enough that their families took vacations together, and Jacobs attended the wedding of Scott's daughter. But he said there was no favoritism. "They pay their way; we pay our way," he said. "I've frequently told Scott, it's very difficult for me to go out with him because he always picks up the check. I'd like at some point to level up. He won't allow that to happen."

A Wal-Mart spokesperson said, "This lawsuit is about Julie Roehm and her misconduct. Her court filing shows how weak her case is. The allegations of impropriety involving our CEO Lee Scott are untrue."

As part of the countersuit, Wal-Mart released what it said were a "series of messages" obtained from Womack's wife and reports from unnamed coworkers who described a torrid affair between him and Roehm. It cited the e-mails and identified Roehm as writing, "I think about us together all of the time. Little moments like watching your face when you kiss me. . . ."

A Wal-Mart spokeswoman said the company decided to air the e-mails and other allegations because Roehm "made disparaging the company a centerpiece of her self-promotion campaign." The company was particularly upset about Roehm portraying herself as a victim of management panic over a sales slump and angst over provocative ad choices. She had criticized the company while entertaining offers for books and movie deals about herself.

Roehm's counterattack included a fierce defense of her short tenure as senior vice president of marketing communications and challenged the company's portrayal of her in its countersuit. She denied accepting gifts, insisted suppliers were told to bill the company for any meals, and said salacious descriptions of her relationship with Womack were false.

Roehm also alleged that Wal-Mart looked the other way when senior executives conducted affairs with subordinates, and allowed executives who owned retail stores to negotiate with subordinates on leases for those properties.

In June 2007, Roehm hired Michael Sitrick, the head of a Los Angeles public relations firm, to help her in her battle against Wal-Mart. Sitrick is known for going atomic on opponents, using "truth squads" (who hunt for inaccuracies in the media), "wheel-of-pain" tactics (negative publicity to quicken settlements), and high-profile journalists (who write profiles). The purpose of hiring the firm was to extract a huge settlement from Wal-Mart in negotiating the case. Sitrick said, "It doesn't take a lot of work to get Wal-Mart to come off as the bully. It's a clear David-and-Goliath situation. Julie is the underdog."

Roehm's suit against Wal-Mart was dismissed by a Michigan judge, who said that the suit would have to be pursued in Arkansas, where Wal-Mart is based. In November 2007, Roehm decided not to pursue the lawsuit against Wal-Mart, and stated that she was not receiving any money or compensation to settle the complaint. She gave the following as her reason for dropping the lawsuit: "I thought that a settlement agreement would be reached in a few weeks. Instead, the lawsuit has expanded into other issues, and has been more difficult and financially draining than I ever imagined."

Case Study Questions

1. Identify any political blunders that Julie Roehm might have committed during her brief tenure with Wal-Mart, and after she left the company.
2. In what way did the behavior of Wal-Mart management invite retaliation by Roehm?
3. How politically astute was Roehm in having accepted a position with Wal-Mart?
4. How politically smart was Julie Roehm in hiring a pit-bull-type public relations firm to help her obtain a big settlement from Wal-Mart?
5. If you were a top-level executive at Target or Kmart, would you hire Julie Roehm as the head of your marketing communications group? Explain your reasoning.

SOURCE: Adapted and excerpted from McWilliams, G., & Covert, J. (2007, May 26–27). Roehm claims Wal-Mart brass defy ethics rules. *Wall Street Journal,* A1, A5; McWilliams, G. (2007, March 21). Wal-Mart details Roehm firing. *Wall Street Journal,* B11; Conlin, M., & Berner, R. (2007, June 25). Out for blood? Who you gonna call? *BusinessWeek,* 39; McWilliams, G., Vranica, S., & Boudette, N. E. (2006, December 11). How a high flyer in marketing fell at Wal-Mart. *Wall Street Journal,* A1, A16; (2007, November 6). Roehm, Wal-Mart war ends. Retrieved 09/01/2007 from www.mediabuyerplanner.com.

POLITICAL SKILL-BUILDING EXERCISE 9

Blunder Recovery and Damage Control

We all make errors, so it is good to practice to plan in advance how you might deal with an embarrassing political blunder, faux pas, or error. In each of the following scenarios, one person will play the role of the person making the error, and the other person the target of the error. Students not participating in the role-play will offer feedback about the sincerity and potential effectiveness of the attempt at damage control.

Scenario 1: You are invited to a new-product development meeting. As friendly chatter during the warm-up phase of the meeting, you comment: "Can you imagine the egg on our faces today? We just released a cologne for men called Barn Musk. Some wacko product developer thought men would enjoy wearing cologne that smells like a barn, and that men wearing the cologne would attract more women." A man you had not known previously turns to you and says, "I am the vice president of research and development, and this product was my idea. So you think I'm wacko?"

Scenario 2: You are at a company picnic on a very hot and dry day. You participate in an intensive jogging activity, and after the jogging is complete you feel dehydrated. So you drink three beers, which is quite unusual for you because you are well aware of the dangers of alcohol, especially if you have to drive home. Somehow you lose your inhibitions, and you approach the CEO and make this comment: "You know, Jim, we all like you. But you have got to change in one way. You are the lowest-technology guy I ever met. Rumor is that you don't even know how to access your e-mail." With a smile on your face, you give Jim a big pat on the back and walk back to your buddies.

Later that night, you have recovered from drinking three beers while dehydrated. Now you wonder what you should do the next day when you report to work—assuming you still have a job.

REFERENCES

1. Rundle, R. L. (2007, April 24). Critical case: How an email rant jolted a big HMO. *Wall Street Journal,* A1, A16.

2. Spector, P. E., Chen, P. Y., & O'Connell, B. J. (2000, April). A longitudinal study of relations between job stressors and job strain while controlling for prior negative affectivity and strains. *Journal of Applied Psychology,* 211–218.

3. Presse Canadienne (2004, May 16). *L'Intimidation menace la productivité selon les chercheurs* [Intimidation threatens productivity according to researchers]. Retrieved 05/16/2007 from www.cyberpress.ca.

4. Quine, L. (1999, January). Workplace bullying in NHS community trust: Staff questionnaire survey. *British Medical Journal,* 228–232.

5. Lublin, J. S. (2007, January 30). How to best supervise internal runner-up for the job you got. *Wall Street Journal,* B1.

6. Quoted in McGregor, J. (2007, January 22). Sweet revenge: The power of retribution, spite, and loathing in the world of business. *BusinessWeek,* 64–70.

7. Aquino, K., Tripp, T. M., & Bies, R. J. (2001, February). How employees respond to personal offense: The effects of blame attribution, victim status, and offender status on revenge and reconciliation in the workplace. *Journal of Applied Psychology,* 52–59.

8. McGregor, J. (2007, January 22). Sweet revenge: The power of retribution, spite, and loathing in the world of business. *BusinessWeek,* 64–70 [pp. 67–68].

9. Cited in Sandberg, J. (2004, February 11). Sabotage 101: The sinister art of back-stabbing. *Wall Street Journal,* B1.

10. Machiavelli, N. (1940). *The Prince* [p. 730]. New York: The Modern Library.

11. Rynecki, D. (2004, April 5). Putting the muscle back in the bull. *Fortune,* 162–170.

12. Lublin, J. S. (2006, November 28). What to do when they don't hire you, but steal your ideas. *Wall Street Journal,* B1.

13. Lublin, J. S. (2006, November 28). What to do when they don't hire you.

14. Sonnenfeld, J. (2007, May 14). The real scandal at BP. *BusinessWeek,* 98.

15. Sandberg, J. (2007, April 17). The art of showing pure incompetence at an unwanted task. *Wall Street Journal,* B1.

16. Guyon, J. (2005, May 16). Jack Grubman is back. Just ask him. *Fortune,* 120; Kadlec, D. (2002, November 25). Did Sandy play dirty? *Time,* 21–22.

17. Furchgott, R. (1992, December). Career-building tactics. *Self,* 102.

18. Brown, G., Lawrence, T. B., & Robinson, S. L. (2005, July). Territoriality in organizations. *Academy of Management Review,* 577–594 [p. 577].

19. Brown, G., Lawrence, T. B., & Robinson, S. L. (2005, July). Territoriality in organizations. *Academy of Management Review,* 577–594 [p. 578].

20. Langley, M. (2006, December 22). Inside Mulally's "war room": A radical overhaul of Ford. *Wall Street Journal,* A10.

21. Kaplan, D. A. (2006, September 26). *Phone-records scandal at HP: To catch a leaker, Hewlett-Packard's chairwoman spied on the home-phone records of its board of directors.* Retrieved 09/06/2007 from www.newsweek/MSNB.com; Horowitz, A., Jacobson, D., McNichol, T., & Thomas, O. (2007, January/February). 101 dumbest moments in business. *Business 2.0,* 105.

22. Bianco, A. (2007, April 30). Wal-Mart's midlife crisis. *BusinessWeek,* 52.

23. Goleman, D., Boyatzis, R., & McKee, A. (2001, December). Primal leadership: The hidden driver of great performance. *Harvard Business Review,* 42–51.

24. Carr, D. (2006, December 18). This time, Judith Regan did it. *New York Times.* Retrieved 12/18/2006 from www.nytimes.com.

25. Elkind, P. (2004, October 18). The fall of the House of Grasso. *Fortune,* 286; Milton, P. (2007, May 9). *NYSE ex-chief wins round on pay bonanza.* Associated Press.

26. Associated Press. (2007, May 31). *Anti-Wal-Mart joke perceived as threat,* gets cashier fired.

27. Sandberg, J. (2005, May 25). Ah, the exit interview: Free at last, is it smart to be really candid? *Wall Street Journal,* B1.

28. Hymowitz, C. (2007, June 18). Personal boundaries shrink as companies punish bad behavior. *Wall Street Journal,* B1.

29. Sills, J. (2007, March/April). Love at work. *Psychology Today,* 64–65.

30. Ely, R. J., Meyerson, D., & Davidson, M. N. (2006, September). Rethinking political correctness. *Harvard Business Review,* 80.

31. Greising, D. (2006, August 27). Impatience no virtue on fast track. *Chicago Tribune,* 5-1, 5-12.

32. Survey cited in Shellenbarger, S. (2005, July 21). Ovulating? Depressed? The latest rules on what not to talk about at work. *Wall Street Journal,* D1.

33. Associated Press (2007, May 27). *Workers fired for gossiping lose appeal.*

34. Conlin, M. (2007, May 21). Do us a favor, take a vacation. *BusinessWeek,* 88–89.

35. Maynard, M., & Fackler, M. (2006, November 29). Low-key chief asserts himself as a leader at Toyota. *New York Times.* Retrieved 11/29/2006 from www.nytimes.com.

36. Cited in Loeb, M. (2007, April 1). A 12-step program that spells job security. Market/Watch syndicated story.

37. Glick, P., Larsen, S., Johnson, C., & Branstiter, H. (2005, December). Evaluation of women in low- and high-status jobs. *Psychology of Women Quarterly, 4,* 389–439; Fisher, A. (2006, November 8). What's wrong with dressing sexy at work? *Fortune,* n.p.

38. Mattioli, D. (2006, December 5). Sober thought: How to mix work, alcohol. *Wall Street Journal,* B10.

39. Joyce, A. (2006, September 10). Fired via e-mail, and other tales of poor exits. *Washington Post.* Retrieved 09/10/2006 from www.washingtonpost.com.

40. Cited in Lublin, J. S. (2005, August 30). How you can survive the dumbest thing you did to your boss. *Wall Street Journal,* B1.

41. Thomas, M. (2005). *A new attitude.* Franklin Lakes, NJ: Career Press.

TEN

THE CONTROL OF DYSFUNCTIONAL POLITICS

LEARNING OBJECTIVES

After having studied this chapter and done the exercises, you should be able to do the following:

1. Understand how employee perceptions of political behavior influence whether the behavior is dysfunctional.
2. Describe the consequences of dysfunctional politics in the workplace.
3. Explain how managers can control dysfunctional political behavior.
4. Recognize what the individual can do to protect himself or herself against negative political tactics.

Top-level management at Custom Research, Inc., of Minneapolis was ecstatic when the firm won the Malcolm Baldrige National Quality Award, administered by the National Institute of Standards and Quality. The award meant that the company, a national market research firm, was recognized as a leader in providing quality research to its customers, and also had outstanding business processes.

The next step was to participate in the award ceremony to be held in Florida. A problem facing management was that it could afford to send only

50 of its employees from multiple locations to the big celebration. It was apparent that every employee wanted to attend the award ceremony. The choice of which 50 employees to send was difficult. One approach was to base the decision on seniority or job title, but this could be unfair. Many less-senior workers contributed heavily to performing quality research, and so did workers whose job titles might not indicate their contribution to quality. Management wanted to avoid showing favoritism in choosing employees for the Florida trip. The nomination of employees for the trip by managers and supervisors was therefore excluded as a method of choosing who would take the trip.

To be as fair as possible, top-level management then put every employee's name in a hat—including the president and the cleaning crew. It was the only way to make certain that every person at every level of the company had an equal chance to attend the celebration.[1] As a result, no employee could complain that "politics" decided which employees would get the perk of a trip to the national award ceremony.

Our final chapter in the book focuses on how the organization and the individual can control excessive, and therefore dysfunctional, organizational politics. First we study the perception of organizational politics because employee perceptions of the extent and type of political behavior often determine whether the behavior is dysfunctional. We then describe some of the consequences of dysfunctional politics that make its control a worthwhile effort. After that, we shift to a discussion of how managers can control dysfunctional politics, and how individuals can counterattack negative politics directed against them.

THE PERCEPTION OF DYSFUNCTIONAL POLITICS IN ORGANIZATIONS

Many workers express dissatisfaction with their jobs and companies because of what they perceive to be excessive politics. Phrases expressing these perceptions include, "This place is a political jungle," "I refused a job as a supervisor because I couldn't take the politics," and "I became a telecommuter so I could avoid the office politics." Dysfunctional politics are often in the eye of the beholder, so the eye or perception is essential in understanding the possible negative impact of political behavior on workers.

The importance of employee perceptions of political behavior has been the subject of many research studies. Researchers have found that perceptions of organizational politics are associated with (a) lower levels of organizational commitment, job satisfaction, and job performance, and (b) higher levels of job anxiety, and intention to leave the organization.[2] Here we look at several studies that illuminate how worker perceptions of organizational politics influence worker behavior.

Organizational and Individual Factors Associated With Perceptions of Politics

A study with 501 regular members, civilian members, and public servants of the Royal Canadian Mounted Police indicated that four situational factors were associated with employees perceiving their organization to be political. Male and female employees were more likely to perceive their organization as being political if they occupied lower job levels, and saw themselves as not having much autonomy or the authority to make decisions independently. A third contributing factor was seeing the workplace as low in formalization (many rules and regulations). The fourth factor contributing to perceptions of politics was a negative evaluation of the climate (or culture) of the organization.

Dispositional variables, or personality factors, also played a role in perceptions of politics. Workers who were more Machiavellian, and had a stronger external locus of control (blaming the environment rather than themselves), tended to view their organization as more political.[3] The implication here is that a person with ruthless tendencies who typically blames fate on personal outcomes is more likely to perceive the work environment as political.

A study conducted with 267 employed undergraduates and their supervisors investigated how feedback on performance influenced perceptions of organizational politics. The students worked an average of 30 hours per week. Perceptions of politics were measured by a questionnaire containing statements such as, "Promotions around here are not valued much because how they are determined is so political." A major finding of the study was that there was an inverse, or negative, relationship between the amount of feedback and perceptions of organizational politics. Specifically, when workers received high levels of informal feedback from their supervisors and coworkers, the workers were less likely to perceive the workplace as political. Supervisory feedback was found to be more influential than coworker feedback. An explanation offered for the results is that when a supervisor gives inadequate or unclear feedback about performance expectations, decisions may appear much more politically driven.[4]

Political skill is another individual factor that might influence how badly a person is affected by perceptions of politics. A group of researchers investigated how political skill influences the amount of depressive symptoms a person develops when he or she perceives the work environment to be political. An example of a depressive symptom is, "Over the past month, things that usually don't bother me have bothered me." Study participants who scored low on political skill developed the most depressive symptoms when they perceived the climate to be highly political. In contrast, those participants with high political skill appeared to enjoy a political environment—and were more likely to have depressive symptoms in a nonpolitical work environment.[5]

The research of Gerald Ferris, G. S. Russ, and P. M. Fandt further explains the role of political skills in softening the potential dysfunctional effects of organizational politics. Individuals high in political skill may view an environment of heavy organizational politics as an opportunity to utilize that expertise instead of as a stressor. In contrast, individuals low in political skill, and therefore low in perceived control, are likely to see a highly charged political environment as a threat. As a result, these people are more likely to be stressed, as the study cited above confirms.[6]

The Impact of Perception of Organizational Politics on Job Performance

Employee age is a key individual or demographic variable affecting how the perception of politics might influence job performance. The age factor is tied in with the **conservation of resources theory**. This theory states that stress occurs with the loss of resources, and that events are stressful to the extent that they make demands that outstrip the resources used to meet those demands. Environmental conditions in the workplace, such as the perception of organizational politics, may threaten to (or actually) deplete resources such as status, position, or self-esteem.

Three studies were conducted with working adults to examine the interaction of perceptions of organizational politics and age on job performance. In other words, does a person's age influence whether his or her perception of politics will influence job performance? Results across the three studies strongly supported the hypothesis that higher perceptions of organizational politics tend to decrease the job performance of older workers. However, the perception of politics did not influence the job performance of younger workers. The authors of the study suggest that the older workers may have fewer resources than younger workers Part of the reason for the depletion of resources is that older workers have faced so much work stress over the years.[7]

Being young may help a person shrug off the impact of politics on performance, and being conscientious might have a similar effect. Data were collected from more than 800 employees in four organizations. A major finding was that when workers perceived average to high levels of organizational politics, the personality factor of conscientiousness was related to job performance. When workers perceived low levels of organizational politics, conscientiousness was not related to job performance. Similarly, perceptions of organizational politics were negatively related to job performance only among workers of average to low levels of conscientiousness.[8] A plausible interpretation of these findings is that a worker who is conscientious will usually not let organizational politics interfere with his or her job performance.

An instrument designed to measure symptoms of dysfunctional politics in the workplace is presented in Exhibit 10.1. Apply the instrument to any workplace familiar to you.

THE CONSEQUENCES OF DYSFUNCTIONAL POLITICS

The consequences of dysfunctional politics overlap with the perceptions of organizational politics because the impact of many political actions only exists in terms of how the actions are perceived. Suppose a division head appoints her favorite niece as a "special executive assistant," a position that carries high pay and a private office. The majority of people who perceive the division head's move to be nepotism will be upset, and perhaps experience job stress. Yet some people may perceive the promotion as making good business sense and not as political because promoting somebody you trust to a key position is sound business practice.

As just implied, a negative consequence of dysfunctional politics is distress for individuals. Many people experience distress, for example, when they are the victim of backstabbing, or when they lose out on a promotion because a rival was shrewd enough to lose to the boss in a golf match.

A high degree of organizational politics becomes dysfunctional when the political activity distracts the worker, and job performance suffers as a

Exhibit 10.1 Symptoms of Dysfunctional Office Politics (the DOOP Scale)

The 10 statements below concern ethics in interpersonal relationships on the job. The more frequently any of these actions take place, the more likely it is that the organization or organizational unit is beset with dysfunctional office politics.

1. A conflict between two or more persons or groups was resolved by who held the most power rather than what would have made sense and would have worked better.
2. A person or group "got even" in some way with another person or group.
3. Information about what was going on at work was withheld from a person or group.
4. Information was reported about a person or group that has been intentionally exaggerated, misconstrued, and/or made mostly untrue by some other person or group.
5. A person or group was led to believe one thing when another was clearly true.
6. A person or group agreed with another person or group solely to "keep the boat from rocking."
7. A person's or group's worthwhile efforts or initiatives were intentionally undermined.
8. Confidential or unfavorable information about a person or group was reported and/or released in order to gain a special advantage.
9. A person or group who looked at things differently and had different points of view was punished and/or silenced by another person or group.
10. An organizational decision was based on self-interest rather than what made sense and would have worked better.

SOURCE: Reproduced with permission from Anderson, T. P. (1994). Creating measures of dysfunctional office and organizational politics: The DOOP and Short Form DEEP Scales. *Psychology: A Journal of Human Behavior, 31*(2), 34.

consequence. The distraction is strongest when the person does not want to engage in political behavior.[9] Instead of concentrating on the job, the person might engage in countermaneuvers against the political players, such as retaliating against an accusatory e-mail. The political victim might feel compelled to send an e-mail explaining his or her side of the story.

Another type of distraction caused by organizational politics is too much focus internally and not enough externally on customers.[10] For example, a manufacturing supervisor might spend a couple of hours during the working day planning a territorial battle against the finance group. A better use of those hours might have been working on adding value for customers. Managers attempting to resolve political disputes may also divert too much attention from positive matters such as dealing with customers and developing strategy.

Two studies with a combined total of over 650 workers including 64 firefighters investigated the relationship between the perception of organizational politics and feelings of disengagement from the job. When workers who perceived considerable politics did not have much emotional support from their supervisors, they tended to become disengaged from their work. When emotional support was high, the tendencies toward disengagement were much less noticeable, despite the perception of politics.[11]

Excessive political behavior in organizations can also be dysfunctional because it slows down decision making. Many meetings end without a decision being made because opposing factions want the decision their way so their side looks stronger. At one chemical company, an ongoing debate raged regarding whether to manufacture a wood sealer that would last three to four years on most fences, decks, and porches. One side argued that the new sealer would be an enormous seller. The other side agreed, but said that the revenue would not compensate for the lost sales from people who purchased and applied wood sealer annually. In the meantime, a competitor entered the market with a thick, long-lasting sealer, and gained a sizable chunk of the market.

MANAGERIAL CONTROL OF DYSFUNCTIONAL POLITICS

To control the negative consequences of politics, managers must minimize or eliminate dysfunctional organizational politics. A far-reaching strategy would be for managers to be aware of the factors contributing to politics as described in Chapter 1, and then minimize those conditions. For example, if the environment is uncertain and turbulent, top-level managers might attempt to stabilize the environment by such measures as eliminating acquisitions and downsizings for two years. This approach would be helpful also because some of the ambiguity that fosters excessive politics would be eliminated. The suggestions for minimizing dysfunctional politics presented in this section and outlined in Exhibit 10.2 relate to some of the causes of politics, and also offer new perspectives.

Create a Prosperous Organization

An ideal approach to minimizing dysfunctional politics is to have a prosperous organization in which people can earn high compensation and be promoted without having to discredit other individuals and organizational units. When people are well compensated financially and are enthusiastic about their work, they tend to concentrate more on tasks and less on posturing. Behaviors such as backstabbing are more prevalent during periods of austerity, including downsizing.

Business writer Jared Sandberg provides an example of how growth and excitement can reduce political behavior. He observed a couple of years ago

Exhibit 10.2 Managerial Control of Dysfunctional Organizational Politics

1. Create a prosperous organization.
2. Set good examples at the executive level.
3. Establish a climate of open communication.
4. Develop congruence between individual and organizational goals.
5. Minimize favoritism and have objective standards of performance.
6. Reward honest feedback.
7. Emphasize the use of teams to reduce self-serving behavior.
8. Threaten to discuss questionable information publicly.
9. Hire people with integrity and honesty.

that the knowledge-outsourcing industry in India was growing so fast that it had not yet fostered the level of backstabbing, turf wars, and stealing credit often found in mature industries. In fact, if a boss plays favorites in India, he or she will be reprimanded by an HR representative.[12]

Set Good Examples at the Executive Level

Organizational culture is a strong determinant of the amount and type of political behavior, and executives help to establish the culture. As a consequence, top-level management that sets a positive example of nonpolitical behavior will encourage nonpolitical behavior throughout the organization. Hundreds of examples of nonpolitical behavior could be cited, but here are two key such behaviors: (1) When filling a key position, the CEO conducts a company-wide internal search, rather than simply handing the position to a crony. (2) Workers who express constructive disagreement about the company strategy are not fired or demoted.

An example of how an executive might attempt to set the stage to decrease dysfunctional political behavior took place when Dieter Zetsche became CEO of DaimlerChrysler AG in 2005. The new CEO said that a gathering of dealers in Las Vegas was "a great chance to set the tone from the beginning," and to make clear that under his leadership "what counts is performance," not internal alliances.[13] (Zetsche is no longer CEO, and Chrysler has been sold, but his message is still valid.)

Establish a Climate of Open Communication

Dysfunctional politics often arise from uncertainty and insecurity. Assume that organizational members are informed truthfully about such matters as the criteria for promotion, whether a merger will take place, or whether a product line will be outsourced. Under these circumstances, they will be less likely to engage in excessive networking in the hopes of forming the right alliance, and discrediting others. Open communication is also helpful for letting everyone know the basis for allocating resources, thus reducing the amount of politicking.

The potential role of open communication in reducing dysfunctional politics is illustrated by the words of Susan Kropf. When she was named president and chief operating officer for Avon Products Inc., she was asked, "How did you avoid being hurt by office politics?" Kropf replied, "I have never really been involved in office politics that much. I try to keep egos out of things and stay focused on doing the best job I can. I'm direct with people, and I let them know that I don't have any hidden agenda. When you demonstrate that, other people play back to you in the same way."[14]

Develop Congruence Between Individual and Organizational Goals

When individuals and organizations share the same goals, dysfunctional organizational politics will often be reduced. Sharing the same goals is referred to as **goal congruence**. If political maneuvering will interfere with the company and individuals achieving their goals, workers with goal congruence are less likely to engage in excessive political behavior. The strategy works much like profit sharing. If workers participate in the profits, they are less likely to waste resources. A political example is that if a marketing specialist wants the company to succeed, he or she is less likely to agree with a bad idea by the marketing head just to please the latter.

A study conducted by L. A. Witt with 1,200 workers in five organizations provides support for the importance of goal congruence as a way of decreasing political behavior that could be dysfunctional. Witt concluded that one way to approach the negative impact of organizational politics is to ensure that group members hold the appropriate goal priorities. In this way, they will have a greater sense of control over and understanding of the workplace, and thus be less affected by organizational politics.[15]

Minimize Favoritism and Have Objective Standards of Performance

For many people, favoritism is synonymous with dysfunctional politics, so any steps managers can take to lessen favoritism will decrease the climate of negative political behavior. Top-level managers not practicing favoritism themselves would be a starting point in minimizing favoritism. If group members believe that getting the boss to like them is much less important for obtaining rewards than good job performance, they will kiss up to the boss less frequently. In an attempt to minimize favoritism, the manager must reward workers who impress him or her through performance-related activities.

A standard antidote to excessive favoritism, as well as other forms of political behavior, is for the organization to maintain objective standards of performance. People have less need to behave politically when their contribution can be measured directly, such as a product development specialist helping create a successful product, or a tech support specialist fixing difficult IT problems. Setting objective standards of performance is not so easy for managerial and professional jobs because subjective evaluations are often used to evaluate performance in these positions. For example, it requires considerable personal judgment to decide whether a public relations specialist has done an effective job of enhancing the reputation of the company. So the specialist would still need to work hard at pleasing his or her manager.

Reward Honest Feedback

A dysfunctional form of politics is for people to say positive things about programs and proposals just to avoid falling into disfavor with managers. To cite the most famous adage about organizational politics, more people will be willing to say that the "emperor has no clothes" if making this statement does not lead to punishment. A suggested way to get rid of yes-people is to reward those who offer you honest feedback, even if it is not what you want to hear. Managers must let people know that they are looking for the unvarnished truth. Here is an example: "Alan, the last thing I wanted to hear today was that we are going to miss another production target. But I had to know. It took some courage for you to come in here. I appreciate that."[16]

Emphasize Teams to Reduce Self-Serving Behavior

As suggested by Jonathon R. B. Halbesleben and Anthony R. Wheeler, organizations might rely on teams to reduce dysfunctional political behavior. Teams sometimes reduce self-serving behavior because the team members identify with the group and may therefore want to be good team players. Team members who act too strongly on their own behalf, such as stealing credit for ideas, risk discipline including ostracism from the group.[17] Although team structures may reduce some aspects of dysfunctional politics, many team members will still go out of their way to gain individual recognition and disparage others.

Closely related to focusing on team structures is top-level management fostering "we" thinking rather than "us against them." Workers throughout the organization should be told frequently that they are stronger working cooperatively rather than engaging in infighting.[18]

Threaten to Discuss Questionable Information Publicly

Dysfunctional politics can sometimes be constrained by a threat to discuss questionable information in a public forum. People who practice devious politics usually want to operate secretly and privately. They are willing to drop hints and innuendoes, and engage in other forms of backstabbing, providing they will not be identified as the source. An effective way to stop the discrediting of others is to discuss the topic publicly.[19] As the team leader, suppose a team member says to you, "I'm worried about Jeanne. She looks so rundown lately that I think her personal problems are beginning to interfere with her work." Using the technique of threatening to discuss questionable information publicly, you might say, "What you say sounds serious. I would like you to bring it up in a team meeting with Jeanne present."

In addition to the manager threatening public discussion of questionable information, workers throughout the organization should be encouraged to do the same. Team member A might inform team member B that team member C said he had terrible IT skills. Following the threat of open disclosure, B would say to A, "Enough of these accusations. Let's meet with C and talk about what she said about me."

Hire People With Integrity and Honesty

A proactive way to decrease dysfunctional political behavior is to hire people whose personality and past behavior predict that they will behave with integrity and honesty. Currently, this approach is emphasized in hiring CEOs and in selecting political appointees. The idea of this careful screening is to minimize the chances that the person will embarrass the company or the political party once in office. Personality testing for Machiavellian tendencies and a lack of conscientiousness can sometimes detect people who might engage in devious politics. Reference checking is likely to be more definitive, and the reference check should search for answers to questions such as: (1) Which type of office politics did this person use? (2) Might you tell me about the most devious things the candidate did during your acquaintance?

In addition to attempting to hire people with integrity, it is also helpful to describe expectations about what types of political behavior will not be tolerated. For instance, job candidates might be informed that making excessive use of e-mail to defend one's position or to criticize others, and turf wars are unacceptable behaviors.[20]

PROTECTING YOURSELF AGAINST NEGATIVE POLITICS

Another key aspect of the control of organizational politics is to defend yourself when you are the target of negative political tactics. Not being able to defend yourself against negative tactics directed at you can result in such negative consequences as day-by-day distress, lowered job performance, and a sullied reputation. Here we describe four ways of protecting yourself against negative tactics.

Understand Political Forces Within the Organization

As with controlling politics from the executive suite, a strong defense is awareness of political forces within the organization. As philosopher Plato advised about 2,500 years ago, "Those who are too smart to engage in politics are punished by being governed by those who are dumber."[21] When workers understand that political forces exist, they are less likely to be distressed by negative politics. This phenomenon is referred to as the *antidote hypothesis* because knowledge helps overcome the problem of negative politics.[22] An awareness of political forces would encompass the type of information presented throughout this book, yet here is a specific example:

> You are making a PowerPoint presentation at a meeting. You have detected that one of the meeting participants is a Machiavellian who enjoys manipulating people by needlessly pointing to their mistakes. During your presentation, he interrupts to say, "I notice that you keep switching the font size on your headlines. What is the problem?" Instead of apologizing to the Machiavellian, you stand your ground and say, "You have made an interesting observation, and perhaps I will standardize my fonts in the future. For now, I would like you to follow the presentation despite the frequent changes in font size."

The point here is that you have observed that the Machiavellian is trying to upset you. Your approach acknowledges the criticism without you losing your cool or counterattacking.

Develop a Clean Record and a Positive Reputation

A major protection against negative politics directed toward you is to have a clean record and a positive reputation. The clean record is particularly useful in protecting against blackmail, such as another person threatening to disclose a kickback you receive unless you grant him or her a favor. Similarly, a person who develops a positive reputation can more readily defend against negative accusations: His or her side of the story is more likely to be believed.

As part of developing a positive reputation, it is useful to document your side of the story on any problem or issue that could be used against you by a rival. Defending yourself in this manner is often referred to as *posterior protection,* but is unfortunately necessary in some highly competitive environments.[23] A loan specialist in a subprime mortgage operation might believe that a particular loan is too risky, even for a company specializing in high-risk mortgages. The specialist might document his or her side of the story, mentioning his or her opposition to the loan. In this way, a Machiavellian in the office cannot blame the specialist if the loan fails.

Developing a good reputation helps a person defend against dysfunctional politics in another important way. With a good reputation, a person has more economic independence. A person with an excellent reputation more readily develops an external network that facilitates finding new employment should he or she lose out in a political battle. A manager might perceive a talented person as a rival, and therefore "tap" him or her to be on the next downsizing list. The person with a good reputation can more readily bounce back from an unwarranted job loss of this type.

Extend an Olive Branch to Rivals

A straightforward approach to defending oneself against attacks by rivals is to make peace with and befriend them. In this way, it is possible that the person attempting to discredit or manipulate you will cease the hostilities. In some cases, it is almost hopeless to win over an enemy, yet extending an olive branch is usually worth a try. Career coach Deborah Brown-Volkman says, "It's harder to be mean to someone you like."[24]

You will recall the example of the person who criticized the variation in font size during a PowerPoint presentation. The person being criticized might meet with the criticizer later, and say, "I enjoy working with you even though you go a little heavy on the criticism. What suggestions do you have so we can work better together?"

Confront Backstabbers

Much has been written in the business press about confronting backstabbers because backstabbing is perhaps the most widespread form of dysfunctional politics. Almost all of the advice centers on calmly and firmly confronting the person who the evidence indicates is backstabbing you. A face-to-face confrontation is usually the best approach to dealing with the backstabber. Even if the confrontation does not repair the damage, talking can prevent resentment from building up and make you feel better. Confrontation may surprise your attacker, who probably assumes that you have not heard the negative things said about you.[25]

Treat the backstabbing incident like a business problem to be solved, instead of getting into an emotional tirade. Present the details in a manner such as, "You have been telling our boss and others that I ignore customer needs when I make suggestions for business process improvement. I want to know why you are criticizing me to others. Let's talk about the problem." The backstabber will sometimes deny having made the criticism, yet will nevertheless discontinue the behind-the-back negative comments.

A proactive approach to dealing with backstabbers is to inoculate yourself against them by expressing genuine admiration wherever you can.[26] In a sense, you build social capital that decreases the likelihood of a negative political actor making you a target. Find honest ways to compliment coworkers—even those you like the least. You might send e-mails to potential backstabbers complimenting them on something that went well, such as having received a recognition award. The person you praise is less likely to look for ways to diminish your standing in the company or unit.

Another perspective on dealing with backstabbers is to recognize your contribution to being backstabbed. Jerry B. Harvey reasons that backstabbing always occurs with the help of the person being slighted. "It is clear that backstabbing is not a crime committed by a solitary individual acting in isolation," Harvey writes. You need to confront yourself about your role in the process of being backstabbed.[27] For example, if you had not said negative things about a second party, the third party would not have had the ammunition to backstab you. As stated above, with a clean record you have less to fear about being attacked by negative politics.

SUMMARY

Employee perceptions of political behavior have been widely studied. One study found that employees were more likely to perceive their organization as political when (1) they occupied lower-level positions, (2) they saw themselves as having limited autonomy, (3) the workplace had low formalization, and (4) the employees had a negative evaluation of the culture. Also, workers who were more Machiavellian and had an external locus of control saw more politics. One study found a negative relationship between the amount of feedback and perceptions of political behavior. Another study found that workers with good political skill were less likely to suffer depressive symptoms as a result of perceiving organizational politics.

Results across three studies indicated that higher perceptions of organizational politics tend to decrease the job performance of older workers, whereas the effect was not found for younger workers. Another study indicated that conscientious employees do not experience lower job performance when they perceive average-to-high organizational politics. Perceptions of politics were negatively related to performance only among workers of average-to-low conscientiousness.

Dysfunctional politics can lead to distress for individuals. A high degree of organizational politics becomes dysfunctional when the political activity is distracting, resulting in lower job performance. Too much politics can also lead to an internal focus rather than paying enough attention to customers. Too much organizational politics can lead to employee disengagement when employees do not receive much emotional support from the supervisor. Excessive political behavior can also slow down decision making.

Suggestions for managerial control of dysfunctional politics include: (1) Create a prosperous organization with ample resources; (2) set good examples at the executive level; (3) establish a climate of open communication; (4) develop congruence between individual and organizational goals; (5) minimize favoritism and have objective standards of performance; (6) reward honest feedback; (7) emphasize teams to reduce self-serving behavior; (8) threaten to discuss questionable information publicly; and (9) hire people with integrity and honesty.

Suggestions for protecting yourself against negative politics include: (1) Understand political forces within the organization; (2) develop a clean record and a positive reputation; (3) extend an olive branch to rivals; and (4) confront backstabbers.

QUESTIONS AND ACTIVITIES

1. Visualize any place in which you have worked where you perceived the environment to be political. What specifically led you to the perception that the environment was political?

2. When subordinates complain about excessive politics, one CEO tells them, "If you can't stand the heat, get out of the kitchen." What does this executive mean, and what do you think of her advice?

3. Explain how a barista at Starbucks might experience goal congruence with the company.
4. Give two examples of objective performance standards in your field that would be useful in minimizing political behavior.
5. Reflect back on several teams you have been part of, either on the job or in school. To what extent was it true that team members tended to minimize self-serving behavior?
6. Identify several behaviors a person might engage in so he or she would be perceived as not engaging in excessive politics?
7. Give two examples of opening lines you might use in a conversation designed to confront a coworker who you heard was backstabbing you.

CASE STUDY: THE NIGHTMARE IN THE LOGISTICS DEPARTMENT

Larry Smits was happy to join the distribution department of his company as a logistics specialist. His position centered on keeping track of shipments to customers and from vendors. A distribution specialist works extensively with computers to track shipments, but part of the job description involves telephone and face-to-face contact with company insiders and outsiders. As Larry enthusiastically explained his new job to his girlfriend, "Here's a great opportunity for me. I'll be using a sophisticated software system, and I'll have lots of contact with a variety of people. I'll be talking to marketing executives, purchasing agents, truckers, package-delivery people, and office assistants.

"Equally good, I'll be learning about a very important part of the business. If the company doesn't ship goods to customers, we can't collect money. And if we don't receive shipments of supplies that we need, we can't produce anything ourselves."

During the first four months on the job, Larry's enthusiasm continued. The job proved to be as exciting as he anticipated. Larry got along well with all his coworkers and developed his closest friendship with Rudy Bianchi, a senior distribution specialist. Rudy said that since he had several more years' experience than Larry, he would be willing to help him with any job problem he encountered. One day Larry took Rudy up on his offer. Larry was having a little difficulty understanding how to verify the accuracy of tariffs paid to several European countries. Part of Larry's job was to make sure the company was paying its fair share of tariffs, but no more than necessary. Larry sent Rudy an e-mail message asking for clarification on three tariff questions. Rudy answered promptly and provided Larry with useful information.

When Larry next saw Rudy in person during lunch, he thanked him again for the technical assistance. "No problem," said Rudy. "I told you that I'm always willing to help a buddy. By sharing knowledge, we multiply our effectiveness." Larry detected a trace of insincerity in Rudy's message, but later thought he might be overreacting to Rudy's colorful way of expressing himself.

Several days later, Larry was reviewing a work assignment with his supervisor, Ellie Wentworth. She said to him, "How are you coming along with the problems you were having understanding how to verify tariffs? That's a key part of your job, you know."

Larry explained to Wentworth that he wasn't having any real problems, but that he had asked for clarification on a couple of complicated rates. He also pointed out that he quickly obtained the clarification he needed. Larry thought to himself, "Oh, I guess Ellie must have misinterpreted a comment by Rudy about my clarifying a few tariff rates with him. I doubt Rudy would have told our boss that I was having trouble. Why should I be paranoid?"

One week later, Rudy stopped by Larry's cubicle. At the moment, Larry had the classified ad section of the *Los Angeles Times* on his desk. "Are you job hunting, Larry? You're a rising star in our department. Why look elsewhere?"

"I'm not job hunting," said Larry. "I was just curious to see what kind of demand exists for logistics specialists. It's just part of my interest in the field. It's reassuring to know we're part of a growing profession."

"That's a great answer," said Rudy. "I was just pulling your chain a little anyway."

A week later, Ellie was reviewing some work assignments with Larry. As the discussion about the work assignment was completed, Ellie said, "I think highly of how you are progressing in your job Larry, but I want to make sure of one thing. Before we give you another major assignment, I want to know if you are happy in your job. If for any reason, you are planning to leave the company, please let us know now."

"What are you talking about?" said Larry with a puzzled expression. "I intend to be with the company for along, long time. I can't imagine what gave you the impression that I am not happy here."

As Larry left the office, he was furious. He began to wonder if someone might be spreading malicious rumors about him. He muttered silently, "It couldn't be Rudy. He's supposed to be my friend, my mentor. But I have to get to the root of this problem. I feel like I'm being sabotaged."

Case Study Questions

1. What devious technique might Rudy, or another coworker, be using against Larry?
2. What motivation might a coworker have for raising questions about Larry's job knowledge and loyalty to the company?
3. How should Larry deal with his suspicions?
4. How effectively has Ellie dealt with her two concerns about Larry?
5. In what ways is Rudy a backstabber?

SOURCE: Reprinted with permission from DuBrin, A. J. (2004). *Applying Psychology: Individual and Organizational Effectiveness,* p. 252. Upper Saddle River, NJ: Pearson/Prentice Hall.

POLITICAL SKILL-BUILDING EXERCISE 10

Confronting the Backstabber in the Logistics Department

The case about the nightmare in the logistics department serves as the background material for this role-play. One student plays the role of Larry Smits, who recently joined the logistics department. Another person plays the role of Rudy Bianchi, the supposedly friendly helper. Larry begins to think that it is Rudy who is spreading those malicious rumors about him. In the role-play scenario, Larry decides to have a"discussion" with Rudy about what has been happening. Larry is quite upset, yet he has no proof that he is being backstabbed by Rudy, and Rudy is defensive about having backstabbed Larry.

Observers of the role-play will look for Larry's confrontation skills, as well as whether the problem appears to be resolved. Look to see if it appears that Larry and Rudy will be able to salvage a working relationship.

REFERENCES

1. Adapted and expanded from McDargh, E. (2007). *Retaining employees and customers is a family affair.* Retrieved 09/20/2007 from the Work 911.com supersite, www.Work911.com.

2. Research reviewed in O'Connor, W. E., & Morrison, T. G. (2001, May). A comparison of situational and dispositional predictors of perceptions of organizational politics. *Journal of Psychology,* 301–312 [p. 301].

3. O'Connor, W. E., & Morrison,T. G. (2001, May). A comparison of situational and dispositional predictors of perceptions of organizational politics. *Journal of Psychology,* 301–312.

4. Rosen, C. C., Levy, P. E., & Hall, R. J. (2006, January). Placing perceptions of politics in the context of the feedback environment, employee attitudes, and job performance. *Journal of Applied Psychology,* 211–220.

5. Brouer, R. L., Ferris, G. R., Hochwarter, W. A., Laird, M. D., & Gilmore, D. C. (2006). The strain-related reactions to perceptions of organizational politics as a workplace stressor: Political skill as a neutralizer. In E. Vigoda-Gadot & A. Drory (Eds.), *Handbook of organizational politics* (pp. 187–206). Northampton, MA: Edward Elgar.

6. Ferris, G. R., Russ, G. S., & Fandt, P. M. (1989). Politics in organizations. In R. A. Giacalone, & P. Rosenfeld (Eds.), *Impression management in the organization* (pp. 143–170). Hillsdale, NJ: Lawrence Erlbaum.

7. Treadway, D. C., Ferris, G. R., Hochwarter, W., Perrewe, P., Witt, L. A., & Goodman, J. M. (2005, September). The role of age in the perception of politics–job performance relationship: A three-study constructive replication. *Journal of Applied Psychology,* 872–881.

8. Hochwarter, W. A., Witt, L. A., Kacmar, K. M. (2000, June). Perceptions of organizational politics as a moderator of the relationship between conscientiousness and job performance. *Journal of Applied Psychology,* 472–478.

9. Hochwarter, W. A., Kolodinsky, R. W., Witt, L. A., Hall, A. T., Ferris, G. R., & Kacmar, M. K. (2006). Competing perspectives on the role of understanding in the politics perceptions–job performance relationship: A test of the "antidote" versus "distraction" hypotheses. In E. Vigoda-Gadot & A. Drory (Eds.), *Handbook of organizational politics* (pp. 271–285). Northampton, MA: Edward Elgar.

10. Martin, C. (2004, May 16). *Office politics.* Retrieved 08/17/2007 from www.nfiresearch.com.

11. Halbesleben, J. R. B., & Wheeler, A. R. (2006). The relationship between perceptions of politics, social support, withdrawal and performance. In E. Vigoda-Gadot & A. Drory (Eds.), *Handbook of organizational politics* (pp. 253–270). Northampton, MA: Edward Elgar.

12. Sandberg, J. (2007, February 27). How long can India keep office politics out of outsourcing? *Wall Street Journal,* B1.

13. Boudette, N. E., & Power, S. (2005, November 28). New Daimler Chrysler CEO targets "infighting, intrigues." *Wall Street Journal,* B1.

14. Quoted in Martinez, M. N. (2000–2005). *Politics come with the office.* Retrieved from www.graduateengineer.com. Copyright © 2000–2005 Career Recruitment Media, Inc.

15. Witt, L. A. (1998, August). Enhancing organizational goal congruence: A solution to organizational politics. *Journal of Applied Psychology,* 666–674.

16. *Manager's Edge* (2006, Spring). Get rid of "yes men." [Special bulletin]. *Manager's Edge,* 2.

17. Halbesleben, J. R. B., & Wheeler, A. R. (2006). The relationship between perceptions of politics, social support, withdrawal and performance. In E. Vigoda-Gadot & A. Drory (Eds.), *Handbook of organizational politics* (pp. 253–270) [p. 266]. Northampton, MA: Edward Elgar.

18. *Manager's Edge* (2006, November). Create "positive politics." *Manager's Edge,* 1.

19. Vecchio, R. P. (2000). *Organizational behavior* (4th ed.) [p. 136]. Fort Worth, TX: Dryden Press.

20. Halbesleben, J. R. B., & Wheeler, A. R. (2006). The relationship between perceptions of politics, social support, withdrawal and performance. In E. Vigoda-Gadot & A. Drory (Eds.), *Handbook of organizational politics* (pp. 253–270) [p. 265]. Northampton, MA: Edward Elgar.

21. Plato (1967). *Plato in twelve volumes,* Vol. 10, trans. R. G. Bury. Cambridge, MA: Harvard University Press.

22. Hochwarter, W. A., Witt, L. A., & Kacmar, K. M. (2000, June). Perceptions of organizational politics as a moderator of the relationship between conscientiousness and job performance. *Journal of Applied Psychology,* 472–478 [p. 273].

23. Sandberg, J. (2005, June 8). Covering yourself is counter productive but may save your job. *Wall Street Journal,* B1.

24. Quoted in Maher, K. (2004, February 10). The jungle: Focus on recruitment, pay and getting ahead. *Wall Street Journal,* B1.

25. Jacobs, D. L. (1995, February). Disarming a back-stabber. *Working Woman,* 52.

26. Rise above office politics: Gain allies without playing hard ball. (1999, August). *Executive Strategies,* 1.

27. Harvey, J. B. (1999). *How come every time I get stabbed in the back my fingerprints are on the knife? And other meditations on management.* San Francisco: Jossey-Bass.

GLOSSARY

Alpha executive An executive who is ambitious, self-confident, competitive, and brash.

Apprising The influence agent explaining why a request or proposal is likely to benefit the target person individually.

Backstabbing A widely known devious political tactic in which another person pretends to be nice to you but is really plotting to damage or ruin your reputation.

Business etiquette A special code of behavior required in work situations.

Buy-in A situation in which workers are willing to go along with an initiative because they feel they will benefit from the change or play an important role in the change.

Centrality Power stemming from being close to power.

Coalition A specific arrangement of parties working together to combine their influence.

Coercive power The power to punish for noncompliance or poor performance.

Connection power The use of people in your network who can influence the person with whom you are dealing.

Conservation of resources theory A theory stating that stress occurs with the loss of resources, and that events are stressful to the extent that they make demands that outstrip the resources used to meet those demands.

Co-optation The merging or incorporating of another power group or individual for the purpose of controlling or silencing a counterpart.

Coworker exchanges Exchanges or interactions among people who report to the same supervisor.

Dependence perspective The explanation that one person accrues powers by others being dependent on him or her for things they value.

Expert power The ability to influence others through specialized skills, knowledge, and ability.

Favoritism Giving preferential treatment to people the manager likes personally.

Goal congruence The individual and the organization sharing the same goals.

Impression management A specific form of social influence behavior directed at enhancing one's image by drawing attention to oneself.

Influence The process of affecting the thoughts, behavior, and feelings of another person.

Information power The power stemming from formal control over the information people need to do their work.

Interpersonal citizenship behavior Citizenship behavior directed toward coworkers and immediate others.

Leader–member exchange (LMX) theory An explanation of leadership stating that the quality of leader–subordinate exchange relationships determines the nature of many outcomes for the organization and subordinate.

Legitimate power The lawful right to make a decision and expect compliance.

Machiavellianism An attitude in which it is acceptable to treat people as a means to an end. A person with Machiavellian tendencies is said to represent the epitome of the negative organizational politician.

Managing up The ability to influence your boss to invest in your ideas and advancement.

Micromanagement The close monitoring of most aspects of a group member's activities by the manager or leader.

Negative affectivity A tendency to experience aversive emotional states. Also, a pervasive predisposition to experience emotional stress that includes feelings of nervousness, tension, and worry.

Nepotism is a form of favoritism based on family membership. The definition sometimes extends to close friends.

Nodes The individuals (or actors) in the network.

Organizational citizenship behavior (OCB) Discretionary individual behavior not directly or explicitly recognized by the formal reward system, which in the aggregate promotes the efficient and effective functioning of the organization. It is also a willingness to work for the good of the organization without the promise of a specific reward.

Organizational culture A system of shared values and beliefs that influence worker behavior.

Organizational politics Informal approaches to gaining power and advantage through means other than merit or luck.

Personal power Power derived from the person rather than the organization.

Political behavior in organizations A wide variety of behaviors including organizational politics, influence processes, and power struggles to gain advantage or resources in the workplace.

Political blunders Insensitive acts also referred to as "putting your foot in your mouth," or committing a faux pas.

Power The ability or potential to influence.

Prestige power The power stemming from one's status and reputation.

Referent power The ability to influence others through desirable traits and characteristics.

Resource dependence perspective An explanation of power stating that the organization requires a continuing flow of human resources, money, customers, technological inputs, and material to continue to function. Subunits or individuals within the organizations who can provide these resources derive power from this ability.

Reward power The authority to give employees rewards for compliance and good performance.

Self-management The ability to control one's emotions and act with honesty and integrity.

Servant leader A comprehensive politically astute, as well as humanistic, method of building downward relations.

Social awareness A part of emotional intelligence that includes having empathy for others and having intuition about organizational problems.

Social capital A resource derived from the relationships among individuals, organizations, communities, and societies. This type of capital in organizations is reflected by the existence of close interpersonal relationships between and among employees.

Social exchange theory The idea that the most fundamental form of social interaction is an exchange of benefits or favors between two parties.

Social network (as opposed to a computer network) A specific set of linkages among a defined set of individuals.

Social network analysis The mapping and measuring of relationships and links between and among people, groups, and organizations.

Social network theory A theory that regards social relationships in terms of nodes and ties.

Spin An influence tactic aimed at hundreds, or even thousands, of people at the same time, placing a favorable face on a negative situation or person.

Strategic incompetence Avoiding work one prefers to shun because it does not fit one's role.

Strategic self-presentation The theory of impression management that categorizes the tactics into ingratiation, exemplification, intimidation, self-promotion, and supplication.

Superordinate goal An overarching goal that captures the imagination of people.

Territoriality An individual's behavioral expression of his or her feelings of ownership toward a physical or social object. Includes behaviors for constructing, communicating, maintaining, and restoring territories around those objects in the organization toward which one feels proprietary attachment.

Ties The relationships between and among the actors in the social network.

INDEX

ABOUT THE AUTHOR

Andrew J. DuBrin is a Professor of Management Emeritus in the E. Philip Saunders College of Business at the Rochester Institute of Technology, where he has taught courses and conducts research into leadership, organizational behavior, influence processes, and career management. He also served as department chairman and team leader in previous years. He received his Ph.D. in industrial/organizational psychology at Michigan State University.

DuBrin has business experience in human resource management, and consults with organizations and individuals. His specialties include leadership; organizational politics, including influence tactics; and career development. DuBrin is an established author of both textbooks and trade books (including *Winning Office Politics*). He contributes to professional journals, magazines, newspapers, and online publications. He has written textbooks on leadership, organizational behavior, management, and human relations.

Printed in the United States
By Bookmasters